Friendship and Peer Culture
in the Early Years

Language and Learning for Human Service Professions

A Series of Monographs
edited by

Cynthia Wallat, Florida State University
and
Judith Green, The Ohio State University

Volumes in the series include:

Friendship and Peer Culture in the Early Years

WILLIAM A. CORSARO

Indiana University

ABLEX PUBLISHING CORPORATION
NORWOOD, NEW JERSEY

Figures 5.1, 5.2, 5.3, and 5.4 are by Tama Robertson, Indiana University, Bloomington.

We are grateful to the following publishers for permission to reprint some of the material contained in this book:

Parts of Chapter 1 appeared in *Ethnography and Language in Educational Settings,* edited by Judith Green and Cynthia Wallat. Norwood, NJ: Ablex, 1981.

Parts of Chapter 3 were published in *Sociology of Education,* 52: 46–59, 1979.

Parts of Chapter 4 appeared in *The Development of Children's Friendships,* edited by Steve Asher and John Gottman, Cambridge University Press, 1981.

Library of Congress Cataloging in Publication Data

Corsaro, William A.
  Friendship and peer culture in the early years.

  Bibliography: p.
  Includes index.
  1. Childhood friendships.   2. Social interaction in children.   3. Play.   4. Participant observation.
  5. Education, Preschool.   I. Title.
  BF723.F68C67   1985   305.2'33   84-28221
  ISBN 0-89391-174-7
  ISBN 0-89391-256-5 (pbk.)

Ablex Publishing Corporation
355 Chestnut Street
Norwood, New Jersey 07648

Contents

Preface to the Series
Language and Learning
for Human Service
Professions

This series of monographs is intended to make the theories, methods, and findings of current research on language available to professional communities that provide human services. From a theoretical and practical point of view, focus on language as a social process means exploring how language is actually used in everyday life.

Communication between and among adults and children, professionals and clients, and teachers and students, as well as the effect of changing technology on communication in all these contexts, has become the object of study in disciplines as varied as anthropology, cognitive psychology, cognitive science, education, linguistics, social psychology, and sociology. The series provides a forum for this research analyzing talk in homes, communities, schools, and other institutional settings. The aim is to shed light on the crucial role of language and communication in human behavior.

The monographs in the series will focus on three main areas:

- Language and Social Relationships
- Language and Helping Professions
- Language and Classroom Settings

We hope that these books will provide rich and useful images of and information about how language is used.

Cynthia Wallat and Judith Green

Acknowledgments

For the past ten years my interests have been primarily in the areas of children's language and socialization processes. This book is based on a detailed ethnography of peer interaction in a nursery school which was carried out in 1974–75. The research was supported by grants from the National Institute of Mental Health and the Spencer Foundation. Throughout the course of data collection and analysis I received encouragement and support from many friends and colleagues. I am especially grateful to Aaron Cicourel, John Gumperz, and Jenny Cook-Gumperz for their theoretical insights, suggestions, and personal support during the course of this project. I wish to thank several of my colleagues at Indiana University, Donna Eder, David Heise, Charles Ragin (now at Northwestern), and Sheldon Stryker, who read and commented on various parts of the manuscript. Special thanks to Allen Grimshaw who first introduced me to sociolinguistics while I was an undergraduate at Indiana and who is now a supportive colleague. Allen carefully read the entire manuscript and offered many useful suggestions. A number of other colleagues have commented on parts of the manuscript. I am especially indebted to Howard E. Becker, Leonard Cottrell, Fred Erickson, Gary Fine, Lawrence Hazelrigg, Nancy Mandell, John McDowell, Hugh Mehan, Geoffrey Schultz, and Ursula Schwartz. I am also grateful to the editors of this series of monographs by Ablex, Judith Green and Cynthia Wallat, who have carefully read the manuscript and offered valuable comments as well as general encouragement throughout the publication process.

A number of people provided invaluable assistance during data collection. These include John Clausen and Dorothy Eichorn and most especially Charlotte Baker, Alice Engle, Thelma Harms, Vi Moulton-Buck, Hannah Saunders, and Barbara Scales. I am also grateful to Alicia Dailey, Michael Fox, Stephanie Sanford, M. Graham Tomlinson, and Peni Volz who helped with typing, transcription, and data analysis. Special thanks to Karen Marie Frane who typed and edited many versions of the manuscript. I wish to thank my wife, Vickie Renfrow, for her patience as well as her constant help, support, and encouragement throughout this project.

Finally, and most importantly, I must express my gratitude to the children who participated in this study. I thank them for allowing me to share a year of their lives which they may not remember clearly but which I will never forget.

William A. Corsaro
Bologna, Italy, December, 1983

CHAPTER 1

Entering the Child's World: Research Strategies For Studying Peer Culture

Two 4-year-old girls (Betty and Jenny) and adult researcher (Bill) in the nursery school:

Betty: You can't play with us!
Bill: Why?
Betty: Cause you're too big.
Bill: I'll sit down. (Sits down)
Jenny: You're still too big.
Betty: Yeah, you're "Big Bill!"
Bill: Can I just watch?
Jenny: Ok, but don't touch nuthin'!
Betty: You just watch, okay?
Bill: Ok.
Jenny: Ok, Big Bill?
Bill: Ok.
(Later Big Bill got to play.)

Doing ethnographic research in a nursery school is not easy. Even after several months of careful field entry and daily participant observation, the researcher can still not completely overcome some obstacles of intrusion. However, as the above dialogue (wherein I received a lasting nickname) indicates, certain of these obstacles can become less problematic with time, patience, and determination.

In this chapter, I describe the ethnographic context and population, and discuss data collection and analysis procedures. My aim is to provide the reader a "natural history" (Becker, 1958) of the data collection and initial analysis phases of the research process.

Prior Studies of Preschool Children's Play and Peer Culture

Although there is a growing interest in peer interaction and play among preschool children (Bruner, Jolly, and Silva, 1976; Garvey, 1977b; Lewis and Rosenblum, 1975; Schwartzman, 1978), there have been few detailed ethnographies of preschool peer environments.[1] There are at least two reasons for the relative sparsity of such research. The first is theoretical. Major theoretical approaches to human learning and development view socialization as the process by which the child becomes an adult. As Speier (1973:141) has so aptly put it, "traditional perspectives have overemphasized the tasks of describing the child's developmental processes of growing into an adult at the expense of the direct consideration of what the events of everyday life look like in childhood." It is the growing concern with children's peer culture as a topic of study in its own right which has prompted a need for ethnograhic studies of peer environments of preschool children.

A second reason for the sparsity of ethnographic research on young children is methodological. Recently, there have been a growing number of observational studies of peer interaction in both laboratory (Bronson, 1975; Garvey and Hogan, 1973; Garvey, 1977b) and natural settings (see Blurton-Jones, 1972, and Hutt, 1971, for naturalistic research by ethologists; Barker, 1966, and Herron and Sutton-Smith, 1971, for ecological studies; and Keenan, 1974, 1977, Meullar, 1972, and Shatz and Gelman, 1973, for naturalistic studies of language development). A major shortcoming of many of these studies is the tendency of the researchers to remove themselves from the social contexts of the peer activities. As a result, the data are interpreted from the adult's perspective, and there is a failure to capture background information on the

---

[1] Denzin (1977a) has presented a series of articles which contain some ethnographic data on his own children and on other children's peer interaction in a nursery school, and Schwartzman (1978) reports on ethnographic data she collected on peer interaction in a nursery school in one chapter of a book which reviews research on children's play.

children's perceptions of their activities and social-ecological environments.

Detailed ethnography, including participant observation, is difficult in peer settings for several reasons. First, there is the general problem of obtrusion. In the case of research with preschool children, this problem is compounded by the necessity of negotiation with adult caretakers before field entry into peer activities can proceed. Once successful negotiation with caretakers is complete, the researcher faces the problems of physical size and perceived power (i.e., adults are much bigger than children and are perceived as being socially more powerful) in his or her initial contacts with children. The latter problem can be reduced substantially with gradual and, what I term, "reactive" field entry strategies; while the problem of physical size can never be overcome completely, but can diminish in importance over an extended period of participant observation.

A second problem in ethnographic work with young children has to do with adult conceptions of children's activities and abilities. As adults, we often explain away what we do not understand about children's behavior as unimportant (i.e., "silly"), or we restructure what is problematic to bring it in line with an adult view of the world. Along these lines, there is a tendency to view children's play as practice at being an adult (anticipatory socialization). This is not to say such interpretations are always incorrect, or that analyses of peer activities from this perspective are without merit. However, these adult interpretations and assumptions about children's behavior are themselves topics for inquiry (see Schwartzman, 1976). One of the central aims of ethnographies of childhood culture is the suspension of such interpretations. The researcher must attempt to free him or herself from adult conceptions of children's activities, and enter the child's world as both *observer* and *participant*. In the following sections of this chapter, I describe the specific methodological strategies I employed to enter and participate in the children's peer activities.

Ethnograhic Setting and Population

The Child Study Center

The data for this research report were collected from direct observations of the children in a nursery school. The nursery school is part of a child study center staffed and operated by a state university for education and research purposes. The center is located in a large metropolitan area near the university campus. There were two groups of children at the school during the research period. One group of children attended morning sessions, and ranged in age from 2 years, 10 months to 3 years, 10 months, at the start of the school year. A second group attended afternoon sessions, and ranged in age from 3.10 to 4.10 at the start of the school year. The majority of children in the afternoon group had attended the school in morning sessions the year before the research was conducted.

The child study center is housed in a fairly large physical complex. There are two physically identical nursery schools in the center, which are separated by an observation booth as depicted in Figure 1.1. Figure 1.2 depicts the university school.

My research was conducted in the university nursery school. The other school, a parent cooperative nursery, was under the supervision of the city school system. Although I made a few initial observations of the cooperative nursery, I decided in the second month of the research to concentrate on the university school. The center also housed offices for the head teachers (one office for each school) and the director of the center. There were also several observational and experimental rooms in the same area of the center where the staff offices were located (see Figure 1.1). I was allowed to use one of the observation rooms as an office for the course of the research.

The university nursery school has an excellent reputation, and only a small percentage of the total applications for admission to the school can be accepted. Acceptance is based on a first-come-first-served policy, with a built-in specification and one exception. The specificiation is related to the research purposes of the center. The acceptance (or recruitment) policy specifies that one boy and one girl be accepted with birthdates representing each month of the year, to insure an ideal sex and age range for each group (see Tables 1.1 and 1.2). The exception to the birthdate specification is for minority group children. Minority children are generally accepted regardless of when their parents applied or the month of their birth, as a way of encouraging minority group participation in the school. As a result of these policies, there were approximately 25 children in each group. Many parents, knowing the first-come-first-served policy, made applications for their children as

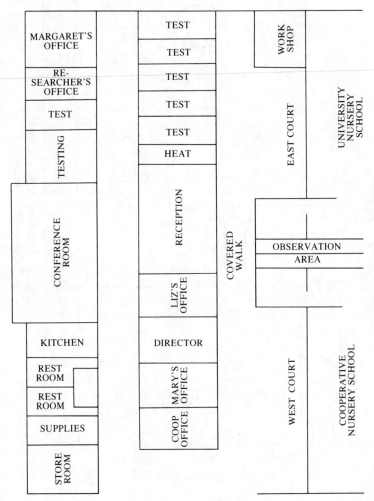

Figure 1.1   Child Study Center

5

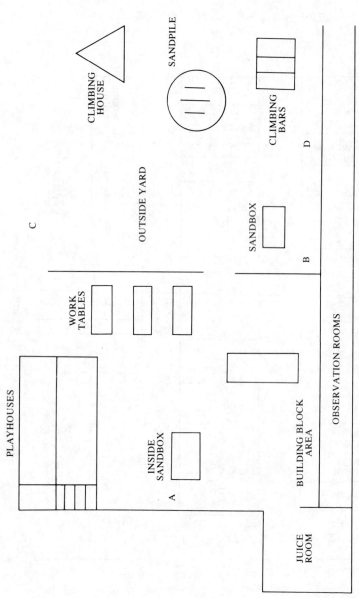

Figure 1.2 University Nursery School
(A-D Camera Placements)

6

early as possible (i.e., on or near the child's birthdate). During my year at the center, almost all of the children who were eventually accepted for admission had applications in at the center before their first birthday.

Population

Tables 1.1 and 1.2 contain a list of the children who participated in the research. Cover names have been used to identify each child. All information beyond age and degree of participation in the research project has been omitted to insure anonymity.

The lists (Tables 1.1 and 1.2) contain all children who attended the university nursery school, with the exception of five cases. In the morning group, the parents of one child did not grant permission for videotaping, and two other children withdrew from the school shortly after the start of the Fall term. In the afternoon group, two children withdrew, and I did not obtain permission from the parents of one other child.

The occupational and educational backgrounds of parents of the children ranged from blue collar workers to professionals (both university and nonuniversity related), with the majority of the children coming from professional (middle and upper class) families. Minority group children (Mexican-Americans, Blacks, and Asians) were represented, but in proportions less than the minority population of the city in which the center is located. This discrepancy was not due to a lack of recruitment attempts, as the exception to the admissions policy demonstrates, but resulted primarily from the tuition fee. This fee, although significantly less than private nursery schools in the area, worked against the participation of many lower class children.

Ethics and Protection of Human Subjects

There is a wide range of positions regarding ethics in observational research (see Barnes, 1967; Becker, 1964; Davis, 1961; Fitchner and Kolb, 1953; Lofland, 1961; Lofland and Lejeune, 1960; Roth, 1962). Ethical questions become more complex when the social actors under analysis are young children (see Fine and Glassner, 1979) and when videotaping procedures are employed. There does seem to be general agreement that overt and informed observations are both more desirable and ethical than covert and disguised re-

Table 1.1   Children in Morning Group at University Nursery School

	Age	Participant* Observation (No. of Episodes)	VTR** (No. of Episodes)
Martin	2.11	73	27
Mia	2.11	31	4
Barbara	3.0	79	21
Dwight	3.1	47	9
Jimmy	3.1	53	9
Nancy	3.1	64	20
Michelle	3.2	58	7
Joseph	3.2	57	22
Leah	3.2	93	16
Concetta	3.3	25	8
Ellen	3.4	69	16
Denny	3.5	107	30
Rita	3.5	65	15
Charles	3.7	63	24
Betty	3.7	77	24
Linda	3.8	76	9
Jack	3.8	59	17
Jenny	3.8	56	15
Roger[a]	3.8	25	11
Cindy[a]	3.9	23	10
Glen	3.9	62	26
Debbie	3.9	89	17
Bill	3.10	65	12
Richard	3.11	53	16

*Refers to total number of episodes in which particular child participated which were recorded in field notes during participant observation. There are 633 episodes in participant observation field notes.

**Refers to total number of videotaped episodes in which particular child participated. There were 146 total videotaped episodes.

[a]These children did not enter school until early January, with the start of the second term.

search (see Barnes, 1967; Becker, 1964). In the present research, the observational procedures were overt, but the respondents' caretakers (parents), rather than the respondents themselves, were informed of the research purposes. In this section, I describe ethical decisions and procedures for the protection of human subjects

Table 1.2　Children in Afternoon Group at University Nursery School

	Age	Participant* Observation (No. of Episodes)	VTR** (No. of Episodes)
Allen	3.9	41	11
Lenny	3.9	39	11
Mark	3.10	59	20
Graham	3.11	81	21
Sue	3.11	31	7
Angela	4.0	18	4
Denise	4.1	37	13
Antoinette	4.1	54	11
Laura	4.1	43	7
Christopher	4.1	27	5
Beth	4.3	28	9
Alice	4.3	36	5
Tommy	4.3	71	8
Brian	4.4	81	20
Sheila	4.4	27	6
Daniel	4.4	89	10
Peter	4.6	97	24
Anita	4.6	39	11
Lisa	4.6	36	13
Eva	4.7	25	9
Dominic	4.7	31	10
Larry	4.7	29	4
Vickie	4.9	63	8
Lanny	4.9	41	10
Frank	4.9	46	7
Jonathan	4.9	57	14
Steven	4.10	35	8

*Refers to total number of episodes in which particular child participated which were recorded in field notes during participant observation. There were 633 episodes in participant observation field notes.

**Refers to total number of videotaped episodes in which particular child participated. There were 146 total videotaped episodes.

as they occurred in the research process. Later in this chapter, I discuss the introduction of the videotape equipment into the school and the children's reactions to the camera and microphone.

Prior to the start of the school term, I talked to the director and head teachers regarding procedures for gaining parental permissions for my research. One of the head teachers suggested I write up a cover page describing my research purposes, attach it to the form, and place it in the students' lockers in the second week of classes. Figures 1.3 and 1.4 are the cover page and permission form I placed in the children's lockers.

Figure 1.3   Cover Letter and Protection of Human Subjects Form

---

TO: Parents of Children Attending the University Nursery School at the Child Study Center

FROM: William A. Corsaro, Post-Doctoral Research Fellow, NIMH

As I have indicated above I am at the Child Study Center this year on a post-doctoral research fellowship from the National Institute of Mental Health. My research involves the observation of pre-school children in a natural setting. I am interested in how children of this age (3-5) initiate, construct, maintain, and terminate social interaction with peers. In short, I focus on what young children "do" and "say" together, especially on how they use language to generate meaning in peer interaction. My work involves only group (age and sex related) comparisons and not the comparison of individual children. Also, the reseaarch does not involve any type of testing of the children or attempts to structure their behavior for observation. I wish, rather, to record samples of the behavior which spontaneously occurs in the nursery school setting for analysis to determine features of peer culture as well as interactive strategies employed by children of this age in peer interaction.

My research involves two types of data collection procedures. One method is the participant observation of the children in the setting, with the main data being field notes. Secondly, I wish to collect videotape data of the children's naturally occurring interactive behavior. Having employed videotape methods in previous research I found that videotape allows for the recording not only of the speech of young children, but also the contextual and temporal features which are of utmost importance in the organization of social interactive events. In the consent form on the next page I discuss the specifics regarding the videotaping procedures and later analysis, use, and disposition of the videotapes. If you have any questions regarding the procedures of the research or data use and analysis I will be glad to discuss them with you. I am usually at the center daily.

Figure 1.4 Consent to Act as Subject for Research

Subject's Name: _____

Date: _____

Name of Project: The Development of Social Interactive Competencies
 Among Pre-School Children

Researcher's Name: William A. Corsaro

I hereby consent to my child's participation in the project named above.
An explanation of the procedures to be followed by provided to me by
Dr. William Corsaro. I was assured that any inquiries concerning the
procedures would be answered. It is also my understanding that the analysis of the videotape data obtained in this study will be confined to the
investigator. I have also been informed that I may inspect any part of
the videotape data upon my request and that I can specify that any part
of the data not be displayed to others. In terms of the final disposition
of the videotapes, it is my understanding that they will remain in the
possession of Dr. Corsaro and that he will use them only for comparative
and instructional purposes along with additional child development data.
Finally, Dr. Corsaro has assured me that a cover name will be used for
my child in any write-up or published report of this research project.

Mother's Signature: _____

Father's Signature: _____

The nature of the research project demanded I get permission
from as many of the parents as possible. If more than one or two
children did not partcipate in the research, there would be severe
limitations on my videotaped observations. Within 3 weeks, I received permission for all but two children (one child in each of
the two age groups). I talked briefly to the parents of these children
at the center, and they voiced hesitancy regarding video recording
of their children's activities. I assured them I would respect their
wishes and would not videotape interactive episodes in which their
children were participants.

During the course of the research, several parents asked me
how things were going and about opportunities for viewing the
data. I responded fully to these queries and told the parents about
my plans for an evening meeting in April where I would show a
few sequences from the videotape data and discuss initial findings.

There were two meetings held in late April (one for each age group). After the meetings, several of the parents (12 in all) set up appointments with me to review data in which their children were involved. During these meetings, I answered any questions they had, and I also asked parents to respond to particular segments of the data. I later matched the parents reactions to these data with my own previously recorded interpretations. Overall, I formed close friendships with several parents during the research, and in a few cases I visited the children and their parents in their homes.

Field Entry and Data Collection

Phase One: Negotiations with Gatekeepers

I arrived in the city where the child study center is located in early September. I was a stranger to this part of the country, and for the first time in my life I felt entirely alone. After finding a place to live near the center, I looked forward to settling in and beginning the research. I had written the director of the center several months earlier, explaining my postdoctoral research plans. In a return letter, the director assured me that my arrival was expected and that I would be provided an office at the center and have access to videotape equipment.

My first visit to the center was frustrating, for two reasons. First, I learned from the secretary, Liz,[2] that the fall term for the nursery school would not begin for another month. This discovery was troublesome, because I was eager to begin observation of the children. A month seemed like a long delay at that time, but as it turned out the extra time was highly beneficial for preparing field entry into the nursery school. A second problem was the absence of the director, who was out of town. As a result, the secretary was not sure what to do with me until the director returned. My arrival was anticipated, but the director had not yet decided exactly where I would be housed in the center. Both of these delays left me a little uneasy, but I had to wait only a few days until the director returned.

During this wait I decided to reassess my strategies for field entry, given the new information regarding the school's timetable. I decided to use the first month to get to know as much about

---

[2]Pseudonyms are used to refer to participants (secretary, teachers, director, children, etc.) throughout this report.

the setting and participants as possible prior to the start of school. I reflected on my conversation with the secretary and wrote down information I had acquired about the setting in that discussion. I now knew the schedule for the fall and spring sessions, as well as the physical layout of the center and the nursery school. I had also obtained information regarding several of the adults who worked at the center (teachers, director, secretary, and teaching assistants). It was clear at this point that the research in the nursery school would be based on what Schatzman and Strauss (1973) have termed "mutually voluntary and negotiated entree," in that my hosts (adult caretakers including the director, teachers, and parents) held "options not only to prevent entree but to terminate relations with the researcher at almost any stage thereafter" (Schatzman and Strauss, 1973:22). During the two days I waited for the director to return, I mapped out initial strategies for building rapport with these various gatekeepers.

The first gatekeeper I talked with at some length was the director of the center, Professor Patricia Smith. I had learned from my first conversation with the secretaries that Professor Smith was not only the director of the center, but also held several other academic positions (high administrative positions in an institute on the university campus where the center is located, and another in a national professional association). The duties associated with these positions required frequent travelling and time away from the center. As a result, the director primarily dealt with major decision making at the center, while the everyday routine activities were assigned to the nursery school teachers and the secretary.

Prior to this initial meeting, I had decided the director would be most concerned with the nature of my research and with how it would fit into the ongoing routine of the nursery school. In the meeting, Professor Smith and I first talked about mutual acquaintances (several of my pervious academic advisors and colleagues). I then broadly outlined my research and specifically addressed the need for videotaping. I assured her that human subjects requirements had been met, and we talked briefly about procedures for gaining parental permission. The director pointed out that detailed videotaping of spontaneous activities in the school had not been attempted in the past, and she seemed quite interested in how it would turn out. The director ended the meeting by noting the informal nature of relations among the staff at the center. It became clear early on in the research that my ability to fit into the "staff family" (director, teachers, secretary, and teaching assistants) would be essential for successful field entry and data collection.

After our meeting, the director and I moved to Liz's office, where we discussed the options of where I might be housed in the center. During my first visit, Liz seemed anxious about the possibility of the director moving me into a large observational room presently occupied by one of the teachers (Margaret). Therefore, I suggested the possibility of occupying a smaller room next to Margaret. The director quickly agreed, and I moved into the center that afternoon. This was a fortunate decision, because it put me in close contact wtih Margaret and prevented her from having to move back into an overcrowded office she had previously shared with the other teacher, Mary (see Figure 1.1).

During the next few days, I discovered that the best source of background information about the nursery school was the secretary (Liz), who had worked at the center since its inception. It was during one of my early conversations with Liz that I made an important discovery about the history of relations between the teachers and past researchers. According to Liz, the teachers were unhappy with much of the research at the center, and often felt used and taken for granted. In many of the studies, the researchers relied on the teachers to entice the children from the school to experimental rooms in the center. In addition, research projects were seldom explained in any detail, and the teachers were seldom asked for advice regarding research designs or procedures. Even more bothersome to the teachers was the frequent failure of researchers to inform them regarding the eventual results of their studies.

This theme of dissatisfaction with much of the previous research at the center was also evident in later conversations I had with the head teachers and teaching assistants. As a result, I attempted to create just the opposite impression for my research. I frequently asked the teachers, assistants, and secretary to respond to my plans for field entry and data collection, and, later in the research process, to help with data analysis and interpretation. During this first month, I often volunteered to help out in the school and the main office, and I soon became part of the "staff family" at the center.

My aim in this approach to field entry was not simply "to come off better" than other researchers, but rather to build an impression of *not being just another researcher*. The people under study in field research should not view the researcher's presence as simply a means to some more important end (i.e., a dissertation, research report, or a monograph). As Becker (1970) has observed, to foster an impression of being important or doing important research can constitute a threat to the people one observes. Throughout the research process, I worked hard to play down my status as a researcher and to emphasize my aim of full time involvement in the daily activities of the school.

For the remainder of the first month, my schedule followed a fairly consistent routine. I would arrive at the center around 8:45 each morning and talk with Liz until around 9:30. I then went to my office where I remained until around 11:15. Before going to lunch I would again talk with Liz for 30 minutes or so, and then again for another 30 minutes when I returned from lunch. I usually got back to my office around 1:30, where I remained until 4:00. At that time, I again visited with Liz for 40 minutes or so, until I left the center for the day.

I acquired a great deal of information which I later used in field entry in these conversations with Liz. Although the actual conversations covered a wide range of topics (my research, academic traning, our families, political views, and leisure activities and interests), they were primarily about the nursery school. I most often used the time spent in my office writing up my recollections of parts of these conversations which were most relevant for later field work. This method of data collection through informal interviewing is beneficial for building rapport and for obtaining needed information in an unobtrusive manner. This informal procedure had the added dimension of providing respondents with the opportunity to volunteer information the researcher may fail to elicit in structured interviewing.

Regarding the head teachers, the information I acquired in conversations with Liz was useful in many ways. For example, Liz indicated that one of the head teachers (Mary) was especially interested in curriculum development in the area of early childhood education. Mary had not only formulated many structured tasks and projects for use in the classroom, but had also authored numerous papers, presented lectures and workshops, and taught courses on early childhood education. Overall, the impression of Mary I received was one of a highly qualified and experienced childhood educator who had invested a great deal of time and energy in formalizing her teaching views and methods.

Margaret's teaching methods were less formalized and structured than Mary's. She was viewed as an excellent teacher who had the ability to perform well on-the-spot. That is, her methods were more informal, and often varied given the characteristics of particular groups of children. The fact that Margaret worked with the younger age group at the center was important, regarding her teaching philosophy and methods. I learned much more about (and grew to appreciate greatly) Margaret's teaching methods after I began participant observation.

In addition to the information about the head teachers, Liz also provided background on the teaching assistants, parents, and children. I acquired some of this information in a more formal manner, by asking to inspect student files. I was provided access to background files which contained information on the children (names and ages) and their families (number, age, and sex of siblings, and parents' names, addresses, and occupations). I spent a great deal of time going over these files during my first month at the center, and had committed much of the information to memory before the first day of class.

Overall, the information I obtained from Liz through informal conversations helped me to establish working expectations of most of the participants in the research setting prior to initial contacts and interaction. In a few cases, the information proved to be highly valuable, for example, the knowledge I gained regarding the teachers' past experience with researchers; while, in others, it helped put me at ease before participant observation began. As a result, my first encounters with the various participants in the study were less stressful and more rewarding regarding the information I obtained.

During the month before the start of the fall session, the head teachers were away from the center most of each day. This time was used for home visits designed to make the children's transition to the school as smooth as possible. Near the end of the month, the teachers were at the center more often and had several organizational meetings with their assistants. It was at this time that the teachers and staff also began to ready the school for the start of the fall session. At this point, I met all of the teaching assistants, sat in on several of the organizational meetings, and observed one day of work in the school itself. It was also during this period that I had my first extended conversations with each of the head teachers.

During my first month at the center, Margaret and I had talked briefly and she had sat in on several of my discussions with Liz. About a week before school started, I had an extended conversation with Margaret during which I gained a great deal of information relevant to strategies for field entry. Initially, we discussed some of the literature on language acquisition and I suggested several recent sources. As the conversation progressed, we moved from my office to hers, where she showed me several articles and books on language and early childhood education. The topic soon shifted to my research plans. I outlined my general interests in peer communication and interaction, and its importance for early childhood socialization. I also described my methodological plans, stressing the necessity for intensive observation and videotaping. Like the director, Margaret noted that this type of research was novel to the center and she displayed a great deal of interest. I asked for her help regarding field entry, and stressed the value of the teacher's interpretations for data analysis. Margaret seemed both surprised and pleased at this request, and said she would be glad to help. She went on to discuss her feelings about being left out of many of the research projects at the center, and noted that some researchers failed to inform the teachers about the outcomes of their studies. I was, of course, not surprised at her descriptions of other research, given my earlier conversations with Liz.

I then moved to a description of my specific plans for field entry, and asked her for reactions. Margaret agreed with my idea to try to become a part of the children's peer world in a gradual manner. However, she suggested I not move into the nursery school itself too quickly. She noted that the first few weeks were usually somewhat traumatic for the younger children, and that the parents and teaching staff were often a little tense during this period. She suggested I could learn a great deal about the children and routine activities in the school by watching from behind the one-way screen in the observation booth (see Figure 1.1) for the first few weeks.

A few days before the start of the fall session, I had my first extended conversation with Mary, the head teacher for the 4- to 5-year-old group. In the meeting, I outlined my research plans and asked for reactions and suggestions. Mary was most interested in the plans for videotaping, and she suggested camera and microphone placements in the school. She also predicted that I would encounter audio problems due to the large amount of background noise in the school. I asked about the possibility of her helping with data analysis later in the year. She agreed, and seemed pleased with the request. Near the end of the meeting, I showed her the human subjects forms for videotaping and asked how I might go about obtaining parental permissions. Mary looked over the forms and suggested I add a brief introductory paragraph describing myself and the project. She also suggested I place the forms in the students' lockers during the first week of classes, since parents often neglected to respond to forms brought home later in the school year.

Shortly after my meeting with Mary, I revised the permission forms and asked Liz to run off copies. With this task completed, I reviewed my field notes and reflected on my first month of observations and informal interviews. Schatzman and Strauss have argued that field entry "is a *continuous* process of establishing and developing relationships, not only with a chief host but with a variety of less powerful persons" (1973:22). At this point in the research, I seemed well into this process. I had established important ties with several of the gatekeepers in the setting, and had obtained a great deal of information about the center. I made up a list of all the information I had acquired in conversations with Liz, Margaret, and Mary, as well as from documents (student rosters and descriptions of the goals of the center) provided by Liz. As I reviewed this material, it became clear that information acquired at one point in the process can be extremely useful at later stages of the research (i.e., information from conversations with Liz for building rapport with the teachers, information from conversations with teachers for initial contact with parents and later entry into the school, etc.) In the next phase of the research, concealed observation, I was to continue this process as I began to acquire background information on the activities in the school and on the children themselves. This information would prove to be essential for later entry into the school and participant observation in peer interaction.

Phase Two: Concealed Observation

Observational routine. A few days after my meeting with Margaret, I looked over my notes of the conversation and decided to follow her advice and begin my research by monitoring activities in the school from the observation booth. The day before the start of school, I inspected the observation area to get an idea of the range of information I could gather from this location. The observation booth ran nearly the entire length of the school, from the inside rooms to the outside courtyard (see Figure 1.1). Although it was not possible to monitor all the activity in the school from a single location, it was relatively easy to move to various places in the observation booth so activities which began in one area and moved to another could be followed with little difficulty.

The physical design of the booth facilitated note-taking, with its running (soda fountain) counter and seats. Although the observation booth was far from ideal for detailed observations of the children's behavior, it was adequate for gaining information on the daily routine of the school and individual characteristics of the children.

On the first day of school, I arrived early and sat in the main office with Liz as the children in the morning group were brought to the center by their parents. The main office was adjoined to a walkway which leads into the nursery school, and the children and parents must pass a large window in the office as they enter the school. As they filed by, Liz waved and occasionally called the names of the children and parents. She also identified each child as I scribbled brief physical descriptions on a copy of the roster of the morning group. With several repetitions of this procedure and my first week of observations, I was able to associate all the children with their names.

Once all the children had arrived, I moved into the observation area. I primarily watched the activities and tried to hear both teacher–child and peer conversations. I was surprised and somewhat overwhelmed by the number, range, and complexity of the interactive events occurring before me. On this first day, I had no clear idea of what to write down in field notes. As it turned out, I recorded only a few observations relating to how long parents remained in the school with their children.

I repeated the same procedure of watching the children and their parents pass Liz's office for the afternoon group. Later, as I watched the activities in the afternoon session, I felt things seemed more structured and defined than they were in the morning session. The children in this group had been at the school the year before, and were familiar with the setting and each other. As a result, several sustained peer activities occurred on the first day. I followed a few of these as best I could, and tried to record some verbal exchanges verbatim. This was a difficult strategy, however, because I did not know the children well at this point and I had some difficulty hearing and understanding many of their utterances. I dropped this strategy after the first day in the observation area, but then readopted it in a modified form near the end of the period of concealed observation. For the remainder of the first week, I concentrated on matching the children with their names and becoming acquainted with the daily routine and schedule for both groups.

Activities in the morning session followed a regular schedule. The children arrived at 9:00 a.m. and were greeted by teaching assistants. The assistants helped the children put their coats in the lockers and also suggested possible activities for the first part of the morning. The children were allowed to move to any area of the school (inside or out), and self-select activities.

At 9:45, a table (large enough to seat seven children and two adults) was set up in the juice room, and "juice time" began. After the initial seven children were recruited and seated, the teaching assistants (TAs) poured fruit juice from large cans into small measuring cups. The children then used the cups to pour juice into smaller paper cups. After the children finished their juice and crackers, they were to dispose of their paper cup and then move into the school and inform other children that there was a space available at the juice table. This procedure continued until all the children had a turn at juice, and normally lasted about 45 minutes (until around 10:30).

Self-selection of activities continued until 10:45, when "clean-up" time was announced. After the children and teachers had returned the play materials to their original places, all the children gathered in the juice room for "meeting time." Meeting time normally began around 11:00 a.m. and lasted until 11:20. A variety of teacher-directed activities occurred at this time, including storytelling, reading aloud from books, and singing participation songs and nursery rhymes.

At 11:20, meeting time ended and the children left the juice room and went to the work tables. Here they played table games with the TAs, or joined small groups of children who sat around individual TAs, listening to stories read aloud from one of the many books in the school. Around 11:25, parents began to arrive, and the last child had normally departed from the school by 11:35.

The schedule for the afternoon session was similar to that of the morning. The children arrived at the school at 1:00 and were free to self-select activities, but only within the inside area of the school. Around 1:45, the doors leading to the outside yard were opened and at this same time the TAs began serving juice in the juice room. Juice time proceeded as it did in the morning group, and lasted until 2:30. Clean up time began at 2:40, and meeting time usually got under way around 2:45.

In the afternoon session, meeting time involved singing, reading stories aloud from books, and question–answer sequences. These sequences involved the teachers asking children a variety of questions about activities at school and home. Children would raise their hands and offer answers, and the teachers attempted to built short dialogues from the initial responses. Meeting time ended around 3:15, and the children played table games or joined story groups until parents arrived at 3:30. Following the departure of the last child, there was a short meeting between the head teacher and the assistants (usually lasting 5 or 10 minutes).

During the first month of school, I followed a fairly routine schedule. I observed from behind the one-way screen from the beginning until near the end of each session. I concentrated mainly on peer activities and moved to and from various locations in the observation booth to monitor behavior in all areas of the school. In field notes, I recorded the topic or nature of peer activities, names of the children involved, and the location, duration, and a running summary of peer episodes.

Near the end of each session, I would leave the observation area, enter the school, and stand near the children's lockers. I waited until parents began to arrive, and then I helped the children gather things from their lockers as they prepared to leave. Occasionally, I talked with the parents and children, but I did not identify myself as a researcher. As I discovered later in conversations with parents, many of them believed I was either a teaching assistant or a father of one of the children at this point in the research. The children seemed to take little notice beyond an occasional "thank you" for my help.

After the children had departed, I helped the teacher and TAs with cleaning up, and when the school was back in order I sat in on the teacher-staff meeting. During the meeting, each of the TAs reported on how they felt the day went and discussed any specific problems they had encountered. The teacher responded to these observations and made specific recommendations on how to handle similar problems in the future. The teacher then ended the meeting after discussing problems she felt merited special attention.

After the meeting, I would return to my office and quickly jot down notes on what had transpired. I then looked over these notes and compared them to notes I had recorded earlier in the day. I was careful to mark both overlaps and differences in interpretations of the same or similar events.

Sampling unit and form of field notes. As I mentioned previously, the field notes I recorded during concealed observation contained information on the participants, setting, and the nature and duration of interactive events. It was at this point in the research that I decided on the *interactive episode* as the collection or sampling unit. In naturalistic research, specimens of behavior are recorded as they occur in the setting under study. The reliability of the data depends upon consistent collection of these specimens into units with specified boundaries throughout the research process. In some naturalistic studies, sampling units are relatively easy to define because boundaries (the beginning and ending of interactive events) are clearly marked. For example, there have been several recent studies of classroom interaction (Eder, 1979; McDermott, Gospodinoff, and Aron 1978; Mehan, 1978) in which formal classroom lessons served as the sampling unit. In work on doctor- and therapist-interaction (Cicourel, 1974; Labov and Fanshel, 1977; and Scheflen, 1973) the professional–client interview session has served as the collection or sampling unit. However, interaction in many social settings can not always be collected in units with such natural boundaries. For example, much interaction in homes, peer settings, informal gatherings, and workplaces is characterized by a continuous flow of conversation. It may well be that the lack of sociolinguistic work in these settings is due to the problem of deciding how to record the interaction into consistent and comparable units.

In the research in the nursery school, I generated a collection or sampling unit from the interplay of theoretical assumptions about units in face-to-face interaction which I carried into the research site, and from information I obtained during the month of concealed information about the social-ecological features of the nursery school setting and the communicative behavior and abilities of the children.

Prior to my participant observation in the nursery school, I (a) reviewed the literature on face-to-face interaction, (b) selected a working definition of a sampling unit from the work of Goffman (1963), (c) established how well the definition captured interactive events I had recorded in field notes during the period of concealed observation, (d) modified the working definition in response to specific features of the setting and peer interaction, and (e) used the resulting revised definition as the collection or sampling unit for field notes and audiovisual recordings.

A brief summary of the five step process is useful to exemplify the generation and characteristics of the sampling unit. After reviewing the literature on fact-to-face interaction, I selected Goffman's (1963) notion of "face engagement" as a working definition for a sampling unit. For Goffman, "face engagements comprise all those instances of two or more participants in a situation joining each other openly in maintaining a simple focus of cognitive and visual attention—what is sensed as a *mutual activity* entailing preferential communication rights" (1963:89). As a result of my review of field notes and knowledge of the literature on children's communicative abilities—Goffman's definition was based on adult communicative competence—I made an immediate extension of Goffman's definition. From field notes, it was clear that interactive episodes in the nursery school began only when children went beyond mutual acknowledgement and initiated or proposed some mode of activity which served as the beginnings of mutual activity. Therefore, I defined the beginning of an interactive episode as the overt attempt(s) to arrive at a shared meaning of what interactants are doing or plan to do.

However, if episodes begin with mutual acknowledgments of copresence and overt attempts to arrive at shared meanings regarding ongoing or planned mutual activity, then when and how do episodes end? Goffman's definition was of little help here. Face engagements were defined in terms of initiations, not terminations, but it can be assumed that they end when people are somehow no longer in each other's presence. Termination implies physical movement out of the ecological area in which the mutual activity occurs. But movement by whom: the original interactants, all but one of any number of interactants, or should termination be defined as that state of a lack of mutual activity which results from the physical movement of participants from a specific ecological area?

Given these questions, I again reviewed the field notes. Although the children did not exhibit a clear understanding of "topics" in their activities, they did seem to organize their behaviors around a set of mutual activities. The initiation and termination of mutual activities were, however, not simple matters. Activities which were initiated in an area of the school by particular children often continued in spite of the departure of the original initiators. Peer activities frequently took on a "life of their own" with alternating participants. Therefore, the eventual definition of a sampling unit had to capture the fact that episodes continued until the leave-taking of participants results in the termination of the originally initiated activity.

Another persistent feature of peer interaction I discovered in field notes was that multiple activities with a range of participants can, and often did, occur simultaneously within the same ecological area. In terms of the eventual definition of a sampling unit, each activity would best be represented as a separate episode, and if two ongoing activities should overlap, the overlapping segments should be included as part of both episodes.

Given this review of field notes and the discovery of consistent features of peer interaction, I generated the following definition of the *interactive episode*. In the nursery school, *interactive episodes are those sequences of behavior which begin with the acknowledged presence of two or more interactants in an ecological area and the overt attempt(s) to arrive at a shared meaning of ongoing or emerging activity. Episodes end with physical movement of interactants from the area which results in the termination of the originally initiated activity.*[3]

The basis of this definition of the sampling unit (interactive episode) was the interplay between theoretical assumptions about basic units in face-to-face interaction and the background information collected in the setting under study. I do not claim, of course, that researchers would generate the same definition in other settings. The important point is that the definition of the collection or sampling unit was based on stable features of the particular setting under study, and that it was used consistently throughout the research process.

---

[3]There was one exception to this definition of the sampling or collection unit, and this was in the case of solitary play. Solitary play rarely occurred in the school, and, for the few cases I included in field notes or on videotape, I sampled solitary play until the child left a specific ecological area or was joined by one or more children. If all but one child left an area, and the one child who remained engaged in solitary play, then I sampled this behavior as a new episode.

For all the data (field notes and videotaped behavior), the interactive episode served as the collection or sampling unit throughout the research process. An example of an interactive episode recorded in field notes near the end of the concealed observation period appears below.

Example 1.1
Date: October 29
Morning—Episode #5
Scene: Outside Sandbox
Participants: Rita (R), Barbara (B), Jack (J), Bill (Bi), Linda (L), Richard (Rich)
FN—Field Note; MN—Methodological Note; PN—Personal Note; TN—Theoretical Note

FN: Five children (R, B, J, Bi, and L) are playing around the outside sandbox. The children are pretending to make cakes, pies, etc., by placing sand in pans and other cooking utensils. There is a toy sink with faucet and a toy oven near the sandbox. Most of the time the children seem to be involved in parallel play, but there is verbal negotiation when the children need to share utensils or props.

B–Bi: I need to get some water. (Bi is standing near front of sink and moves to one side as B approaches)
Bi–B: There's no water in there. (Referring to fact that faucet is not real)
B–Bi: Well, it's *pretend water.*
Bi–B: Ok.
B–Bi: We all have to share the only one.

Later another instance involving cooperation and sharing occurred.

B–J: Jack?
J–B: What?
B–J: I'm putting this in the oven.
J–B: Ok. (B puts pan in the oven)
B–J: Here, this is mine, J. (J now holds pan as B puts sand in it)

(J now reaches for a scoop in the sandbox)

J–B: Mine.
B–J: No, you can have this (B hands a spoon to J)

(Shortly after this exchange B leaves the area with no verbal marking and goes inside the school)

Now only R, J, and L remain playing around the sandbox. Rich now approaches and watches the other children for a few minutes. Rich then walks near J and says:

Rich–J: It's clean up time!

Richard then reaches for Jack's pan filled with sand and tries to dump it out. J resists Rich and dumps the sand himself. J then goes inside the school. Rich remains a few minutes and plays in sandbox and then leaves. R and L play (there are several verbal exchanges) until a teaching assistant announces that it is clean-up time.

PN: I found earlier that any attempt to record everything the children said was fruitless. As a result, I often relied on summaries here. It seemed Richard said it was clean-up time so that he could dump Jack's sand, but it was apparent that Jack did not fall for his ploy.

MN: I will want to observe interaction around the outside sandbox when I begin participant observation. This should not be difficult, since I could sit down by the sandbox and be at the same height as the children. Obtrusion would be less of a problem around the sandbox than in the playhouses or climbing bars.

TN: (1)   The fact that the children moved from seemingly parallel play to social interaction to negotiate sharing of objects is interesting and should be investigated further. It suggests the importance of contextual factors in the children's use of social and ego-centric speech.

(2)   As in earlier episodes, the children did not verbally mark leave-taking, and after they departed they did not seem to be missed by the other children.

(3)   Play around the outside sandbox is similar to play in the play-houses in that the children go through or produce household routines (i.e., cooking, cleaning, etc.). However, specific roles (mother, father, baby, etc.) are not assigned in the play around the sandbox, as they often are in role play in the playhouses.

The recording conventions employed in the above example were first suggested in Strauss (1964) and are quite similar to those presented in Schatzman and Strauss (1973:99–100). The chief advantage of the convention is that it allows the researcher to separate out different types of information in the data (FN, PN, MN, TN) while insuring that varying types of data are tied to the specific interactive context in which they occurred. As the study proceeds, the researcher can search for patterns in field notes over time and across and within interactive episodes.

During the period of concealed observation, I reviewed my notes twice a week, searching for early patterns in the data. As Greer (1967) has noted, one can draw few conclusions from patterns in early field notes, but they may have far-reaching effects on the rest of the study. Many of the patterns I isolated in notes during the period of concealed observation were discovered by focusing on theoretical notes, and were often the basis of later sampling decisions as well as the eventual generation of hypotheses regarding peer activities in the school.

Advantages of concealed observation. Overall, the period of concealed observation was useful for several reasons. First, since the teachers, parents, and children were all somewhat tense at the beginning of the year, my presence as an observer in the school would have been quite obtrusive. From the concealed observation area, I was able to learn a great deal about the children, daily routines in the two groups, and features of peer interaction *before* actual entry into the school itself. Secondly, if I had attempted entry at the start of the school year, the chidren might have defined me as a teacher as they did the other strange adults (i.e., TAs). A third advantage of concealed observation was that it allowed me to follow activities in all areas of the school without difficulty or disruption.

Cicourel (1964) suggests that any knowledge of the research setting, independent of that which might be obtained in the actual field work, should be secured prior to field entry. All of the above advantages tie into this central aim in field research. The knowledge I gained in my first month at the center and during concealed observation was of major importance for later entry into peer activities, participant observation, sampling decisions, and eventual data analysis and interpretation.

Phase Three: Participant Observation

Entry into the nursery school. At the start of the second month of the school year, I moved into the school itself. My goal was to become an active participant in the children's peer activities. Participant observation was necessary for several reasons. First, it was essential that the children perceive me as different from the teachers and other adults in the nursery school setting, so that they would not suppress certain behaviors for fear of negative reactions. Secondly, once videotaping began I felt the children would find the equipment less obtrusive if they had become accustomed to my presence in their daily activities. Finally, becoming a participant in the children's activities was necessary to gain insight into *what mattered most to them* in their everyday interaction in the school. This knowledge was of central importance for isolating patterns in field notes, analyses of video-taped episodes, and the generation of hypotheses.

In preparation for entry into the school, I reviewed the methodological notes collected during concealed observation. In these notes I had continually reminded myself *not to act* like other adults when I moved into the school. During concealed observation I discovered adults primarily initiated contacts with the children; that is, they were primarily *active* rather than *reactive*. The teachers directed and monitored the children's play, helped in times of trouble, or told the children what they could or could not do. Other adults (parents and researchers) mainly watched the children, often while standing over and peering down at them. The adults would frequently move from one group of children to another, and initiate conversations without any real intention of engaging in extended interaction. Adult contacts with children were restricted to specific areas of the school. Adults seldom entered the playhouses, outside sandpile, climbing bars, or climbing house (see Figure 1.2).

Given this knowledge of typical adult–child interaction, I adopted a simple, what I term "reactive," entry strategy. For the first week in the school, I continually made myself available in peer-dominant areas and waited for the children to react to me. For the first few days, the results were not encouraging. I would enter the school shortly after the children arrived and sit down in a peer area. A number of peer interactive episodes developed and progressed as I sat nearby. I observed seven episodes in each session over a 3-day period without any overt response from the children beyond several smiles and a few puzzled stares. Of all the many hours observing in this setting, these were the most difficult for me. I wanted to say something ("anything") to the children, but I stuck with the strategy and remained silent.

On my fourth afternoon in the school, I stationed myself in the outside sandpile directly behind a group of five children who were digging in the sand with shovels. They had defined their activity as "construction work" with two "bosses" and three "workers" (four boys and one girl). I watched for over 40 minutes, and first two of the children, and then the remaining three, dropped their shovels and ran inside with no verbal marking. I suspected the construction project was completed or abandoned, but was not sure, since termination had not been marked explicitly.

I was feeling ill at ease and debating my next move when I saw Sue watching me from a distance. She was standing alone near the sandpile about 20 feet from where I was sitting. I smiled and she smiled back, but then to my dismay she ran over near the sandbox and stood watching a group of three other girls. My attention was then diverted by a minor disturbance near the climbing bars. Peter had (or so Daniel shouted) stolen Daniel's truck, and a teacher had just arrived to settle the dispute. When I looked back to the sandbox, Sue was gone.

I then decided to move inside, but as I started to stand up I heard someone say "What 'ya doing?" Sue had approached me from behind and was now standing next to me in the sandpile. I said, "Just watching." "What for?" she asked, and I answered, "Cause I like to." Then she asked my name. I said, and this turned out to be an important reply, "I'm Bill and you're Sue."

She took two steps back and demanded, "How did you know my name?" Remembering my methodological notes, I now did something I noticed adults do not often do in conversations with young children—I told the truth with no attempt to simplify. "I heard Laura and some other kids call you Sue," I said. "But how do *you* know my name?" was Sue's response. I again pointed out that I had heard other children call her by name. Sue then turned and ran inside.

I had just decided I had blown it when Sue re-emerged from the school, accompanied by Jonathan. When they reached me, Jonathan asked, "What's my name?" I told Jonathan his name, and then he, like Sue, asked how I knew. Again I was truthful." I heard Peter [one of Jonathan's most frequent playmates] and some other kids call you Jonathan."

"See, I told you he knows magic," said Sue. "Wait a minute," cautioned Jonathan, and then, pointing to Lanny and Frank, he asked, "Who are those kids?" I was able to correctly identify both Larry and Frank, as well as several other children Jonathan pointed out. Jonathan then asked, "Ok what's my sister's name?" Jonathan thought he had me here, but I actually knew his sister's name. As I mentioned earlier Liz had provided me with rosters which listed the children's names, parents' names, and number and names of siblings. I had memorized much of this information and I remembered Jonathan's sister's name which was "Alicia." So I told Jonathan his sister's name and he was now very impressed. However, two months later Jonathan asked me to name "his friend who lived down the street." He did indeed have me at this point, and I told him I needed to think about it for awhile. He accepted my cop out, but with an air of triumph that he had stumped me.

After my performance, Jonathan turned to Sue and said, "I can't figure this guy out." He then ran off and joined Peter, Daniel, and Graham, who were playing in the climbing bars. I noticed he turned and pointed to me after he reached the other three boys.

Sue then handed me a shovel. "You wanna dig?" "Sure," I said, and we shoveled sand into buckets. Later we were joined by Christopher and Antoinette. This activity ended when one of the TAs announced "clean-up time," whereupon we put away our shovels and went inside for meeting time.

For the next several days, children in both sessions began to react to my presence (ask who I was) and invite me to play. Although I was able to observe, and in many cases participate in, peer activities, the process was a gradual one. For nearly the first month, the children were curious about me and why I was around every day. Table 1.3 summarizes the frequency of several "types" of questions which the children asked in attempts to identify my role in the school during the first 3 months of participant observation.

Table 1.3 indicates a gradual process of identification. There is a movement from general questions centering around adult characteristics to the last question about siblings, which is a question most typically asked of another child.

Children's questions provide data on attempts at identification. They do not, however, directly support the contention that the children had accepted me into peer activities. The reference, or nickname, "Big Bill," which surfaces near the end of the first month of participant observation, indicates a marking of the size difference between me and the children, but also differentiates me from other adults.

In addition to the questions and the nickname, there were three other types of data which demonstrated my acceptance as a peer. First, I was allowed to enter ongoing peer activities with little or

Table 1.3 Children's Questions Regarding Researcher's Identity During Participant Observation

Question	N	Number of Children	Temporal Range
Who are you?	48	32	November 7–22
Are you a teacher?	40	28	November 7–December 1
Are you gonna play a game with me (us)?*	21	20	November 15–December 17
Are you a daddy?	13	10	November 7–January 28
Do you have any brothers or sisters?	10	5	November 20–March 4

*Other researchers at the center often asked children, "Do you want to play a game with me?" as a device to encourage children to participate in an experimental study.

no disruption. In most instances, the children simply acknowledged my entry by addressing me in the course of unfolding events. In only a few cases were activities stopped and my presence questioned.

A second cue to the children's perceptions was my lack of authority. Given the nature of the research, attempts to control behavior were few and produced only when I felt there was a chance that a certain activity might lead to physical injury. On these occasions my "Be careful" warnings were always countered with "You're not a teacher!" or "You can't tell us what to do!"

A third type of data is more indirect, but occurred with a great deal of consistency. Throughout the school year, the children insisted I be a part of the more formal peer activities. At birthday parties, for example, the children demanded I sit with them (in a circle) rather than on the periphery with the teachers and parents. Also, several of the children demanded their mothers write my name, along with the names of the other children, on cookies, cupcakes, and valentines which were brought to school on special days.

Observational routine and sampling procedures. Participant observation followed a fairly routine schedule. I would enter the school every morning shortly after the children arrived, watch as episodes emerged, and then place myself in the area where an episode was underway. My ability to enter into peer activities improved as the study progressed, due to practice and my reviews of personal and methodological notes. My participation in peer activities can best be described as "peripheral." I entered an ecological area, moved when necessary, responded when addressed, and occasionally offered verbal contributions when they seemed appropriate. My activity was peripheral in that I never attempted (a) to initiate or terminate an episode, (b) to repair disrupted activity, (c) to settle disputes, or (d) to coordinate or direct activity. What I did do was try to play, to become a part of the activity without affecting the nature or flow of peer episodes.

When recording field notes, I would enter short summaries of episodes into a small notebook shortly after the end of each episode, and then fill in and expand the notes at the end of each day. Every weekend, I would review my notes, searching for both negative cases and/or additional support for earlier patterns, as well as indications of new patterns, in the data.

Daily participant observation continued for 3 months (November through January). In late January, I began videotaping, with taping sessions occurring twice a week while participant observation continued on the other 3 days until the end of the school year in June. I recorded a total of 633 episodes in field notes during this period.

Earlier, I defined the *interactive episode* as the collection or sampling unit. Actual sampling procedures involved decisions regarding which units (interactive episodes) to sample from the continuous flow of interaction in the nursery school. The interactive episodes recorded in field notes and on videotape were representative of typical activities in the setting and had potential for the development of theoretical propositions. In short, sampling decisions *were both representative and theoretical.*

When a sample is representative, it captures the overall texture of the setting under study. Since it is impossible to record all interaction in a given setting, field researchers often attempt to insure representativeness by collecting data across several dimensions, including people, places, time, and activities (cf. Denzin, 1977b; Mehan, 1979; Reiss, 1971; Schatzman and Strauss, 1973). A typical strategy is to draw up an inventory of the range and number of elements in each of the dimensions in early phases of field entry, and then modify the inventory as needed at various points in data collection. When using more than one data collection technique (e.g., observational field notes, interviewing, audiovisual recording, etc.), data obtained at one point in time with one technique can serve as a basis for identifying dimensions in the setting which are then sampled using another technique later in the collection process.

I used data collected during the period of concealed observation to develop an inventory of the participants, activities, social-ecological areas, and schedule of the nursery school. The inventory then guided the sampling of interactive episodes in participant observation during the next 3 months. At the end of this period, I reviewed the field notes, and added and deleted items to and from the inventory. The revised inventory was then used to guide sampling decisions in later participant observation, and for the audiovisual recording of interactive episodes.

Once the videotaping phase of the research began, I checked the representativeness of the sample of audiovisual data in two ways. First, after each taping session I reviewed and summarized the data. In the summaries, I specified the number of episodes, where and when they occurred, their duration, the participants, and the nature of the activity. At the end of each week, I compared the summaries with the sampling inventory and checked off items (features of the behavior recorded in the episodes) as they were collected. Secondly, on several occasions I asked the teachers to look over the summaries and to respond to their representativeness of typical activities in the school. The teachers' responses, as well as my comparison of the audiovisual data with field notes, resulted in the collection of additional videotaped episodes which improved the overall representativeness of the recordings.

In addition to representativeness, sampling procedures in field research should also generate data which have theoretical relevance. The concern with theoretical relevance of sampling in field research has been discussed at length by Glaser and Strauss (1967) and Denzin (1977b). However, general reactions to the Glaser and Strauss notion of "theoretical sampling" have not been favorable. The procedure is often labeled as vague and unstructured, thereby limiting the generalizability of eventual conclusions. Furthermore, some argue that all sampling procedures (in both qualitative and quantitative research) are theoretical, in that the data collected are a reflection of theoretical questions or issues the researcher wishes to address.

I feel critics of "theoretical sampling" are correct in pointing to some of the obvious shortcomings of this procedure; however, they often tend to overlook the central importance of a theoretically directed sampling procedure for ethnographic research. As I have pointed out, sampling procedures in field research should be both reliable and representative. But the nature of ethnographic research demands that sampling procedures also be reactive to developments in the course of research. As Hymes notes, "for many ethnographers, it is of the essence of the method that it is a dialectical, or feed-back (interactive–reactive) method. It is of the essence of the method that initial questions may change during the course of inquiry" (1978:8). Thus, sampling procedures must, in part, reflect the dialectical nature of ethnographic research.

It is precisely along these lines that ethnographic research differs from hypothesis-testing approaches. It is not that field research is more theoretically oriented than hypothesis-testing approaches (i.e., surveys, experiments, etc.), but rather that field research differs in that theoretical concerns guide sampling decisions *both initially and throughout the study*. The ethnographer must be sensitive to theoretical leads as they emerge, and pursue them through theoretically directed sampling procedures.

Phase Four: Videotape Recording

Introducing the videotape equipment into the setting. Although there have been several recent studies involving the audiovisual recording of adult–child and peer interaction (see reports in Lewis and Rosenblum, 1975; also Garvey, 1974, 1977a; Keenan 1974, 1977; Keenan and Klein, 1975), these studies (with the exception of Keenan's work with her own children) have not been grounded in extensive ethnographies of the settings and participants involved. In the present research, audiovisual recording was based on initial patterns isolated in the prior field work.

In early January, I reviewed my notes and drew up a list of the types of peer activities I planned to capture on videotape. The activities on this list, as well as those selected for recording in later reviews of notes as participant observation progressed, were directly related to emerging patterns in the field notes. In this sense, patterns in the ethnographic data were the basis for the sampling of videotaped interactive episodes.

During the evening hours in mid-January, I began initial testing of the equipment. I set up the camera and determined the video range and quality of several possible placements. I discovered I could capture activities in all areas of the school with four camera placements (see Figure 1.2, letters A–D).

Audio recording, however, was a much more difficult problem. During participant observation, I placed an audio recorder in several areas of the school. The playback of these tapes was not encouraging, and it was apparent high quality audio recording would be difficult to attain in this setting. I tested microphone locations in all areas of the school, and eventually placed microphones in the playhouses and over the building block area, inside sandbox, and work tables. In the remaining areas inside the school and in the outside yard, I stored microphones in unobtrusive places (inside cupboards, on top of bookcases, and on posts of the wall which encloses the outside yard). When videotaping began, I would move to these areas, pick up the microphones, and join ongoing peer events.

During the testing period, I completed the training of my research assistant. The assistant (Jane) was a graduate student in linguistics who had prior experience in the collection and transcription of audiovisual data. A research assistant was necessary for two reasons. First, I had become a participant in the school, and it would be highly obtrusive for me to withdraw from peer activities and move behind the camera when videotaping began. Secondly, due to the audio problems it was imperative I enter certain areas with a microphone and get as close as possible to the ongoing interaction.

I spent several sessions with Jane going over my general research aims, demonstrating the operation of the camera, VTR unit, and microphone mixer, and working out a hand-signal communication system. When videotaping began, I used this system to relay instructions to Jane regarding when to begin and end recordings, and when and how long to record children's departures from interactive episodes. The system became more complex as the study progressed, and by the last month of the study Jane was excellent in her ability to anticipate my directions.

During the last week of January, Jane and I set up the equipment in the school. On the first 2 days, Jane stayed near the camera and I engaged in participant observation as usual. During the next 3 days, we did some audio and video recording for testing purposes. I was pleased with the video quality of these recordings, but it was obvious that audio was to be a persistent problem.

I also used the first week to gauge the children's initial reactions to the equipment. A few of the children posed when Jane stood behind the camera, and later asked if we got any good pictures of them. However, since the camera was stationary and Jane only occasionally stood behind it, the children soon accepted this new addition to their environment.

The children also paid little attention to microphones which were hanging above several areas of the school. They did, however, want to talk into the microphones I held during participant observation. Since background noise in the school often necessitated my using microphones in this fashion, I had to devise strategies to minimize obtrusiveness. Here again I relied on information gained earlier in the research as the basis for my strategy. When the children asked about the microphone, I did not act surprised or upset, but simply told them I wanted to hear and record what they were saying. When the children wanted to talk, I simply let them talk. When I handed them the microphone they usually laughed, sang, shouted "hello," or became shy and said nothing at all. After each child had a turn, they went back to what they were doing before they noticed the microphone.

After the break-in period, we videotaped twice a week and I continued participant observation on the other 3 days until the end of the school year. After each day's taping, I reviewed and summarized the interactive episodes which were recorded. Although I transcribed several episodes prior to the termination of data collection in May, the bulk of transcription and data analysis occurred over the summer months. I collected 27 hours of videotaped data which contained a total of 146 interactive episodes.

Estimating obtrusiveness. There are several ways that the obtrusiveness of audiovisual recording can be estimated in field research. First, researchers should be prepared both to answer and make a record of all questions participants may ask about the equipment. The frequency, range, and duration of questions are all indicators of the participants' awareness of and sensitivity to the equipment. I recorded all the children's questions about the equipment, as well as my responses shortly after they occurred. When I looked over these notes during the third month of recording in the school, I was surprised to find that the children actually asked fewer questions about the camera than I had believed. In fact, there were only 12 such questions recorded, and and only two had occurred after the third day the camera was in the school. On the whole the children showed little interest in the camera and seemed more concerned with the cameraperson, Jane. Several of the children asked if she was my sister, wife, or girl friend. I explained to the children that Jane was my friend and was in the school to help me take some pictures. Since the camera was stationary and Jane only occasionally stood behind it, the children soon accepted this new addition to their environment and went back to their everyday activities. As I noted earlier, however, the children were more concerned with the microphones, and the notes showed that they asked several questions each taping session about the audio equipment. Given the fact that the disruption regarding microphones was almost always brief and the chidren would then return to their normal activities, I felt the frequency and range of questions about the microphones was not a major problem.

Many of the children's questions and comments about the equipment contained phrases which directly linked the equipment to me (i.e., "Did your mommy buy that camera for you?" "Can I talk in your microphone, Bill?" "Bill, Jenny's got your microphone and she's gonna break it."). In a sense, the equipment may have been less obtrusive because it was introduced into the setting long after I had been accepted and it came to be defined as an extension of me.[4] When the equipment was first introduced, I was like the child who brings one of his own toys to school. On these occasions, all the other children want to examine and play with the toy rather than the school toys, simply because it is different. But when the new object is in the setting daily (like my camera), the novelty begins to wear off. One day near the end of the school year, one of the children was showing a neighborhood friend who was visiting around the school. The visitor was quite curious about the camera and asked his friend why it was in the school. The

---

[4]On one occasion when I was using a very long, directional microphone for the first time, I was quite conscious of its possible obtrusiveness. I was sitting in the sandpile and pointing the microphone in the direction of a group of children who were digging canals. After a few minutes, one of the children (Rita) stopped play and stared at me for a few seconds. I was all prepared to explain the purpose of the "big microphone" and to let her examine it when she said: "You don't look like Bill with glasses on." I was at first surprised at this statement, but then realized I was wearing my glasses. I then used glasses mainly for reading, and before this particular occasion I had never had them on in the school. In this instance, the microphone, which was a normal part of my appearance in the school, was less obtrusive than my glasses, which were not.

other child shrugged and simply responded: "Oh, that's just Bill's camera and stuff."

A second way to estimate obtrusiveness of audiovisual equipment and recording is to compare videotaped events with similar activities which have been recorded in field notes. Here, the researcher can directly address the possibility that certain behavior in the videotaped episodes may be reactions to the presence of the recording equipment. I found no disparity in the children's behavior between videotaped episodes and field notes. However, the value of this strategy is more than just a test for obtrusiveness. The strategy can lead to the identification of disparities (if they exist) which can serve as the basis for attempts to eliminate, or at least be aware of, their effects on valid interpretations of the data.

A third procedure for estimating obtrusiveness is to have participants in the research setting assess videotaped materials (cf, Cicourel, 1975, and Mehan, 1979). This strategy is, of course, greatly enhanced by the retrievability of audiovisual data. I asked the teachers (Margaret and Mary) to view segments of videotaped episodes at two points in time after audiovisual recording was underway. The first time was 1 week after the initial taping and the second was several weeks later in mid-April. The teachers' independent assessments confirmed correspondence between what they felt was typical behavior in the school and what I had captured on videotape.

Data Analysis

In the analysis process, I also moved through a series of steps or phases. The phases involved: (a) identification of consistent patterns in field notes and the development of working hypotheses, (b) organization and transcription of the videotaped data, (c) microsociolinguistic analyses of videotaped episodes and initial testing and refinement of working hypotheses, and (d) validity estimation and indefinite triangulation of theoretical interpretations of the data.[5] The various phases of analysis are exemplified in

---

[5] I should point out that the first three phases of data analysis often overlapped. In some instances, I began the transcription and microsociolinguistic analyses of segments of videotaped data in line with a certain pattern, while transcription of data in line with other patterns occurred at a later point in time. For most of the analysis, there was a movement through the four phases for each major pattern in the data.

varying degrees in Chapter 3 through 5. In these chapters, I discuss substantive issues and patterns regarding structure and process in peer culture, and present and analyze supportive data. In discussing data analysis in this chapter, I will briefly summarize and discuss each of the phases, and refer to patterns and data which are discussed in more depth in later chapters.

Phase One: Stable Patterns and Working Hypotheses

The initial phase of data analysis involved three processes: (a) the identification of consistent patterns in field notes, (b) the generation of working hypotheses, and (c) the theoretical sampling of additional field observations and videotaped episodes. Once participant observation began, I reviewed theoretical notes once a week and isolated a number of patterns regarding peer interaction and culture. Several of these patterns (i.e., children's conception and use of social knowledge, children's communicative strategies, and peer activities, values, and concerns) were stable and consistent over time and were the basis of a set of hypotheses about peer culture which are presented in Chapters 3 through 5.

Once patterns were identified, I documented their consistency, frequency, and distribution across participants and interactive settings (cf. Becker, 1958). For example, early in participant observation a review of theoretical notes led to the discovery of a relationship between the children's references to friendship and their defense of play areas in the school during peer interaction (see Chapter 4). When I examined field notes, I found references to friendship often preceded or accompanied defense of play areas. Also, this relation between friendship and defense of play areas appeared consistently over time and across participants, activities, and areas of the school.

The next step in analysis was the formation and initial testing of working hypotheses. I hypothesized that the children were primarily concerned with control over play areas and used friendship as a device to gain control and exclude others. To test the working hypothesis, I examined the structure of social contacts (who played with whom) in peer interaction as recorded in field notes and in the initial videotaped episodes. If the hypothesis was correct, I expected to find two patterns in the data: (a) peer episodes would most often be initiated and maintained by children who frequently played together, and (b) acceptance into or exclusion from ongoing episodes would most often be based on the frequency of prior contacts.

The analysis of social contacts did not support the hypothesis. First, there were very few stable core groups or cliques in the nursery school. The most typical pattern of social contacts was one where children consistently interacted with several playmates (usually from 5 to 8 of the 25 children). Second, I found no clear relation between frequency of contact and acceptance into (or exclusion from) play groups. In many instances, initial reactions to access attempts were uniformly negative regardless of interactive history (see Chapter 4).

Although the children did restrict entry of others into ongoing episodes, a further analysis of field notes and initial videotaped episodes suggested that they were more concerned with *maintaining the stability of the interaction than with the control of territory or play materials*. The data also indicated that the children were aware of the relation between group size and stability and attempted to restrict the size of play groups to two or three interactants.

Given these findings, I paid careful attention to references to friendship and the chidren's access strategies and resistance to access attempts in later participant observation. I was also careful to have all access attempts and their outcomes recorded in episodes which were videotaped.

These theoretical sampling decisions led to the collection of additional data which were important in the eventual generation of hypotheses regarding the relationship among social organizational features of the nursery school as a peer environment, stable patterns in peer relations, and the children's developing conceptions of friendship. These hypotheses are discussed at length in Chapter 4.

Phase Two: The Organization and Transcription of the Audiovisual Data

Before I could begin microsociolinguistic analysis, it was necessary to catalogue and transcribe the videotaped episodes. These operations are often seen as mechanical rather than analytic, and in some research studies they are delegated to assistants. Although the importance of data organization can vary given the goals of the research, I would argue that cataloging and transcription are important steps in data analysis. In fact, they are key operations for linking background information about the setting and participants to the audiovisual data. This linkage process, which I refer to as "framing the raw (videotape) data," is essential for insuring valid interpretations of patterns isolated in later analysis.

What I am arguing here is in line with what many sociolinguists have recently emphasized; that is, the need to go beyond individual speech acts or even sequences of discourse to include background information on the participants and settings in the analysis of social interaction (Cicourel, 1978a; Gumperz, 1977, 1978; Goffman, 1974; Labov and Fanshel, 1977). My main point, however, is that not only should such information be included in the analysis, but that methods of data organization be designed so that this information is attained and linked with audiovisual data in a consistent and valid manner. The following description of cataloging and transcription processes demonstrates the importance of the temporal linkage of different types of data and the researcher's memory and cognitive processes (cf. Cicourel, 1979) in the acquisition, summarization, and utilization of background information in data analysis.

Cataloging. In cataloging the data, I first viewed each day's recordings the evening after collection. In this process, I concentrated on one episode at a time and numbered, dated, and listed the names of all participants as well as the location, duration, and general nature of the activity (i.e., role play, block play, fine arts, etc.). I also wrote out running narratives of what transpired in each episode and added information which was relevant to understanding the meaning of ongoing activities, but which was not captured on videotape. Adding information of this type was frequently necessary, and it varied from specifying where children who left a play group went in the school to facts about past events which had a bearing on the meaning of ongoing activity. I also occasionally composed theoretical memos about features of the data which I felt overlapped with patterns isolated in field notes or summaries of prior videotaped episodes.

As it turned out, there were several unanticipated advantages associated with the cataloging process. First, since the data were precisely cataloged it made representative sampling relatively easy. It was much simpler to check on what participants and activities had been recorded, and when the activities had occurred, by inspecting the cataloged summaries than it would have been to gain the same information from reading through transcripts. In fact, the examination of cataloged summaries was the basis of decisions regarding the temporal order in which episodes were transcribed for analysis.

The most important advantage of the cataloging and summarization procedures, however, was that they improved the validity of my interpretive processes in data analysis. Since background knowledge was recorded at the time it was first perceived, it was not necessary for me either to rely totally on my own memory search or the elicitation of a similar search from informants at some point later in data analysis. The chief advantage here is that there was much less chance of selective memory. Selective memory of this type can be a problem, because, as Becker (1970) argues, data interpretation in field research depends on the construction and initial testing of "analytic models" which specify interrelations among patterns in the data. Given these analytic procedures, there is a tendency to make "things fit together." It is important, therefore, that the background information the field researcher relies on in constructing analytic models is linked to audiovisual data by procedures which minimize the probability of distortion and selective memory. It is my contention that the cataloging and summarization procedures described above are less susceptible to these validity problems than researchers' delayed memory searches or unstructured interviews with informants.

Transcription procedures. Most microanalyses of audiovisual data begin with transcription of all verbal information. In my research, the rather uneven technical quality of the audio portion of the data demanded that I personally transcribe the videotaped episodes. Although this procedure involved a major investment of time, I found that there were several advantages to the method of transcription I developed.

At first, I transcribed several of the episodes without any assistance. In this procedure, I would stop the recorder with each utterance, rewind and replay the tape when necessary, and eventually write out all the recoverable verbal information in longhand. This approach was not only tedious and time consuming, but also left me unsure about the accuracy of some parts of the transcripts. As a result, I hired an assistant, who had a background in linguistics, to help with transcription. I then developed a revised system in which the assistant operated the recorder and I wrote out the transcript. With each addition to the transcript, I asked for verification from the assistant regarding the accuracy of my understanding of what the children had said. Although the assistant found it difficult to understand the children at first, over time she not only became proficient enough to supply verification but also to detect specific transcription errors. Wherever there were alternative interpretations, we would review the sequence as many times as necessary to arrive at mutual agreement.

Transcription involves continual decision making on the part of the researcher in his or her reconstruction of the data from visual–auditory signals to a written description of interactive events. In a general sense, transcription is an interactive process between the researcher and the data. However, the data can not respond to or judge the validity of the transcriber/researcher's understanding of the interaction. In numerous cases, my assistant and I had to watch and listen to segments of the data over and over, with each of us offering various possible interpretations, until the puzzle was solved (or partially solved) and we reached agreement on a correct or highly probable transcription.

Finally, the transcription process is not only interactive, but also analytic. To arrive at a correct transcription of a sequence, it is often necessary for the researcher to make some inferences about the intentions of social actors. These inferences should be based on both knowledge of the interactive history of the individual in the setting or group under study, and background knowledge about the individual's life outside the setting, such as one's network of obligations in family, occupational, and other settings (cf. Labov and Fanshel, 1977), among other things. When such information was needed, I kept an explicit record of the linkage of such knowledge to the intentions of the actors involved in the form of analytic memos (cf. Glaser and Strauss, 1973) which were then available for consultation in later phases of data analysis and interpretation.

Transcription notational system. Recently, Ochs (1979) addressed the importance of the transcription process and notation system in research on language use in natural settings, and argued that transcripts should meet both practical and theoretical considerations. Ochs noted that a transcript should not discourage the reader from integrating verbal and nonverbal acts, but should be readable and display clearly and systematically all utterances and contextual information (Ochs, 1979:59). Ochs also discussed the advantages and disadvantages of several transcription formats previously used in sociolinguistic research, and presented a transcription system which she felt best presents sociolinguistic data involving young children. Although the transcription system I used in data collection and to display the sociolinguistic data in this book varies somewhat from the system recommended by Ochs, the system was influenced by the issues discussed in her article.

The transcription format I use throughout the book involves placing all verbal transcription on the left side of the page and a running description of nonverbal and other contextual information on the right side. To illustrate the notational system, I first present an example of transcribed data and then discuss the features of the transcription system.

Example 1.2—Spontaneous Play in the Outside Sandpile
Tape 14—Episode 3
Morning Group
Scene: Outside Sandpile
Participants: Joseph (J), Roger (R) and Concetta (C)

Transcription	*Description*
	J, R, and C have been burying objects in the sand and then digging them up. J and R are kneeling in sand while C stands nearby. This sequence begins about 5 minutes into the episode.
(193) J–R: I'll do it. I'll take this up.	J has placed a fire hat in the sand and hit down on top of it. J then lifts hat and a design (imprint) remains in the sand.
(194) J–R: A road! V-rr-o-om!	J traces around the rim of the imprint of the hat, pretending it is a road.
(195) R–J: //Let	
(196) J–R: //Wanna// do it again?	
(197) R–J: Yeah.	
(198) J–R: Ok	J now places the hat on the sand again and presses down hard.
(199) R–J: Now it's a deep road.	J lifts hat after this utterance from R. They both then look at resulting imprint.

Transcription, cont'd	*Description, cont'd*
(200) J–R: They'll go Vrr–om-pa!	J says this as he traces around the rim of the imprint with his finger.
(201) R–J: No, watch me. Watch this.	J places hat back down on the sand and taps it. R now also taps the top of the hat and then pushes down hard on the hat as he produces this utterance.
(202) J–R: Ok.	After saying "Ok," J lifts the hat from the sand.
(203) R–J: Oh—Ha!	
(204) J–R: Ha—ah—Ha! It's a fire engine hat!	Since R pushed down hard on the hat, the design of the fire hat is now clearly visible in the sand.
(205) J–R: Now let's (flat) it up.	After this utterance, both J and R pat on hat design.
(206) J–R: Flat it up. Now. No— No—That's—	Before he says "now," J pushes R's hand away to stop his patting.
(207) R–J: Oh, it looks like a cowboy hat.	After this utterance, J puts the hat back on the sand and he and R push down on it again.
(208) R–J: There.	After this utterance, J lifts the hat from the sand.
(209) R–J: Yea!	
(210) R–J: Now we have to make—cover it all up to make it bigger.	R smoothes out the design in the sand as he says this.
(211) R–J: Now. //Now	
(212) J–R: //Now// put it on.	J puts hat on the sand as he says "put it on." J then pushes very hard on the hat.
(213) R–J: Now, you're smuching it.	
(214) J–R: Kush!	J makes this sound as he removes the hat from sand.
(215) R–J: Now, now, now—Let me have it. Have it!	R reaches for the hat and J holds it out of R's grasp.
(216) J–R: Let me use it. Because I had it first.	J puts the hat on the sand as he says "use it."
(217) R–J: I <u>had</u> it first.	
(218) J–R: There.	J says this as he removes the hat from sand.

Transcription, cont'd	*Description, cont'd*
(219) J–R: Now let me get some sand in. There. (K-k-krush).	J now puts sand in the hat as he says "sand in." J then dumps sand as he says "there," and places empty hat on sand as he says "k-k-krush."

The first thing to notice in Example 1.2 is that the transcript should be read from right to left and top down, with each numbered entry as a turn at talk for the various speakers. Both the speaker and addressee are designated with the notation A–B, meaning A is addressing B. In cases where the addressee is not clear, only the speaker is identified. The transcription of utterances is not represented phonetically; rather, I employ a modified orthography which was recommended by Ochs (1979) and used in conversational analysis by Sacks, Schegloff, and Jefferson (1974). This system includes the use of items like *gonna, wanna, for'ya,* etc. I also attempted to capture sounds ("kush") and the children's invented words ("smuching") in modified orthography. Finally, regarding metatranscription markings, (   ) signified an utterance of about the designated length could not be clearly heard, and (there is) signified a tentative or probable translation.

Paralinguistic features of the children's speech were marked with specific notations on the left side of the transcript and/or specified in prose on the right side. The notations used in Example 1.2 and in transcripts throughout the book are specified below.

_____	(underlining) Marks stress, as in: "It's going to be <u>fun</u>!"
?	Marks high rise and questions, as in: "and you can too, Ok?"
!	Marks exclamatory utterance, as in: "It's a fire engine hat!"
—	Marks both self-interruptions and interruptions by others, as in: "Now, now, now—Let me have it," and "No—that's—"
//	Marks overlapping speech. When placed at the beginning and ending of overlapping speech, as in: R-J: //Now J-R: //Now// put it on.

Paralinguistic cues consistently described in the right hand column of the transcripts include: *intonation, pitch, rhythm,* and other voice qualities such as *laughing, singing, crying, whining, baby talk,* and *animal accents or voices.*

In all the transcripts which appear in the book, nonverbal information is provided in prose in the right column. I have decided to literally specify how verbal and nonverbal behavior are integrated rather than to rely on subscript notaton (see, for example, utterance 219 in Example 1.2). Nonverbal behaviors consistently referred to in the transcripts include (a) body movement and gross motor activity, (b) manipulation of physical objects, (c) eye contact, (d) facial expression, (e) gesture, and (f) body orientation. Although I consistently refer to nonverbal information in the transcriptions, I make no attempt to systematically include and analyze every occurrence of nonverbal behavior or paralinguistic cues. The general strategy is to mark the occurrence of nonverbal and the co-occurrence of verbal and nonverbal behavior which I felt was necessary to capture the nature of the activity and/or which had an apparent bearing on the interpretation of the meaning of specific sequences of interaction.

Phase Three: Microsociolinguistic Analysis and the Refinement of Working Hypotheses

I use the term "microsociolinguistic analysis" to refer to the analysis of communicative processes in face-to-face interaction. In line with Kendon (1975), I see the primary aim of microsociolinguistics to be the description and understanding of how occasions of interaction are organized and maintained. Procedures for the microanalysis of audiovisual data have been greatly advanced in the recent work of Labov and Fanshel (1977) on comprehensive discourse analysis; Gumperz (1976, 1977, 1978; also see Cook-Gumperz and Gumperz, 1976) on conversational inference; Cicourel (1974, 1978a, 1978b) on cognitive processing in social interactions; and several researchers (Erickson, 1978; Erickson and Schultz, 1982; Kendon, 1977; McDermott and Roth, 1978; Scheflen, 1973, 1974) on nonverbal elements in communicative processes. In this study, I have borrowed from several of these systems of microanalysis, but I have been influenced primarily by the work of Gumperz.

In the present research, the first step in microsociolinguistic analysis involved the identification of *contextualization cues* the children routinely used in attempts to communicate about the social activity they were engaged in achieving (see Gumperz, 1976, 1978; Cook-Gumperz and Gumperz, 1976). Contextualization cues refer to specific communicative elements (linguistic, paralinguistic, and extralinguistic) which the children employed in the interactive process. Examples of contextualization cues referred to in analyses presented in Chapter 3 through 5 include: linguistic communicative functions containing phonemic, syntactic, and semantic elements; paralinguistic features (intonation, stress, and pitch); gesture and proxemic features; and the manipulation of physical objects in the ecological setting.

The identification of contextualization cues is a methodological strategy for determining how children link linguistic information with propositional content, on the one hand, and extralinguistic cues and background expectations on the other. Cook-Gumperz and Gumperz (1976:12) have referred to this articulation of various elements of communicative events as a *process* of contextualization "in which contextual information is both coded as semantic information, and signalled as part of the interaction. The signalling of context makes the context available to the participants as a potentially shareable *cognitive construct* which frames the range of possible interpretations both in terms of the relevance of presuppositions and as guides to further action."

Following the identification of contextualization cues, the analysis moved to an examination of the children's production and use of cues across social activities and situations. In this phase, there was a search for patterns in the children's articulation of contextualization cues, with both the accustomed expectations of various social-ecological areas of the school and conventionalized expectations based on sociological or cultural knowledge.

Phase Four: Validity Estimation and Indefinite Triangulation

Even with the advantages of prior ethnography, participant observation, and videotape recording, I still found it necessary to estimate the validity of my interpretations of the data by involving others in the analysis process. Cicourel (1975) has referred to this procedure as "indefinite triangulation." Indefinite triangulation is a procedure in which the researcher creates "circumstances whereby the same and different respondents react to information obtained on a previous occasion." With indefinite triangulation "the role of attention and memory becomes paramount, as does the respondent's ability to utilize specific lexical items or vocabularies" (Cicourel, 1975:97).

The validity of my interpretations of the children's use of contextualization cues, and my conclusions regarding the more general patterns in the data, were checked by way of indefinite triangulation. I asked different respondents (research assistants, teachers, parents, and the children themselves) to offer both general interpretations and specific judgments of playbacks of videotaped sequences or entire episodes. In this procedure, the respondents' reactions were audiotaped and later compared to my own interpretations which had been recorded prior to the indefinite triangulation process. Indefinite triangulation led to the generation of background data which confirmed or disputed my interpretations of specific events. In those instances (see especially Chapter 4) where interpretations of the data varied, I refined and/or expanded my original conclusions.

Overall, indefinite triangulation is an important methodological technique for estimating the validity of interpretations of qualitative data. It is also an important tool for the initial testing and refinement of hypotheses, and is, in this sense, a vital part of theory generation in field research.

Summary

In this chapter I have described the research setting, participants, and methodological procedures upon which this study is based. My purpose has been (a) to provide the reader with a clear picture of what I did in the research and (b) to construct a "natural history" of the research process which traces key decisions in field entry, data collection, and the recognition and categorization of basic patterns in the data and their linkage to theoretical propositions and conclusions.

As Cicourel (1964) has noted, social scientists have come to place such a premium on "objectivity" that the conditions for research are explored not for theoretical and methodological potential but as vehicles for obtaining substantive results. This concern for substantive results has had two important effects. First, it "has obscured the fact that such results are only as good as the basic theory and methods used in 'finding' and interpretating them'' (Cicourel, 1964:54). Secondly, it has caused social scientists, and especially field researchers, to overlook an important source of data. As Cicourel (1964) has observed, the research setting, as well as methods for field entry and participation, serve as data which can contribute to our knowledge of methodology and theoretical properties of social structure and process.

It is my hope that the detailed description and discussion of the methods employed in this research will enable the reader to better understand and evaluate the substantive findings and interpretations presented in the subsequent chapters. I also hope the discussion provides the reader with a sense of the methodological problems encountered in this attempt to enter the child's world.

CHAPTER 2

Theoretical Issues in Research on Peer Culture

Buddy and his mother are at lunch. Buddy is still curious about blood from his cut finger the day before:

Buddy: Mom?
Mother: What?
Buddy: Chips [Potato chips] have blood on them. Do they have blood on 'em?
Mother: No, I don't believe so.
Buddy: Kids and people do.
Mother: Um-hum.
Buddy: And monsters.
Mother: Yeah.

As the above brief exchange from lunchtime talk between a mother and her 2 ½-year-old son indicates, children and adults do not always share the same view of the world. Although young children are often unaware of this difference in perspectives, they (like Buddy) are aware of differences between kids and grown-up people. A recurrent finding in my 10 years of work with pre-school children is that they are aware that they are different from adults and like other children. This awareness of "being a child" becomes even more apparent when children begin to spend time with peers. In the preschool years, children's life-worlds and social development are dramatically affected by their entrance into peer culture.

The purpose of this book is to present and develop the implications of a year long microethnography of a nursery school which reveal the importance of peer relations and culture for theories of childhood socialization. In this chapter, I will first review three general approaches to human development embodied in the work of Piaget, Vygotsky, and G. H. Mead, as well as the more recent theoretical contributions of Aaron Cicourel. Following this review, I present an emerging theoretical perspective which integrates features of these constructivist approaches with an emphasis on the importance of children's life-worlds and peer cultures.

Constructivist Approaches to Human Development

The socialization process has traditionally been viewed in one of two ways. One perspective defines socialization as children's *internalization* of adult skills and knowledge. This view is primarily behavioristic, with an emphasis on modeling (or imitation) and reinforcement as the key mechanisms in human learning and development. As a result, this approach stresses the importance of adult caretakers, whose inputs to children are seen as crucial to the developmental process. It is not surprising, then, that researchers who take this position attempt to measure and to discover consistencies and variations in adult inputs or socialization practices. From the behavioristic perspective, the child is relegated to a passive role. The socialization process is basically unilateral, with the child shaped and molded by adult caretakers.

A second perspective on socialization stresses the active role of the child. Although there are a number of variants of this position, there is a shared belief that children interpret, organize, and use information from the environment and in the process *acquire* or *construct* adult skills and knowledge. This perspective has been termed both *interactionist* (because children acquire skills and knowledge in interaction with others) and *constructivist* (because children actively construct their social worlds).

It should be pointed out that the constructivist approach is not in direct opposition to behavioristic theories, as is often believed. Constructivists do not deny that children imitate adults (and other children), or that reinforcement is a factor in socialization. Constructivists do, however, believe that these mechanisms cannot, in and of themselves, account for the complexity of the socialization process. Adult models and reinforcement are important inputs to children. However, constructivists believe that there are numerous other informational inputs as well, and that information *is always interpreted, organized, and acted upon from the child's point of view.* For constructivists, children's perspectives are continually changing and are related both to the child's level of cognitive development and to stable features of the child's life-world.

Piaget and Cognitive Developmental Theory

There have been a number of detailed reviews and evaluations of Piaget and cognitive-developmental theory (see, for example, Brown, 1965; Flavell, 1963; Furth, 1969; Gardner, 1981; Ginsburg and Opper, 1979; Kholberg, 1969; Youniss, 1980). I will not attempt an in-depth review in this context. My purpose here is to consider two central features in Piaget's theory and discuss the importance of these features, as well as some of the recent work of cognitive developmental theorists for theory generation in the area of childhood socialization.

As Gardner (1981) has suggested, Piaget is perhaps most renowned for his view that cognitive development unfolds in a series of steps or stages. For Piaget, intellectual development is not the quantitative accumulation of facts or skills, but is best seen as the child's progression through a series of qualitatively distinct levels of cognitive ability. Piaget's conception is important for theories of childhood socialization because he argues that children should not be viewed as immature or incomplete when compared to adults. In the Piagetian perspective, children perceive and organize their worlds in ways qualitatively different from adults. Therefore, any theory of childhood socialization must consider the child's level of cognitive development in attempts to explain children's understanding and use of information from the adult world, and children's participation in and organization of their own peer worlds. To discount Piaget's notion of levels of cognitive development, as some interactionists advise (cf. Denzin, 1977a), can lead to interpretations of children's worlds which distort the actual conceptual abilities of young children.

Probably the most important element in Piaget's theory of cognitive development is his conception of equilibrium or equilibration. As Piaget (1968) himself has noted, the concept of equilibrium has frequently been employed in both the physical and social sciences. However, unlike many sociological and psychological theorists who use the concept of equilibrium to predict behavioral or attitudinal change (i.e., an occurrence which creates disequilibrium will be followed by attempts on the part of the individual to regain balance), Piaget is more concerned with the *process of equilibration*. For Piaget, equilibrium is not conceived as a balance of forces in a state of rest, but is seen rather "as the compensation resulting from the activities of the subject in response to external intrusions" (Piaget, 1968:101). In Piaget's model, external intrusions are compensated only by *activities,* and the "maximum equilibrium will not involve a state of rest but rather a maximum of activity on the part of the subject which will compensate both for the actual intrusion and for virtual intrusions" (1968:101). Along these lines, Piaget developed a probabilistic model of equilibration where the child's activities in response to an external intrusion can be seen as strategies with increasing probability of occurrence (1968:12).

Although I can not address the complexity of Piaget's probabilistic notion of equilibrium in this context, it should be clear that equilibrium is the central force which propels children through the stages of cognitive development. However, Piaget's conception of equilibrium should not be seen simply as a form of biological determinism. Although equilibrium is seen as a tendency to compensate for environmental intrusions, the nature of compensations are dependent on the *activities* of children in their social-ecological environments. The form the child's activities take is a reflection of (a) characteristics of the source of the intrusion, (b) the cognitive developmental level of the child, and (c) specific features of the child's life-world in which the intrusion and the child's compensation are imbedded.

Throughout his work, Piaget focused primarily on the second of these factors, at time addressing the sources of intrusion, and rarely identifying specific features of children's life-worlds. In his work with infants, Piaget carried out careful, detailed, naturalistic observations of a small sample of children (see, for example, Piaget, 1952). In these observations, Piaget described both sources of external intrusions and patterns in the infants activities to compensate for disequilibrium. From these observations, Piaget addressed his main concern: the identification of the nature of child's cognitive abilities during the infancy period. It should be noted, however, that Piaget focused almost entirely on physical intrusions. For example, there were few references to the role of social factors, including the everyday activities of caretakers for children's cognitive development.

In his research with children who had moved beyond the infancy or sensory-motor stage, Piaget relied less on naturalistic observations and more on the clinical method. In using this method, Piaget would often create external intrusions and both observe and question children regarding their attempts to compensate for the intrusions. The clinical method has definite advantages over naturalistic observation for identifying specific features of children's perspectives and stages of cognitive development. The method is, however, less useful than naturalistic observation for identifying the concrete experiences which bring about disequilibrium, and for specifying how these experiences and the resulting equilibrations are embedded in children's everyday life-worlds.

Recently there have been a number of attempts to extent Piagetian theory to consider the development of social cognition. Most of this research involves attempts to identify levels of development of social concepts (e.g., friendship, distributive justice, social conventions, etc.) by primarily relying on variants of Piaget's clinical interviewing method. In the case of researchers like Selman (1976, 1981) and Damon (1977), the clinical method is seen as appropriate because they share the assumptions that physical, logical, and social concepts are interrelated and that logical and physical concepts as outlined by Piaget (1950) are the basis on which children develop social concepts.

Turiel (1978a, b) takes a different position and argues that logical, physical, and social concepts are not necessarily interrelated. According to Turiel, "thought is organized (and changes sequentially) within a domain and not necessarily across domains" (1978b:4). Given this position, Turiel argues that the fundamental task of theorists of social development is to identify both the different domains of social knowledge and the levels of conceptual development within domains. In addressing these ends, Turiel has relied on both clinical interviews (1978a) and naturalistic observations coupled with the questioning of children about specific events (see Nucci and Turiel, 1978). Turiel's work is particularly relevant to theories of childhood socialization because he argues that the effects of specific experiences (i.e., intrusions, disequilibriums, and compensations) in one conceptual domain may have minimal effects in other domains. Turiel's position is an important extension of Piagetian theory in that he accepts the basic notion of stages of cognitive development and equilibrium, but argues that there is a need to look more closely at the nature and type of environmental intrusions and their effects on the development of social concepts.

Another recent extension of Piagetian theory can be seen in the work of Youniss (1975, 1978, 1980). Youniss (1980) presents a synthesis of the views of Piaget and Harry Stack Sullivan in which he argues that social development occurs as the result of children's interpersonal interactions in two distinct social worlds. In parent–child relations, interdependency is established within a system of complementary exchange where children trade conformity for adult approval. According to Youniss, the parents' pervasive role as evaluator in interaction with children "gives rise to children's belief that parents must know society well," and "in adopting their parents' views, children believe that they have entered this privileged view themselves" (Youniss, 1980:274). Although resulting in a somewhat limited view of the social world, children's relations with parents and other adults provide "a sense of an ordered social reality and launch [children] along a relational path" (Youniss, 1980:20).

It is, argues Youniss, children's entry into peer relations which gives development an innovative direction. Peer relations are, according to Youniss, best characterized as involving the cooperative use of direct reciprocity. When interacting with peers, children's "particular behaviors are no longer predetermined as right or wrong or better or worse. Behavior can be tested and submitted to mutual definition." Finally, "unlike the system which children believe adults already know, the one created by collaborating peers has no definite endpoint. It is open to redefinition through a democratic process founded in methods of reciprocity" (Youniss, 1980:19).

Youniss' work is an important extension of Piagetian theory in that he suggested that the child's activities in response to disequilibrium most often involve social interaction with others. According to Youniss, the child's construction and conceptualization of the social world is not a private event. Instead, conceptualization is seen as a social event involving an exchange of actions. This exchange involves the contribution of the child and another person, with the other representing "the socializing influence which enters the child's own conception" (Youniss, 1980:278).

Youniss' view of peer relations is directly relevant to the analyses of peer culture presented in this book. Youniss' research, however, was with older children (preadolescents and adolescents) and he relied on clinical interviews rather than naturalistic observations. As I discuss at some length later, preschool children's peer activities are best characterized as involving communal rather than reciprocal action, and can be seen as an intermediate point between adult–child relations and the peer relations of older children described by Youniss. Regarding methodology, Youniss' reliance on clinical interviewing does lead to interesting findings regarding the identification of children's conceptions of various types of social knowledge. However, the clinical method can not directly uncover the *interactive processes* from which these concepts emerge. Although interesting and useful for identifying levels of conceptualization, children's accounts or story telling in response to hypothetical questions or dilemmas cannot fully reflect features of peer culture in which interactive events are embedded in children's everyday life-worlds.

Vygotsky and Soviet Views of Human Development

Vygotsky is the main contributor to the Soviet view of socialization and human development. Although Vygotsky did not present a detailed and well-integrated theory of development in his work (as compared to Piaget), he has offered a number of important concepts. Since Vygotsky died at an early age, it is difficult to predict what may have emerged if there had been time for him to integrate many of his wide-ranging theoretical concepts and ideas. Vygotsky is most widely known in the West for his book *Thought and Language*. However, the recently translated *Mind in Society* is probably the best collection of Vygotsky's views.

In the introduction to *Mind in Society,* Michael Cole and Sylvia Scribner (1978) argue that Vygotsky, unlike many Soviet scholars, was not merely attempting to make his theory conform to the standard Marxist line. According to Cole and Scribner, Vygotsky clearly viewed Marxist theory as a valuable resource from early in his career. The Marxist influence can be seen in a number of aspects in Vygotsky's work. However, there seem to be three important principles which predominate.

First is the notion of dialectical change. Vygotsky's view of social psychological phenomena, and his research methods, share an emphasis on process and change. Vygotsky believed that it was "the scientist's task to reconstruct the origin and course of development of behavior and consciousness" (Cole and Scribner, 1978:7). Further, Vygotsky believed that the key motivating factor for development and change is conflict and problem-solving.

The influence of the Marxist notion of historical materialism is best seen in Vygotsky's views regarding the relation between practical activity and human development. From Vygotsky's perspective, changes in society, especially changes in societal demands on the individual, require changes in strategies for dealing or coping with these demands. These coping strategies can be seen as practical actions which lead to both social and psychological development. For Vygotsky, the emphasis is on both changes in societal demands and the practical activities which result. Practical activity in this sense leads to the acquisition of new skills and knowledge which can be seen as transformations of previous skills and knowledge.

A third Marxist principle which plays a central role in Vygotsky's views involves the individual's internalization or appropriation of human society and culture. Vygotsky argues that sign systems and language, like tool systems (i.e., material objects), are created by societies over the course of history and change with cultural development. The acquisition of language by children enables the child, through interaction with others, to appropriate cultural elements of society. This appropriation brings about "behavioral transformations and forms the bridge between early and later forms of individual development." Thus for Vygotsky, in the tradition of Marx and Engels, "the mechanism of individual development is rooted in society and culture" (Cole and Scribner, 1978:7).

Vygotsky's notion of internalization, which he defines as "the internal reconstruction of an external operation" (1978:56), has received a great deal of attention in recent work on human development and education (see Hood, McDermott, and Cole, 1980; Hood, Fiess, and Aron, 1982). According to Vygotsky, "every function in the child's development appears twice: first on the social level, and later on the individual level; first, *between* people *(interpsychological)*, and then *inside* the child *(intrapsychological)*" (1978:57, emphases as in original). For Vygotsky, the transformation of interpersonal processes to intrapersonal processes occurs gradually over an extended period of time. During this period, "the process being transformed continues to exist and to change as an external form of activity—before definitely turning inward" (1978:57). Finally, Vygotsky argues that some functions may not be internalized and, therefore, remain forever at the external level.

Before pursuing Vygotsky's notion of internalization and its role in his conception of children's play which is most relevant to the purposes of this book, it is necessary to compare briefly the theoretical views of Vygotsky and Piaget. Both theorists view development as resulting from the child's activities on the environment. However, Vygotsky makes no nativistic assumption similar to Piaget's notion of equilibrium to account for the motivating factor which generates the child's activities. Vygotsky sees "practical" activities developing from the child's attempts to deal with everyday problems or difficulties. In dealing with these problems, the child develops strategies in cooperation with others. While Vygotsky stresses the social nature of human development, Piaget sees the child moving toward equilibrium primarily as the result of individual activity (both overt and mental). For Piaget, human development is primarily individualistic, while for Vygotsky it is primarily collective.

Other differences between the two theorists are primarily ones of emphasis. Piaget tends to concentrate more on the nature and characteristics of cognitive (or higher-order) processes and structures, while Vygotsky emphasizes their developmental contexts and history. As a result, Vygotsky is less interested in identifying abstract levels or stages of cognitive structures and more interested in specifying the social *events* which lead to practical activities and the internalization and transformation of these activities over time.

This emphasis on the practical activities of children in everyday social events is most evident in Vygotsky's work on language and thought, and in his views regarding the importance of play in human development. Vygotsky's conceptualization of language and thought have received a great deal of attention in psychology (see, for example, Kholberg, Yeager, & Hjertholm, 1968). It is Vygotsky's views on play and development which are most relevant for the purpose of this review and the analyses of peer play and culture presented in later chapters of the book.

According to Vygotsky, the very young child tends to gratify his or her desires immediately, but at the preschool age a number of unrealizable tendencies and desires emerge. Therefore, preschool children face an important tension. They encounter a large number of desires which cannot be immediately gratified or forgotten and they retain the tendency for immediate fulfillment of desires from the infancy period. "To resolve this tension," argues Vygotsky, "the preschool child enters an imaginary, illusory world in which the unrealizable desires can be realized, and this world is what we call play" (1978:93).

For Vygotsky all play is imaginative and all imaginative play involves the use of rules. However, the rules of imaginative play are not formulated in advance, but rather stem from the imaginative situation. That is, the very organization and coordination of imaginary play events lead children to abide by close approximations of real life rules (e.g., what mothers, sisters and babies are to do and not to do in relation to each other; see Chapter 3) and to invent new rules which define the proper behavior of imaginary characters and objects (e.g., what monsters and threatened victims are to do in relation to each other; see Chapter 5).

Vygotsky's emphasis on the underlying rules of children's play is the basis of his position regarding the positive effects of play for development. For Vygotsky, imaginative play liberates the child from situational constraints because, in play, objects and situations lose their determining force. In play, argues Vygotsky, "the child sees one thing but acts differently in relation to what he sees. Thus, a condition is reached in which the child begins to act independently of what he sees" (1978:97). For Vygotsky, imaginative play is a transitional stage between the purely situational constraints of infancy and adult thought, which can be totally separated from real events. For example, when a child pretends that a wooden stick is a horse, the stick, according to Vygotsky, serves as a "pivot for detaching the meaning of 'horse' from a real horse" (1978:98). The preschool child cannot detach a meaning or word from an object except by finding such pivots. But by *acting* with such pivots in play—acting with the stick as though it were a horse—the child begins to separate meaning from objects. But, argues Vygotsky, the child is not aware of the significance of his or her actions because "in play a child spontaneously makes use of his ability to separate meaning from an object without knowing he is doing it" (1978:99). For Vygotsky, this is one of the paradoxes of play in that in play children take the line of least resistance (by doing things they like to do) while simultaneously following the line of greatest resistance (by adhering to the rules of play).

Although Vygotsky stresses the importance of play in development, he does not see play as a prototype of children's everyday activities. In fact, Vygotsky argues that play "is not the predominate feature of childhood but it is a leading factor in development" (1978:101). For Vygotsky, play is the child's way of dealing with and more firmly grasping the meanings of real life situations and problems. Although children's play involves the construction of imaginative situations, it is often based on real life events. In this sense, Vygotsky has referred to play as memory in action rather than as a novel imaginary situation.

But we should not see play as the mere imitation of real life events. For in play "a child," argues Vygotsky, "always behaves above his average age, above his daily behavior; in play it is as though he were a head taller than himself" (1978:102). In play, children go beyond recollection and imitation of events from their everyday lives to the recognition and use of implicit rules of social organization and action. In this way, preschool children make important strides toward the development of abstract thought.

Vygotsky's views of children's play and social development have had an important influence on the theoretical model I present below and the analyses of peer play and culture in Chapter 3 through 5. Like Vygotsky, I see social development as resulting from children's everyday practical activities in their life worlds. Although peer play is an important part of children's worlds, it should not be seen as the "predominate feature of childhood" (Vygotsky, 1978:101). Children's worlds involve consistent and sustained interaction with adults (especially parents), and children are also continually exposed to the adult world by the media (especially television). However, also in line with Vygotsky, I see peer play as essential for children's acquisition of social knowledge and interactive skills. The theoretical perspective I present below does, however, extend Vygotsky's views in that I see play as something preschool children do together. Play in this sense is a *shared feature of peer culture*. Therefore, to understand the importance of peer play we must enter and achieve an understanding of peer culture. From this interpretive perspective, I have discovered that play is not simply a reproduction of the adult world, it is rather a *reproduction within peer culture*. In this process of reproduction, children come to more firmly grasp, refine, and extend features of the adult world in the creation of their own peer world.

The Views of Mead and Cicourel

The social philosophy of G. H. Mead has had a profound influence on sociological approaches to social psychology in the U.S. Symbolic interactionist theory, which had its origins in Mead's (1934) pragmatic philosophy, has been the basic perspective underlying many theoretical developments in the areas of deviance and mental illness, adult socialization, and collective behavior. Given Mead's influence and his interest in children and their development of self-consciousness, it is surprising that there has been so little research in American sociology in the area of childhood socialization.

There have, however, been two recent attempts (Cicourel, 1974, and Denzin, 1977a) to address the theoretical neglect of childhood socialization in sociology. Denzin (1977a) presents a detailed examination of children's language, socialization experiences, and development of self-conceptions from the symbolic interactionist perspective. I will not attempt to duplicate Denzin's analysis here, but rather focus on those aspects of Mead's views of the development of self which are most directly related to my concerns in this review. Cicourel's (1974) work, on the other hand, can be seen as an extension of Mead and symbolic interactionist theory, and his views have had a major influence on the theoretical model I present below. I will begin, then, with a consideration of Mead's views regarding the genesis of self and then go on to consider Cicourel's more recent work on children's acquisition of a sense of social structure.

Mead's Views of the Genesis of Self

For Mead, the self has a central characteristic ''that it is an object to itself, and that characteristic distinguishes it from other objects and from the body'' (1934:137). According to Mead, the individual experiences himself indirectly from the standpoints and responses of other members of the same social group. In this sense, the individual acquires a sense of self ''not directly or immediately, not by becoming a subject to himself, but only in so far as he first becomes an object to himself just as other individuals are objects to him or in his experience; and he becomes an object to himself only by taking the attitudes of other individuals toward himself within a social environment or conetxt of experience and behavior in which both he and they are involved'' (Mead, 1934:138).

It is not surprising, then, that Mead sees the genesis of self-consciousness as beginning with the child's initial attempts to step outside him or herself by imitating others, and reaching completion when the child, through participation in games with rules, develops the ability to take on or assume the organized social attitudes of the group to which he belongs. However, a careful examination of Mead's stages in the genesis of self reveal that the child is acquiring more than a sense of self. In both Mead's play and game stage, children are acquiring (or in Vygotsky's terms ''appropriating'') conceptions of social structure and organization, and, I will argue, are developing a collective or group identity which is maintained throughout childhood.

Although there is some debate about Mead's views of imitation (i.e., incipient role-taking) as composing an initial stage in self-development, it is clear that Mead was most concerned with the child's movement from the play to the game stage. In the play stage, the child (sometimes without tangible others, but in the nursery school, most often, with peers) assumes different roles. In these activities, the child goes beyond mere imitation in that the roles assumed act as a set of stimuli to which the child and his playmates respond. As Mead argues, the children's responses organize the emergent activities.

For example, a child may take the role of mother and tell her baby ''to go to bed'' (see, Chapter 3, Example 3.1). This role-taking calls out a response from a playmate, who, taking the baby's role, resists the mother and crawls away from the crib. This response in turn calls out a new response from the mother, who blocks the baby's path, steers him back into the crib, and covers him with a blanket. The baby then responds by kicking off the blanket which the mother replaces, trying to soothe the baby by rocking the crib and humming a lullaby.

The importance of role play of this type—which is common among preschool children—is that in such play the child produces ''a set of stimuli which call out in himself the sort of response they call out in others.'' In play, the child takes ''this group of responses and organizes them into a certain whole" (Mead, 1934:151).

We see, then, that children are not merely imitating the specific acts of mothers and babies, but rather are responding to and organizing these activities into interactive events. In so doing, the child not only takes the role of another but also responds to the reactions of others to his behavior. The child begins to understand that mothers (or fathers, or babies, or firefighters) do not simply do certain things, but that they *do certain things with others.* The child is adopting the role as it is embedded in an organized social structure. However, the child's firm grasp of this social structure and his or her place in it is, as Mead argues, dependent on his or her participation in organized games with shared rules.

However, before turning to a discussion of the game stage, I wish to consider an additional element of peer play that is important but often overlooked in studies of child development. In role play with peers, children are *jointly producing socially ordered events.* Many of these play events or routines involve people, objects, and ideas of which children lack a firm cognitive grasp. It may be for this reason that Mead compared the role of children to the myths and rituals of primitive people. According to Mead, the rituals of primitive people belong, not to the activities of their daily lives where they have definite self-consciousness, but rather to their attitudes toward forces of nature upon which they as a people depend. "In their attitude toward this nature which is vague or uncertain," Mead argues, there is a more primitive response "which finds its expression in taking the role of the other, playing at the expression of their gods and their heroes, going through certain rites which are the representation of what these individuals are supposed to be doing" (Mead, 1934:153).[1]

For Mead, these rituals are similar to the situation where young children "play at being a parent, at being a teacher—vague personalities that are about them and on which they depend. These are personalities which they take, roles they play, and in so for control the development of their own personality. This outcome is just what the kindergarten works toward. It takes the characters of these various vague beings and gets them into such an organized

---

[1] One could, of course, argue that many of the religious rituals and other festivals of people from modern, industrial societies are quite similar to those of primitive people.

social relationship to each other that they build up the character of the little child'' (Mead, 1934:153).

In making this comparison, Mead is not implying that the play attitude of primitive people in myths and rituals is the same as that of young children, since adult participants are aware of the interpretive nature of their rituals in advance of their performance. However, the comparison is an important one because it draws attention to the ritual and communal nature of children's activities in the play stage. Although preschool children seldom initiate dramatic role play or other peer play routines (see Chapter 5) with definite plans of action or preconceived interpretive schemes, *plans and interpretive themes are jointly produced and shared during the course of play*. In this sense, peer play among preschool children does not involve individual self-consciousness, but I argue in an extension of Mead's view that peer play does involve the children's development and use of a group or collective identity. During the course of peer play, children, like adults in the production of ritual events, experience a sense of communal sharing and group identity.[2]

For adult members of primitive societies, participation in rituals was a way of collectively dealing with forces of nature of which they had only a limited understanding but which had important effects on their daily lives. For young children, paticipation in peer play is often an attempt to make sense of and deal with the adult world. But, in both cases, the activities are communally produced and lead to the development of a collective identity. For children, this collective identity can be seen as the shared recognition of their membership in a peer culture.

Although preschool children develop a firmer grasp of social knowledge and acquire a group or collective identity in peer play, they have still not developed full self-consciousness. For Mead, full self-consciousness results, not from communal sharing, but from cooperative interdependence among individuals to reach a common goal. Young children's first experiences of this type result

---

[2] This notion of children's movement from group identities to individual identities within a group or society is also apparent in the recent theoretical work of Habermas on childhood socialization. According to Habermas, ''Identity is produced through *socialization,* that is, through the fact that the growing child first of all integrates itself into a specific social system by appropriate symbolic generalities; it is later secured and developed through *individuation* that is, precisely through a growing independence in relation to social systems'' (1979:74).

from their participation in games with rules. Games differ from play and ritual in that there is a definite end to be obtained. As Mead points out, the actions of individual participants in a game "are interrelated in a unitary, organic fashion" (1934:159). To participate competently in a game, the child must "have the attitude of all others involved in the game" (Mead, 1934:154). That is, he or she must take the general attitude of all the participants which is embodied in the rules of the game. Mead has referred to this process of simultaneously taking the role of all participants in the game as taking the role of the generalized other. Mead defines the generalized other as the common set of standpoints or attitudes of the group or community as a whole.

According to Mead, self-consciousness reaches its completion in the game stage. For Mead, "the self reaches its full development by organizing [the] individual attitudes of others into organized social or group attitudes, and by thus becoming an individual reflection of the general systematic pattern of social or group behavior in which it and others are all involved" (1934:158).

On the surface, it may appear that the notion of collective identity (which I have claimed emerges in peer play) is similar to Mead's generalized other. This is not the case. In peer play, children come to develop an initial sense of social structure in which they come to see themselves as "children" and as distinct from adults. They come to develop a collective identity with an emphasis on what they as children *share in common*. But they have yet to develop a distinct individual identity or self. In peer play, the preschool child has a rudimentary sense of society as composed of two groups (adults and children), but he or she does not have a full awareness of being an *individual in society*.

When children begin to participate in games with rules, they not only develop a generalized other, they also develop an awareness of how their individual actions, attitudes, and desires are in line with or differ from the general attitudes of the group. In play, there is a stress on communal sharing and doing things together; in games, there is a stress on cooperative interdependence and competition. In the play stage, the group is the self; in the game stage, the self is part of a group.

The Child's Acquisition of Social Structure

The recent work of Aaron Cicourel (1974, 1978a, 1978b, 1980, 1981) is important not only for childhood socialization but also for sociological theory in general. Cicourel has presented an approach to social action or discourse which integrates major theoretical developments in cognitive psychology, anthropology, and linguistics (see Corsaro, 1981a, for a detailed discussion of Cicourel's interactive model of discourse). This interdisciplinary emphasis is also apparent in Cicourel's work on socialization Cicourel argues that "recent work inlinguistics, language socialization, and research on the properties of everyday practical reasoning suggest radical changes in conventional sociological conceptions of norms, socialization and the acquisition of rules by children" (1974:12).

Cicourel is critical of traditional views of socialization in sociology which emphasize children's internalization of norms, roles, and values. Cicourel argues that the notion of internalization is not well developed and is often glossed by casual references to the importance of language and social interaction (see, for example, Clausen, 1968; Ritchie and Koller, 1964). Cicourel maintains that sociologists have traditionally "endowed their model of the actor with the ability to assign meanings, but only after assuming that attitudes and norms provide automatic guides to role-taking. The internalization of norms is assumed to lead to an automatic application of rules on appropriate occasions" (1974:75). But, as Cicourel points out, the traditional approach does not specify how actors recognize appropriateness, nor the interpretive procedures social actors use to link general rules to specific situations. Finally, there is a failure in traditional approaches to consider the developmental history of these interpretive abilities.

In addressing the deficiencies of traditional sociological approaches to social action and socialization, Cicourel has offered several properties of interpretive procedures which are primarily drawn from the phenomenological view of Schutz (1953, 1955) and Garfinkel (1967). I will not attempt a detailed review of the properties of interpretive procedures in this context (see Cicourel, 1974:33–38, 52–56), but rather briefly consider the general nature of interpretive procedures, how they are acquired by young children, and their importance in the peer culture of preschool children.

For Cicourel, interpretive procedures "are invariant properties of everyday practical reasoning necessary for assigning sense to the substantive rules sociologists usually call norms" (1974:52). According to Cicourel, norms (or "surface rules") "carry an open structure or horizon vis-à-vis some boundable collection of meanings until they are linked to particular cases by interpretive procedures" (1974:52). Some of the properties of interpretive procedures discussed by Cicourel include notions first developed by Schutz and Garfinkel: the reciprocity of perspectives, the et cetera assumption, and the retrospective-prospective sense of occurrence (see Cicourel, 1974:52–56). When discussing properties of interpretive procedures, Cicourel also borrows from work in linguistics and sociolinguistics. For example, when discussing the notion of "talk as reflexive," Cicourel extends the work of Garfinkel, who has argued that the mere presence or absence of talk in interaction is meaningful, to introduce the ideas of Gumperz (1982) and others who have argued that the way speech is produced (e.g., intonation, prosody, stress patterns, etc.) is as important in communication as the substantive content of utterances.

In more recent work, Cicourel (1978, 1980, 1981) has presented an interactive model of discourse. Cicourel argues that both top-down and bottom-up models of discourse, which rely primarily on references to *autonomous* syntactic, turntaking, or macro-level rules, "must be understood as aspects of a general processing system that reflects on and interacts with information from a local communicative context" (1978:26). In generating an interactive model to account for how participants use several types of logical reasoning, and for their ability to articulate multiple levels of information, Cicourel builds on Pierce's (1957) classical notion of abduction. Cicourel argues that for Peirce abduction "seems to be an inferential step that occurs in first stating and then reflecting on a hypothesis that would choose among several possible explanations of some set of facts" (1978:28). Applying this notion to discourse, Cicourel maintains that the particular circumstances that exist during discourse provide for "the recognition or creation of facts that contextualize the inferential step of making guesses about what is happening" in the social exchange. From this perspective, the analysis of discourse must include references to autonomous rules, recognition of local features of the interactive setting, and properties of the logical reasoning and cognitive strategies participants employ to link formal rules and higher order predicates or knowledge to specific features of ongoing interative events.

Cicourel's notion of interpretive procedures, and his interactive model of discourse, have important implications for childhood socialization. However, in line with the developmental perspective of Piaget, Vygotsky,and Mead, Cicourel argues that models of adult knowledge and interactive competence should not be imposed upon the child. In the process of acquiring adult interactive competence and social knowledge, children actively move through stages of child grammars, interpretive procedures, and assumptions of the social world. Cicourel suggests that the best source of data for understanding the socialization process is the child's everyday social interactions with adults and peers. Recently, there have been a number of important studies of interaction between preschool children and adults in natural settings. However, the study of peer interaction among preschool children in natural settings and, most especially, the importance of peer culture in children's worlds, have been relatively unexplored.

Regarding adult–child interaction, there have been a number of studies of adult communicative styles with young children. These studies demonstrate how adult speech and interactive styles expose children to basic characteristics of social action and language (see Bruner, 1975; Ervin-Tripp and Miller, 1977; Gelman and Shatz, 1977; Newport, Gleitman, and Gleitman, 1977; Shatz, 1981; Snow, 1972). Other work (Cicourel, 1978b; Corsaro, 1977, 1979b) focuses directly on how adults routinely expose children to the normative order.

Adult–child interaction not only facilitates children's acquisition of language and interpretive skills, it is also important for the child's acquisition of a sense of social structure. As Mead maintained, the development of self-consciousness involves children's differentiation of themselves from other objects in their social world. This process of differentiation often results from adults' attempts to expose children to membership categories (see Sacks, 1972). In work on adult–child interaction, Cicourel found that adults and older children made continuous attempts "to elicit utterances from younger children that express and confirm the developmental acquisition of knowledge associated with membership in some groups and the transition to adult status in the larger society" (1978:274). These findings led Cicourel to conclude "that the attribution of membership in social groups and the differential ranking that can be achieved by or assigned to children is in large part revealed by performance in interactional settings" (1978:274).

Many of these performances involve young children's participation in typical adult–child play and games (see Bruner, 1975;

Bruner and Sherwood, 1976; Ratner and Bruner, 1978) and adult responses to the frequent "why" questions of young children. A good example of adult descriptions of the "why" of everyday life can be seen in the short exchange between Buddy and his mother which serves as an introduction to this chapter. This exchange is part of a longer sequence which went beyond the "why" question about blood to a consideration of the distinction between animate and inanimate objects and between real and pretend features of the child's social world (see Corsaro, 1979b).

Thus, adult–child interaction continually involves categorization, and two of the earliest social categories grasped by young children are those of "adult" and "child." Through interaction with adults, preschool children come to realize that they (as "kids") differ from adults in terms of size, power, and responsibility. Much more work needs to be done in the area of adult–child interaction. But as the sequence between Buddy and his mother indicates, the distinction between "kids" and "grown up people" arises early in life and is an important feature in children's acquisition of social structure.

Although adult–child interaction is of central importance for childhood socialization, the main contention of this book is that preschool children also acquire and use interactive and interpretive abilities and social knowledge in intraction with peers. Cicourel shares this belief. He argues that "although initial interpretive procedures do not permit the child to comprehend adult humour, *double entendres,* antinomies, and the like, but [they] do generate esoteric childhood social structures in which it is possible to fear stuffed animals on display in a museum, be whisked away by witches at night, and believe in the existence of Batman and Robin" (1974:50).

In Chapters 3 through 5, I present numerous examples which demonstrate "that the child's sense of social structure (his interpretive abilities and surface rule competence) generates childhood conceptions of social organization" (Cicourel, 1974:50). For example, in Chapter 5 I describe children's approach–avoidance routines, and I argue that such play is a stable feature of peer culture in the nursery school. In approach–avoidance play, children often spontaneously label or define other children as monsters, wild animals, or other threatening agents who are then approached and avoided. Since these play routines develop spontaneously with little or no verbal negotiation, the children must rely on their interpretive abilities to link specific signals or cues (voice intonation, facial expression, avoidance behavior, etc.) to shared knowledge about monsters, mad scientists, etc., to participate competently in the routine.

In one enactment of an approach–avoidance routine described in detail in Chapter 5, several boys (Denny, Jack, Joseph, and Martin) were playing in the upstairs playhouse. The boys had been wrestling and laughing on the bed. Suddenly Joseph pointed at Martin and yelled: "Watch out for the monster!" Denny and Jack responded: "Oh, yeah, watch out!" Then the three boys ran downstairs, pretending to flee from Martin.

Martin was, at first, a bit bewildered by what was happening. He moved to the stairway to see where the others had gone, and, then, not seeing them, returned near the bed and looked down into the school. Meanwhile, the other boys huddled together in the downstairs playhouse and pretended to be afraid. Denny suggested: "Jack, go see where the monster is." Jack carefully moved out of the playhouse, looked up, saw Martin, and then ran back inside screeching loudly. Martin now began moving down the stairs and eventually reached the bottom, turned, and saw the other boys in the playhouse. The three boys screamed and ran back upstairs, and as they passed Martin, Joseph yelled: "You can't get us, monster!"

At this point, Martin began walking mechanially (somewhat like a "mummy") and followed the other boys back upstairs. The approach–avoidance routine was then recycled several times, with Denny becoming the monster later in the episode.

We see in this example that the children were relying on interpretive procedures and childhood beliefs to generate a shared behavioral routine. In this interactive event, the child first designated as the monster (Martin) had to employ his developing abductive reasoning abilities to link the behavioral displays of his playmates with shared knowledge of childhood culture to produce and share in the performance of this routine. This interpretation is in line with Cicourel's contention that "the child is able to link immediate experiences to learned sociocultural rules systems, while simultaneously providing for a creative activity that is tied to the perception of an unfolding scene with problematic features. The child can thus imagine and believe in activities or objects for which no clear normative adult categories exist" (1978:276).

The importance of preschool children's participation in peer culture for their acquisition of interpretive procedures is developed at length in later chapters. Here I should point out that, in line with Cicourel, although preschool children can produce socially ordered events in peer interaction, we cannot assume that they are able to summarize reflexively the significance of these productions upon questioning from adults. This distinction between the ability to produce and share in social events in real time, and to reflect upon and summarize these same events in the abstract, is important for theory and method in the study of childhood socialization. It is a point I will develop in some detail in the next section, where I present an interpretive theory of childhood socialization.

The Production of Social Order in Children's Life Worlds: An Interpretive Approach to Childhood Socialization[3]

I began this chapter by contrasting behavioristic and constructivist approaches to socialization. I argued that the constructivist approach is best suited to deal with the complexities of human development, and I went on to discuss the importance of several well-known constructivist theories (Piaget, Vygotsky, Mead, and Cicourel) for the study of peer culture. In this last section, I present an emerging theoretical perspective that, although in line with constructivist theory, extends the constructivist view in important respects.

Constructivist approaches to socialization emphasize the importance of the child's *activities* on the environment. This emphasis can be seen in Piaget's stress on activity to compensate for disequilibriums, Vygotsky's emphasis on children's practical activities, and the importance Mead places on children's abilities to take the role of the other. The emphasis on the child's activity in constructivist theory is an excellent starting point. However, as Cicourel has suggested, the child's activities are always embedded in social context and always involve the child's use of language and interpretive abilities. The approach offered here is essentially interpretive, in that the child is viewed as the discoverer

---

[3] This section is heavily influenced by the ideas of Jenny Cook-Gumperz. See Cook-Gumperz, Corsaro, and Streeck (in press) for an elaboration of this approach to childhood socialization.

of a world endowed with meaning. From this perspective, the child begins life as a social being within an already defined social network and, through the growth of communication and language, the child, in interaction with others, constructs a social world.

The interpretive approach extends the constructivist view by arguing that children not only act on their environment, they participate in a social world. From the interpretive perspective, children help to shape and share in their own developmental experiences by their interactive responses. Moreover, their interpretive search is essentially part of their developing control of language and discourse skills.

What is important from the interpretive perspective is not that shared understanding is always achieved in adult–child or peer interaction, but rather that attempts at interpretive understanding are always made (see Ryan, 1974; Shotter, 1974). Often, especially in adult–child intraction, children are exposed to social knowledge and discourse styles they do not fully grasp during the course of interactive events. However, interaction normally continues in an orderly fashion, and ambiguities are often left to be pursued over the course of children's interactive experiences. A frequent pattern for preschool children involves the child's exposure to social knowledge and communicative demands in everyday activities with adults which raises problems, confusions, and uncertainties which are later reproduced and readdressed in the activities and routines making up peer culture (see Chapter 5). These communicative activities and routines offer children the opportunity to control and actively deal with problems, confusions, and concerns jointly or communally with peers. For this reason the interpretive approach demands direct entry and involvement in children's life-worlds.

The interpretive view offered here also extends the constructivist conception of the nature of the developmental process. The constructivist view that human learning is transformational and occurs generally in a stage-like fashion is an important improvement over the strictly accumulative or additive views of behaviorists. However, constructivists and behaviorists share a primarily *linear* view of the developmental process. In the linear view, it is assumed that the child must pass through a transition from a biological being, through a period of childhood, into a socially competent member of society. In this view, the period of childhood is a set of developmental stages in which cognitive skills, self or identity, and social knowledge are acquired in preparation for adult life. Sociologically, the linear view depicts childhood as the period during which the basic skills of cooperation, exchange, and moral values are acquired through progressive experience in different institutional settings.

Although the notion of stages is clear in the work of Piaget, the linear view is also apparent in Mead's model of the development of self-consciousness. Vygotsky, on the other hand, offered the basis for an alternative to a purely linear view of development with his emphasis on language and his belief that individual development is rooted in society and culture. For Vygotsky, human development is dialectic, and involves the child's appropriation of culture through interaction with others. In this sense, Vygotsky's views, although still emphasizing the outcome of the developmental process (i.e., becoming an adult), provide an important starting point for the extension of the linear model of socialization.

In the interpretive approach offered here, the view of development is reproductive rather than linear. From this perspective, the child is seen as interactively responsible for constructing activities within social contexts from the beginnings of life. Central to the reproductive view is the belief that language provides a socio-cognitive apparatus for the child and others to use. Language and discourse become the most critical tool for the child's construction of the social world, because it is through language that social action is generated. From this reproductive view of development, the child enters into a social nexus, and through interaction with others builds up a social understanding which becomes a core of social knowledge on which the child builds throughout the life-course.

Thus, the interpretive model extends the constructivist view by emphasizing the microprocesses through which interaction takes place and is stored for future use. The interpretive model extends the notion of stages by viewing development as a productive–reproductive complex in which an increasing density and reorganization of knowledge marks progression. The nature of this reorganization of knowledge changes in accordance both with children's developing cognitive and language abilities and with changes in the peer cultures making up children's life-worlds. In this sense, childhood socialization can be viewed as children's participation in and production of a series of peer cultures in which childhood knowledge and practices are gradually transformed into the knowledge and skills necessary for participation in the adult world.

The interpretive approach to childhood socialization demands the careful study of children's life-worlds throughout childhood and adolescence. Of special interest is children's acquisition and use of language and discourse skill with adults and peers. Recently there has been research which demonstrates that language learning begins before children produce and combine words, and that the *joint activity* of the caregiver and infant plays an important role in the development of communicative competence (Bruner, 1975; Halliday, 1974; Snow, 1977). In fact, mother–infant interaction can be seen as the social basis of language learning, because it is a context that provides children with frequent reactions and interpretations of their speech by adults who are highly motivated to understanding them (see Ryan, 1974; see also Corsaro, 1981c, for a review of research in this area). Some of the most impressive work on adult–child interaction in the early years demonstrates how children actively affect their movement from nonspeech to early speech through their participation in adult–child (especially mother–child) play and games (see Bruner, 1974, 1975, 1977; see also Ratner and Bruner, 1978). However, the interface of further language learning with social developmental experiences, once the child has begun to speak, is as yet a relatively unexplored area.

In particular, we know little about the role of language and the types of social learning that occur in the routine activities making up the peer cultures of young children. It is the purpose of this book to chart a beginning for needed research on peer cultures throughout childhood and adolescence, by focusing on friendship and peer culture in the early years. As we shall see in later chapters, the peer culture of the nursery school children in this study is best seen as a *joint or communal* attempt by the children to acquire *control* over their lives through the establishment of a collective identity. In this sense, the peer culture of preschool children is best seen as the children's continual, communal attempts to grasp and control a social order first presented to them by adults, but one which eventually becomes their own reproduction.

CHAPTER 3

Children's Conceptions of Cultural Knowledge in Role Play

Given the influence of Mead's (1934) social psychology, particularly his broad outline of stages in the development of self, it is surprising that there has been so little research on children's development of social knowledge by sociologists.[1] Several recent studies of this type have been done by developmental psychologists (cf. Damon, 1977, 1978; Selman, 1976; Shantz 1975; Turiel, 1978b; Youniss, 1975). The main goal of this work is the identification of levels of social knowledge in childhood through experimentation and clinical interviewing. What is often missing in these studies are adequate descriptions and theoretical incorporation of children's social-ecological worlds. Naturalistic studies of adult–child and peer interaction are essential for an understanding of how children acquire social knowledge and the interactive and conversational skills necessary to link such knowledge with ongoing interactive events.

Naturalistic studies of children's spontaneous role play are crucial for the discovery of how children acquire and use social

---

[1]A recent exception is Denzin, who claims in the introduction to his book that "there does not exist, nor has there ever existed, a sociology of childhood" (1977a:1). Denzin's work, although a contribution to a neglected area, is purposely differentiated from recent research in developmental psychology and language development. A position I do not adhere to in this monograph, which can be described as a micro-sociolinguistic study of peer interaction in a nursery school.

knowledge. Symbolic interactionists (Cooley, 1922; Cottrell, 1969; Denzin, 1977a; Mead, 1934; Stone, 1956) have stressed the importance of role play for the development of self. Taking the role of others in play enables the child to reflect back upon his or her own actions from the viewpoint of others. But role play is also important for children's development of cultural knowledge, including their conception and use of social information like status, roles, and norms. In role play, children do not simply imitate adult models, but rather use information acquired from observation and interactive experience with adults to reproduce social events. These reproductions are not exact replicas of the adult models, because they are influenced by features of peer culture (i.e., they are pretend or play), and because children's observations of interaction between actors occupying various social positions in the adult world are filtered through the children's developing conceptions of social knowledge and their repertoire of linguistic skills for realizing them (cf. Corsaro, 1979a). Role play is serious business in that it is practice in the production of social reality, and through role play children's conceptions of social knowledge and interactive skills become more diverse and logically integrated. In addition, role play activities are often a reflection of the desires of the children "to play at reality" or "experiment" with developing social knowledge. It is on these occasions when role play is a definite part of peer culture.

Type, Range, and Nature of Role Play Activities

Throughout the discussions in this book I refer generally to play as activities not performed for the sake of any result beyond their own production (see Dewey, 1938).[2] Role play is play which involves taking on social positions which exist in society (family roles, teacher, doctor, etc.) This definition of role play is similar to what Stone (1956) termed "anticipatory childhood drama," and differs from "fantastic childhood drama." Fantastic drama, ac-

---

[2]Although there are limitations to Dewey's (1938) definition of play, I feel it is concise and serves as a good working definition for my purposes in the monograph. However, the reader should see Schwartzman (1978) for a detailed review and evaluation of definitions of children's play.

cording to Stone, involves children's taking on roles which they cannot reasonably be expected to enact or encounter in later life (i.e., pirates, monsters, etc.). All fantasy play of this type was not included in the present analysis, with one exception. I did count as role play all the cases where the children adopted the positions of family pets ("kitties," "doggies," etc.) and all instances of "animal family" play (see below) where the children pretended to be animals *and* designated social positions such as "mother lion," "baby lion," etc.

The role play episodes which were recorded in field notes and on videotape are listed and summarized in Table 3.1. Role play occurred frequently in the nursery school and, therefore, I recorded a rather large number of role play episodes (36 of the 146 episodes recorded on videotape). In the videotape data, there were a total of 33 different role alignments involving 31 different social positions ranging from mother and baby to lion trainer and lion.

In the following sections of the chapter, I discuss the importance of role play for the children's development and use of social knowledge and the relationship between role play and peer culture. Regarding social knowledge, analyses of the children's role play revealed a great deal about their conceptions of status and role, as well as about how children use this knowledge to organize and maintain peer interactive episodes.

Children's Conception of Status

To identify the children's conceptions of status and role, I performed micro-sociolinguistic analyses (see Chapter 2) of the videotaped role play episodes. The analyses involved both a static and processual phase. In the static phase, I attempted to discover a relationship between the children's speech styles and the status alignments of the various social positions they enacted in role play. Table 3.2 contains data on the frequency of occurrence of a set of communicative functions or linguistic contextualization cues (Cook-Gumperz and Gumperz, 1976; Gumperz, 1976) in the role play episodes. In this table, I have classified the data, originally summarized in Table 3.1, in terms of speaker–addressee alignments of the various social positions (i.e., superordinate → subordinate, subordinate → superordinate, superordinate → su-

Table 3.1 Type, Range, and Number of Role Play Episodes Recorded in Field Notes and on Videotape

Type of Role Play	Field Notes[c]		Videotape[d]		Average Number of Participants	Videotaped Episodes Average Duration in Minutes	Average Number of Turns
	M[a]	A[b]	M	A			
Family (Roles Defined)	26	7	10	4	3.5	17	42
Household Routines	7	3	4	3	3.5	14	21
(Roles Not Defined)							
Salesperson	7	4	0	2	2.5	18	31
Fireman	2	8	1	1	5.0	9	18
Animal Family	0	9	0	2	3.0	8	16
Police	2	4	1	1	3.5	13	28
Workers	1	4	1	1	3.5	8	19
Doctor	1	0	1	0	3.0	11	20
Teacher	0	0	1	0	3.0	15	27
Liontrainer-Lion	0	1	0	1	2.0	20	32
Hunters	0	0	0	1	3.0	17	36
Campers	0	1	0	0	...	...	...
Fishing	1	1	0	0	...	...	...
Puppet Show	0	0	0	1	6.0	18	43
Bakers	0	2	0	0	...	...	...
Astronauts	1	0	0	0	...	...	...
N	48	44	19	17	3.5	14	27.8

[a]Morning
[b]Afternoon
[c]Majority of Field Notes Were Recorded from October 1 to January 30
[d]Videotapes Were Recorded from January 31 to May 31

Table 3.2   Production of Communicative Functions Across Status
Alignments in Role Play

	Cross-Status		Same-Status	
	Sup→Sub[a]	Sub→Sup[b]	Sup→Sup[c]	Sub→Sub[d]
Imperatives	293 60.8%	6 3.0%	16 4.0%	9 9.9%
Informative Statements	98 20.3%	92 46.5%	226 56.6%	42 46.1%
Request for Permission	0 0.0%	24 12.1%	3 .8%	1 1.1%
Request for Joint Action	46 9.5%	10 5.1%	50 12.5%	3 3.3%
Answers (Account)	8 1.8%	32 16.2%	32 8.0%	7 7.7%
Information Requests	23 4.8%	6 3.0%	23 5.8%	9 9.9%
Directive Questions	5 1.0%	0 0.0%	0 0.0%	0 0.0%
Tag Questions	4 .8%	0 0.0%	34 8.5%	0 0.0%
Greetings	0 0.0%	8 4.0%	15 3.8%	4 4.4%
Baby Talk	5 1.0%	20 10.1%	0 0.0%	16 17.6%
N	482 100%	198 100%	399 100%	91 100%
Total N = 1,170	41.2%	16.9%	34.1%	7.8%

[a]Superordinate→Subordinate (i.e., Mother–Baby)
[b]Subordinate→Superordinate (i.e., Baby–Mother)
[c]Superordinate→Superordinate (i.e., Husband–Wife)
[d]Subordinate→Subordinate (i.e., Baby–Baby)

perordinate, subordinate → subordinate).[3]Although the set of communicative functions presented is a product of the present analysis, several of the functions were presented in my own and other sociolinguistic studies of child language and adult–child interaction (cf. Broen, 1972; Cook-Gumperz and Corsaro, 1977; Garvey, 1975, 1977a; Ervin-Tripp, 1976, 1977; Gleason, 1972; Holzman, 1972; Mitchell-Kernan, 1977; Newport, 1976; Shatz and Gelman, 1973; Snow, 1972, 1977).

Imperatives are direct commands or warnings which are produced with heavy stress at the end of the utterance and overloud emphatic tone. The main function of the imperative is to control the behavior of other interactants. *Informative statements* are

---

[3]In episodes with both superordinate and subordinate positions all interaction between or among those of equal rank was classified in line with one's position in the specific episode. For example, speech among children (babies) was classified as subordinate → subordinate, while speech between mother and father was classified as superordinate → superordinate. There were relatively few episodes with no obvious status differences. For those cases the speech was classified as superordinate → superordinate. Although one could group all these data together as conversation between equals (cf., Mitchell-Kernan and Kernan, 1977), I used the above scheme to investigate the possibility of differences between subordinate → subordinate and superordinate → superordinate relations as defined within specific episodes.

declaratives produced to provide information relevant to the acknowledged topic or activity, to comment on on-going interaction, or to express personal feelings toward specific features of the interactive scene. *Requests for permission* are communicative functions which involve the speaker's seeking of permission to engage in specified behavior, *while requests for joint action* refer to the speaker's suggestions for joint activity. *Requests for permission* and *joint action* differ from *imperatives* in that they (a) normally take the interrogative form, (b) are declaratives without heavy stress patterns, or (c) contain syntactic elements which signify the suggestion of joint action (i.e., "Let's go shopping, Mommy."). *Answers (accounts)* are declaratives in which the speaker is responding to a previous question or imperative from another interactant, or is accounting for a past action or failure to act (i.e., in response to a *request for joint action,* "I can't, I'm too tired."). *Directive questions* are interrogatives which function as directive speech acts (cf. Hudson, 1975). Ervin-Tripp refers to directive questions as imbedded imperatives where "agent, action, object, and often beneficiary are as explicit as in direct imperatives, though they are embedded in a frame with other syntactic and semantic properties" (1976:29) (i.e., "Could you pick up that blanket?"). *Tag questions* are generally declaratives which have been transformed into interrogatives by a tag marker at the end of the utterance. In peer interaction, children often employ *tag questions* to gain shared understanding of the emerging scene (i.e., "We're cleaning the house, right?"). *Tag questions* differ from informative statements in that they tend to insure auditor feedback which signifies mutual understanding. *Information requests* are interrogatives employed by the speaker to obtain information from other interactants which is relevant to the ongoing activity. *Greetings* are self-explanatory, while *baby* and *animal talk* refer to phonetic strings often produced with high pitch which are prevocabulary babblings ("goo-goo," "gee-gee") or animal sounds ("meow," "grr-grr").

All the data were transcribed and coded by the author. A subsample of the data (8 episodes, 647 conversational turns over the three settings, and 5 types of role play) were coded independently by a coworker who had also helped with some of the transcription. The reliability (proportion agreement between coders) was .904. Although the categories in Table 3.2 did not exhaust all the speech in the role play data, all but 9 utterances (less than 1% of the total) were coded into one of the above categories.

Table 3.2 shows that role-taking has dramatic effects on speech style.[4] Children occupying superordinate positions produced a larger percentage of utterances than subordinates (75.3% to 24.7%), with superordinates producing the highest percentage of utterances when talking to subordinates (41.2%). Superordinates were much more likely to produce *imperatives* with subordinates than with other superordinates, and subordinates rarely produced *imperatives* at all. *Imperatives* accounted for 60.8% of the superordinates' speech to subordinates. Clearly, the children used language to exert authority depending on the social positions they occupied in role play.

The frequent use of *imperatives* by superordinates in role play is consistent with previous research on variation in speech styles across status alignments for adults and children. Green (1975) and Ervin-Tripp (1976) have described several types of directives in adult English. My definition of *imperatives* is similar to Ervin-Tripp's and to Green's definition of "orders." Green maintains that "the giver of an order believes that he has the authority to control the intentional behavior of the recipient and he expects to be obeyed" (1975:120). Ervin-Tripp (1976) found that *imperatives* were most often used downward in rank or between familiar equals. The children's use of *imperatives* in role play is in line with both Green's prediction and Ervin-Tripp's findings.

Regarding children's speech, Sachs and Devin (1976) found that preschool children used significantly more imperatives when speaking to a real baby and doll (in elicited role play) than with peers, their mothers, or as a baby (in elicited role play); while Martlew, Connolly and McCleod (1978) found that a 5-year-old produced a higher percentage of imperatives in solitary play than with a peer friend or his mother. In an elicited role play procedure with Black American children (age 7 to 12), Mitchell-Kernan and Kernan (1977) found that imperatives were directed to persons of lower rank more than five times as often as they were directed to persons of higher rank. In the role play data in this report (Table 3.2), *imperatives* were directed to subordinates 15 times as often, which suggests the

---

[4] In this report, I first present the entire data set in terms of distributions of communicative functions, with the data broken down into cross-status and same-status positions alignments. It should be remembered, however, that grouping the data in this fashion means relying on adult conceptions of the status properties of the various social positions adopted in role play, and that the procedure also removes the data from the interactive contexts in which they were collected. For this reason, I also present frequency distributions of communicative functions and the processual analyses of selected episodes.

authority and power dimensions of status may be even more salient for younger children. Although the studies of children's speech were not explicitly concerned with children's knowledge of status and did not include data on spontaneous role play among peers, the children were found to use a greater number of imperatives in situations where they were in a superordinate role—a finding consistent with the children's use of imperatives in this report.

Returning to Table 3.2, we see that all the children produced a sizeable percentage of informative statements. Informative statements are produced with high frequency in peer interaction across a range of situations and activities (cf. Cook-Gumperz and Corsaro, 1977). Children use the declarative in this way to structure emerging activity by informing coparticipants of what they are doing—a communicative strategy which reflects the emergent, here-and-now features of much of children's play. What is of interest in Table 3.2 is that status differences reduce reliance on this communicative strategy for children in the superordinate position who produce a high frequency of imperatives. Subordinates in cross-status alignments produce more informative statements than superordinates (46.5% to 20.3%), and the children produce a high frequency of informative statements in same-status interaction regardless of social position. While superordinates gave orders in the role play, subordinates spent a great deal of time showing deference. Showing of deference was evident in two ways: (a) the subordinates produced numerous answers (16.2%) in response to superordinate *imperatives* (i.e., Mother: "You get in bed, baby!" Baby: "Yes, Mama."), and (b) the subordinates produced a sizeable percentage of *requests for permission* (12.1%) before engaging in certain types of behavior (i.e., "Can I go outside, Mommy?"). *Requests for joint action,* on the other hand, appeared more often in superordinate → subordinate interaction than vice versa (9.5% to 5.1%), and most frequently in same-status interaction among superordinates (12.5%).

These patterns are also consistent with the work of Green and Ervin-Tripp on adult speech. Ervin-Tripp (1976), for example, found that "permission directives" were most often directed upward in rank and were very common in the speech of young children. Green's (1975) "pleas" are similar to *permission directives* except for her insistence that subordinates have no real expectation that they will be granted. Green maintains pleas are made from a position of subordinancy, and again her prediction and Ervin-Tripp's data are consistent with the findings in Table 3.2.

Regarding *requests for joint action,* it is difficult to compare the results in Table 3.2 with the work on adult directives because of the structuring rather than controlling function of this form in peer interaction. *Requests for joint action* were used by the children to offer up plans for action or "scripts," and, if approved, an attempt was generally made to enact the script. In family role play, superordinates often produce *requests for joint action* with high pitch and exaggerated intonation typical of adult "baby talk" to small children (cf. Ferguson, 1964; Garnica, 1977). *Requests for joint action* produced with these prosodic features by superordinates not only suggest activity, but also are used to show affection to subordinates (i.e., "Let's go for a walk, little baby."). When *requests for joint action* were used in same-status interaction, the joint (sharing) aspect of the request was often stressed. In short, *requests for joint action* were used primarily to encourage "doing things together."

Regarding *information requests,* Table 3.2 shows that this type of question was produced more frequently in same-status than in cross-status interaction (15.7% to 7.8%). This finding is consistent with recent work by Goody (1978) on questioning. Goody maintains questions "are speech acts which place two people in direct, immediate interaction. In doing so, they carry messages about relationships—about relative status, assertions of status and challenges to status" (1978:39). In ethnographic work in Gonja, Goody found the information and command functions of questions are fused, making it difficult for members of unequal rank to ask or receive genuine information questions. The situation in role play is similar to Goody's data in that status is a central factor. However, I would not argue that the information and command functions are fused in role play; rather, superordinates and subordinates are so busy giving, eliciting, or following orders that they have little time or occasion for *information requests.* The salience of status in role play seems to limit the number of *information requests* which could appear in cross-status alignments.[5]

---

[5] A similar pattern also appears in Sachs and Devin's (1976) data. All the children asked more questions of peers than of mothers or babies, and two of the four children asked more questions of babies than their mothers. This finding was opposite of the authors' predictions, but was explained to be the result of their focus on syntactic form rather than the social functions of questions. This explanation does not, however, account for the consistent pattern of the children producing more imperatives and fewer questions in cross-status than in peer relations.

Finally, differences also exist in the production of the communicative functions across same-status alignments. In superordinate → superordinate relations, *tag questions* and *requests for joint action* were used more frequently than in any other alignment. Both *tag questions* and *requests for joint action* were employed to offer up plans of action or organize ongoing activity. What is of interest is the children's infrequent use of these communicative functions in subordinate → subordinate interaction in the presence of superordinates. This pattern, along with the difference in proportion of total number of utterances (34.1% in superordinate → superordinate, compared to 7.8% in subordinate → subordinate) suggests the children may be developing a rule which restricts conversation between subordinates in the presence of superordinates.

Processual analysis.. Although the data in Table 3.2 reveal consistent features of children's conceptions of status in role play, it is not possible to capture how the children articulate their conceptions to ongoing interactive scenes by focusing only on static frequency distributions of communicative functions. Therefore, I selected two sustained role play episodes for processual analysis.[6]

Table 3.3 contains data on the frequency distribution of the communicative functions for a family role play episode involving three children from the morning group (Barbara, Debbie, and Charles). Barbara, who occupied the highest status position (Mother), produced the largest proportion of utterances (45.8% of the total, to 41.2% for the Big Sister, Debbie, and 6.9% for the Baby, Charles). It is particularly striking that Charles did not stray from the communicative style appropriate to the subordinate position even though he was one of the most verbal children in the school.

Another interesting pattern in Table 3.3 is that the mother addresses a high proportion of imperatives to the baby (65.2% of all utterances addressed to the baby), but none to the big sister. Several of the children defined the "big sister" position as "being

---

[6] Although these episodes were selected because of their length and sustained role play activity, Tables 3.3 and 3.4 show that the distribution of communicative functions is consistent with the total data set presented in Table 3.2. In short, these episodes were not randomly selected, but are representative of the total data source (i.e., 36 videotaped role play episodes).

Table 3.3 Production of Communicative Functions in One Family Role Play Episode (Mother, Big Sister, Baby)

	Mother		Big Sister		Baby	
	To Baby	To Big Sister	To Mother	To Baby	To Mother	To Big Sister
Imperatives	30 65.2%	0 0.0%	0 0.0%	0 0.0%	0 0.0%	0 0.0%
Informative Statements	7 15.2%	11 50.0%	34 68.0%	1 25.0%	2 28.6%	0 0.0%
Requests for Permission	0 0.0%	0 0.0%	8 16.0%	1 25.0%	2 28.6%	0 0.0%
Requests for Joint Action	0 0.0%	3 13.6%	2 4.0%	0 0.0%	0 0.0%	0 0.0%
Answers (Accounts)	0 0.0%	3 13.6%	4 8.0%	0 0.0%	1 14.3%	2 100%
Information Requests	2 4.4%	4 18.3%	0 0.0%	1 25.0%	1 14.3%	0 0.0%
Directive Questions	4 8.7%	0 0.0%	0 0.0%	0 0.0%	0 0.0%	0 0.0%
Tag Questions	0 0.0%	0 0.0%	0 0.0%	0 0.0%	0 0.0%	0 0.0%
Greetings	1 2.1%	1 4.6%	2 2.0%	1 25.0%	0 0.0%	0 0.0%
Baby Talk	2 4.4%	0 0.0%	0 0.0%	0 0.0%	1 14.3%	0 0.0%
N	46 67.6%	22 32.4%	50 92.6%	4 7.4%	7 77.2%	2 72.8%
	Mother N = 68 46.8%		Big Sister N = 54 41.2%		Baby N = 9 6.9%	

Total N = 131

able to do whatever you want,'' and this definition is a good characterization of the big sister's behavior in this episode.[7] She moves in and out of the scene while the mother almost continually directs and disciplines the baby. Upon reentering the interaction, the big sister would tell the mother all the things she had done while away, resulting in the large number of informative statements (68% of her total utterances).

The following sequence is drawn from the role play episode presented in Table 3.3.

Example 3.1   Family Role Play (Mother, Baby, and Big Sister)

Transcription		*Description*
(1)	B S: Mommy, I had lunch. Then I am going to ( ).	Big Sister (BS) has just returned from shopping.
(2)	B: Goo-goo.	The baby (B) gets out of bed and crawls on the floor.
(3)	BS: Hi, little baby.	Hugs B.
(4)	M: Ah-this—	BS moves toward stairs.
(5)	BS: I gotta go—h—I—I'm gonna buy you something mama. I'm gonna bu-buy baby my book. I'm gonna—bye, Mommy.	BS turns and leaves scene.
(6)	M: Baby—you shouldn't take my money! Crawl baby!	B crawling on floor. M moves close to him, then B crawls toward stairs.
(7)	M: Don't go out of the house!	B moves away from stairs and crawls up on table.
(8)	M: Baby get off the table!	M pulls B from table to floor.
(9)	M: Crawl!	B crawls toward bed.

---

[7] Of the 14 family role play episodes, there were 4 which included the big sister or big brother position. Four children enacted this social position (three girls and one boy) in role play in the nursery school. In one other episode, there was a "sister kid" position whose behavior suggested she was not a baby, but she was also not "allowed to do anything she wanted." In addition to the videotaped behavior of the children in these positions, I also questioned two of the girls who took the big sister position, and the boy who enacted the big brother position, about behavioral expectations (i.e., "what do big sisters/big brothers do?"). All the children said "whatever she/he wants," and one of the girls also added: "big sisters stay up late."

Transcription, cont'd			Description, cont'd
(10)	BS:	I brought you some-thing—	BS returning to playhouse.
(11)	M:	Dee-dee-dee.	Singing and tickling baby.

This sequence reflects a pattern in which the mother disciplines the baby while listening and at times responding to reports from the big sister. In all the role play episodes where clear status differences were exhibited, the higher status interactant always spent a great deal of time maintaining control over lower status interactants. In this episode, we also see that the baby does not merely respond to commands, but often directs the flow of the interaction with purposeful misbehavior (6–10). Misbehavior which challenges the authority of superordinates occurred routinely in all the role play data, and definitely contributes to the continual exertion of authority which typified cross-status interaction.

Table 3.4 reports the frequency of occurrence of the communicative functions for four children from the morning group in another family role play episode. The two positions with the higher status (husband, Bill, and wife, Rita) produced about the same number of utterances (around 55 each), while the family pets (two kitties, Charles and Denny) produced a total of 40 utterances. Of course, kitties, like the baby in the previous episode, cannot talk; they mainly "meow" (animal talk). It should be remembered, however, that adopting the subordinate position entails relinquishing control of power in interaction. If one decides to be a kitten, he or she cannot say much, and expects to be ordered around.

The kitties are indeed ordered around. As we see in Table 3.4, there is a marked difference in speech style for superordinates and subordinates. When talking to each other, the husband and wife primarily employed informative statements and questions, but when interacting with the kitties, they relied overwhelmingly on imperatives.

But what else can you say or do with kittens? Could it be that the majority of speech to pets in real life is made up of directives and the children are simply imitating adult models? Surely there is imitation, but the exertion of power dominates in role play. Although affection is displayed, we would expect to see at least nearly as much nurturant behavior toward the pets as discipline, but this was not the case—neither here nor in the earlier interaction between the mother and the baby.

Table 3.4 Production of Communicative Functions in One Family Role Play Episode (Husband, Wife, Pet Kitties)

	Wife		Husband		Kitties		
	To Husband	To Kitties	To Wife	To Kitties	To Husband	To Wife	To Other Kitty
Imperatives	0 0.0%	17 63.0%	1 4.0%	25 86.3%	1 5.9%	2 13.4%	1 12.5%
Informative Statements	20 71.4%	7 25.9%	15 60.0%	2 6.9%	5 29.3%	4 33.3%	0 0.0%
Requests for Permission	0 0.0%	0 0.0%	0 0.0%	0 0.0%	0 0.0%	1 5.9%	0 0.0%
Requests for Joint Action	1 3.6%	1 3.7%	0 0.0%	0 0.0%	0 0.0%	0 0.0%	0 0.0%
Answers (Accounts)	3 10.7%	0 0.0%	4 16.0%	0 0.0%	1 5.9%	0 0.0%	0 0.0%
Information Requests	1 3.6%	0 0.0%	0 0.0%	1 3.4%	1 5.9%	0 0.0%	0 0.0%
Directive Questions	0 0.0%	0 0.0%	0 0.0%	0 0.0%	0 0.0%	0 0.0%	0 0.0%
Tag Questions	3 10.7%	0 0.0%	4 16.0%	0 0.0%	0 0.0%	0 0.0%	0 0.0%
Greetings	0 0.0%	0 0.0%	1 3.4%	1 3.4%	0 0.0%	0 0.0%	0 0.0%
Animal Talk	0 0.0%	2 7.4%	0 0.0%	0 0.0%	9 53.0%	8 53.3%	8 87.5%
Total Utterances	28 50.9%	27 49.1%	25 46.3%	29 43.7%	17 41.5%	15 36.5%	9 22.0%
	Wife $N = 55$		Husband $N = 54$		Kitty $N = 41$		
	36.7%		36.0%		27.3%		

Total $N = 150$

Finally, in interactive scenes where both superordinates and subordinates are participating, status dominates the interaction. Although the data in Table 3.4 indicate that the husband and wife addressed each other as often as the kitties, the fact is that the kitties were not present when the majority of the husband–wife interaction occurred. The wife produced a total of 32 utterances when the kitties were present, and 27 of these were directed to the pets; for the husband, the proportion was similar—29 of 33 utterances directed to the kitties.

Not only was there a shift regarding who the husband and wife addressed, there was also a shift in speech style from informative statements and questions to imperatives, as illustrated in the following sequence. In this sequence, there is movement through three phases: (a) the claiming of the playhouse; (b) "setting the scene" by arranging the objects in the setting and offering up plans of action; and (c) the direct involvement in role play, with strict adherence to status differences and the exertion of authority.

Example 3.2   Family Role Play (Husband, Wife, and Pets)
The husband (H), Bill, and the wife (W), Rita, have just entered the upstairs playhouse carrying purses and suitcases. They have allocated the social positions of husband and wife as they gathered the materials before going upstairs. They also saw two boys (Charles and Denny, K1 and K2) pretending to be kitties in front of the downstairs playhouse. As they move upstairs, H referred to K1 and K2 as "our kitties," but there was not, nor had there been previously, any formal negotiation between H and W or among H, W, K1, and K2 regarding who the kitties belonged to. We pick up the interaction early on in the episode.

Transcription		*Description*
(20) H–W:	This is our special room, right?	H has placed blankets on the bed and suitcases and purses on floor in front of bed. H then gets a crib and places it along-side of bed blocking off the area from the rest of the room.
(21) W–H:	Right.	
(22) H–W:	This is our little room we sleep in, right?	H is now sitting on the bed.

Transcription, cont'd		
Description, cont'd		

		Transcription	Description
(23)	W–H:	Our little room. Our—	W is holding a doll. At this point K1 and K2 enter playhouse and H and W turn to look at them.
(24)	K1–WH:	We're the kitty family.	K1 and K2 are crawling and meowing.
(25)	W–K1, K2:	Here kitty-kitty, here kitty-kitty.	K1 and K2 are crawling and meowing.
(26)	W–H:	Yeah, here's our two kitties.	
(27)	H–K2:	Kitty, you can't come in this room.	K2 crawls near bed as K1 knocks something from the table.
(28)	W–K2:	Here do-do.	K2 scratches at W as K1 crawls into the blocked-off area.
(29)	H–K1:	No! No!	K1 leaves the area and crawls to stairs, with K2 following.
(30)	H–K1,K2:	Go on! Get down in the backyard!	
(31)	W–K1,K2:	Get down in the backyard, you two cats!	K1 begins crawling down stairs. K2 follows but then hesitates at top of stairs. W is standing behind K2.
(32)	W–K2:	Go down! Down! Down!	
(33)	K2–W:	No, I'm the kitty, I'm the kitty.	H has joined W at the top of the stairs.
(34)	W–K2:	Go! Rr—	
(35)	H–K2:	Go! Back!	
(36)	W–K2:	Rrr-Rrr!	
(37)	H–K2:	Go back in the backyard!	
(38)	W–K2:	You get in the backyard. Ya! Ya!	
(39)	H–K2:	Chow! Chow! Go!	K2 starts downstairs.
(40)	W–K2:	Go! Go! Chow!	K2 now downstairs with K1.
(41)	H–K2:	Go in the back-yard, we're busy!	

Transcription, cont'd

(42) W–K2:   Yeah.

(43) W–H: They was—rough
                on us.

Description, cont'd

H has moved to front of house and
is looking down at K1 and K2. W
is standing behind H.

In this sequence (20–24), the children are "setting the scene"
and preparing for the arrival of the kitties. The language style
they employ in this stretch of dialogue is typical of peer interaction.
The children are continually offering up plans of action for con-
firmation by way of the tag question (20, 22). The temporal aspects
of what is happening are important here: H's blocking off the room
has implications for the activity which emerges with the arrival
of the kitties.

The kitties enter at 24 and identify themselves as the "kitty
family" for purposes of initiation, then only "meow" except for
one exception (33). The children readily fall into behaviors which
illustrate the importance of status in role play. The kitties immediately become a nuisance, doing exactly what they are told
not to do (28–30). The husband and wife switch speech styles and
take on the authority which is embedded in their statuses as masters of the pet kitties. The intonation and stress patterns in these
commands make this claim to authority clear to all the interactants.
The kitties finally leave (41) and, with W's remark at 43, we get
the impression that she expected the kitties to give them a hard
time, but that in this instance they were especially difficult.

Although the data in Tables 3.1–3.4 demonstrate the effects of
status on speech style for the total sample of peer role play, a
comparison of individual children's speech across social positions
in role play and in other peer activity could strengthen the argument that status is a determining factor in language use. Table
3.5 contains the frequency distributions of the communicative
functions for two of the nursery school children (Rita, age 3 years,
9 months, the wife and master of pet kitties for the episode in
Table 4; and Barbara, age 3 years, 6 months, the mother in the
episode in Table 3) in several role play episodes and one episode
of sand play. In sand and block play, the children frequently engage in "spontaneous fantasy" (cf. Cook-Gumperz and Corsaro,
1977) during which activity emerges in the process of verbal negotiation, and conventionalized expectations (including status and

role characteristics of social positions), although referred to at times, are not relied upon continually to structure the activity as they are in role play.[8]

Table 3.5 shows that both children were much more likely to use imperatives in the superordinate → subordinate relation than in any other alignment or in sand play (over a 55% difference for both children). *Informative statements* are used more often in same-status alignments and sand play by both children, while *requests for permission* are used primarily when occupying a subordinate position in role play. *Requests for joint action* and *tag questions* were used with some regularity by both children in superordinate → superordinate role play alignments and in sand play, but rarely in cross-status role play. *Baby* or *animal talk* was primarily confined to the subordinate position in role play, but was used quite often by Rita in sand play. In this particular episode, Rita was pretending to be the toy horse she played with in the sandbox. Although animal talk was appropriate in this case, it is clear Rita was not limited to this form of speech and produced a wide range of communicative functions. Overall, this sample of data involving two children's speech in a range of social positions and two types of play is consistent with the general pattern of the data in Table 3.2.

Children's definitions of status.. To this point, I have inferred children's conception of status from their role behavior and interpreted the effects of this knowledge on the interaction. I will now examine data which more directly support my conclusions regarding young children's conceptions of status. The data, also drawn from role play sequences, involve the children's own interpretations of status and its implications. When talking about status, children usually talk about bosses.

---

[8]The two children were selected because they had enacted a range of social positions in several sustained, videotaped episodes. Although comparisons of this type (i.e., across several social positions) were not possible for the majority of the children, analyses of data for each child where at least one comparison was possible revealed a pattern consistent with the findings in Table 3.5. Also a more general comparison of the frequency distributions of the communicative functions for the total role play data set and 12 episodes of spontaneous fantasy (sand and block play) led to findings consistent with those in Table 3.5, where the speech style in sand play is similar to that in same-status role play but quite different from that in cross-status role play.

Table 3.5 Production of Communicative Functions for Two Children in Various Social Positions in Role Play and in Sand Play

| | Rita | | | | Barbara | | | |
| | Role Play | | | Sand Play | | Role Play | | Sand Play |
	Sup→Sub[1]	Sub→Sup[2]	Sup→Sup[3]		Sub→Sub[4]	Sub→Sup[5]	Sup→Sup[6]	
Imperatives	63.0%	5.7%	0.0%	2.8%	65.2%	0.0%	3.3%	7.5%
Informative Statements	25.9%	34.3%	71.4%	47.6%	15.2%	23.1%	63.4%	50.0%
Request for Permission	0.0%	8.6%	0.0%	0.0%	0.0%	23.1%	3.2%	0.0%
Request for Joint Action	3.7%	0.0%	3.6%	17.1%	0.0%	0.0%	6.5%	20.0%
Answers (Accounts)	0.0%	8.6%	10.7%	12.7%	4.4%	15.3%	12.9%	5.0%
Information Requests	0.0%	0.0%	3.6%	1.0%	8.7%	0.0%	3.2%	2.5%
Directive Questions	0.0%	0.0%	0.0%	0.0%	0.0%	0.0%	0.0%	0.0%
Tag Questions	0.0%	0.0%	10.7%	0.0%	2.1%	0.0%	6.5%	10.0%
Greetings	0.0%	0.0%	0.0%	0.0%	0.0%	0.0%	0.0%	2.5%
Baby Talk/Sounds	7.4%	42.8%	0.0%	16.5%	4.4%	30.5%	0.0%	2.5%
Other*	0.0%	0.0%	0.0%	2.3%	0.0%	0.0%	0.0%	0.0%
N	27	35	28	103	46	13	31	40

*These utterances were not classifiable in the set of communicative functions. The two occurrences in sand play for Rita were similar to requests for joint action, but more specific in that they were requests for aid or help.
[1]Superordinate→Subordinate (Master–Pets)
[2]Subordinate→Superordinate (Kitty–Master)
[3]Superordinate→Superordinate (Wife–Husband)
[4]Superordinate→Subordinate (Mother–Baby)
[5]Subordinate→Superordinate (Kitty–Master)
[6]Superordinate→Superordinate (Teacher–Teacher)

Example 3.3 Digging Canals

Three children are digging canals and building dams in the outside sandpile. Social positions had been established earlier. Charles (C) is the "dam stopper," Bill (B) is the "canal digger," and Rita (R) is the "boss." This sequence begins after Rita has briefly wandered off from the work area.

Transcription			*Description*
(1)	C–R:	R! R!	R turns to look.
(2)	R–C:	What?	R returns and stands near C.
(3)	C–R:	You're the boss.	
(4)	R–C:	Yeah.	
(5)	C–R:	Well, you're the boss, so you're suppose to stay here and order us around.	
(6)	R–C:	Oh. Stop up the dam over there!	Points to other side of canal.
(7)	C–R:	Ok.	

Stratified role alignments such as the one above often emerge spontaneously in role play. In this episode, there was no inherent need for a boss. There could have been two dam stoppers or canal builders, but the children jointly agreed a boss was necessary. Further, when the boss strayed away she was reminded of her duties (i.e., bosses give orders). Here we have direct support for the contention that, for children, higher status means power and giving orders. It may be many years before the children understand that bosses have other duties besides giving orders, the legitimacy of the bosses' authority, or the integrative function of "order giving" in the work place.

A second sequence of peer interaction collected in a home in conjunction with the nursery school research[9] is even more revealing of children's conception of status.

---

[9]The children in the following sequence (Tea Party) of peer interaction in a home setting are two girls, Jean (J) and Karen (K). Jean was 4 years, 4 months old and Karen was 5 years old when the data were collected. The children did not attend the nursery school. The data were collected for comparative purposes (i.e., dyadic peer interaction in the home, compared to multiparty, peer interaction in the nursery school). I have included this sequence of the home data because the children's conversation reveals a great deal about their conception of status.

Example 3.4   The Tea Party (Jean, J, and Karen, K)

Transcription	*Description*
(1) J: Yeah, and let's pretend when Mommy's out till later, ok? (and these two can be off but she didn't want we eat—one—and pretend ate one—later), ok?	J sitting next to K. Both are drinking milk from tea cups. J points to two cookies left on table as she said "these two can be off."
(2) K: Ooooh. Well, I'm not the boss around here, though. Cause Mom—mommies play the bosses around here.	
(3) J: Yeah.	
(4) K: And us children aren't.	K shakes head no as she says this.
(5) J: So long age—and when I grow up and you grow up, we'll be the bosses.	
(6) K: Um—hum.	Shakes head yes.
(7) J: A-A-ah!	Swallowing some milk.
(8) K: But, maybe we won't know how to punish.	
(9) J: I will.	
(10) K: How?	
(11) J: I'll put hand up and spank 'em. That's what my mom does.	Swings hand in air.
(12) K: My mom does sometimes too. Um, spilled some milk.	Spills milk as she starts to take a drink.
(13) K: Look how much I got?	

Jean initiates the discussion of bosses (1), but there is some difficulty in interpreting the meaning of this utterance. Given that this statement leads into the direct discussion of status, I feel its inclusion and some speculation about its meaning is important. Since I observed this sequence when it occurred and have reviewed the tape numerous times, I have reasonable confidence in my interpretation. It seems J is referring to the two cookies which are left on the plate when she says, "and these two can be off but she didn't want we eat—one—." Earlier, J's mother told the girls they could have one each of three different kinds of cookies, six in all. In this utterance, it appears J is proposing that "mommy's out till later" and that they can go ahead and eat the remaining two cookies.[10] In any event, the issue is one of authority and whether they should eat the rest of the cookies now as opposed to later.

J's proposal leads to the interesting exchange which follows. Karen does not confirm J's suggestion, stating she is not the boss and does not have the right to make such a decision. The fact that she says "Mommies play the bosses around here" is difficult to interpret, because she uses the verb "play" as opposed to "are." The utterance suggests that she could confirm J's proposal, but only if she pretends to be the Mommy. In (3), J confirms K's signification of mommies as bosses, and then K goes on to differentiate mommies from children (i.e., "mommies are bosses and children aren't"). J then notes that, when children grow up, they become bosses (5); here we can see that J understands the relationship between status (power) and age. K first affirms J's recognition of this relationship (6), then becomes worried about their ability to exert authority (i.e., punish). The fact that K is concerned with the exertion of authority, rather than the many other rights and duties of being a mother, is in line with earlier findings where the higher-status interactants spent the majority of their interactive time exercising authority over subordinates.

Summary. Overall, the data suggest the children have clear conceptions of status as power. In all the role play episodes, there were no violations of status expectations; that is, the baby never told the mother what to do, the kitties never chased their masters from the house, workers never gave orders to the boss, etc. Children may develop crystallized notions of status early in the developmental process because of frequent and sustained interaction with adults. As a result, children seem to internalize the superordinate position of the adult–child self-other system (cf. Cottrell,

---

[10]One complication in the children's discussion is the mixture of play and reality in this sequence. The cookies are in both realities for the children. It seems K is hesitant to pretend because of the possibility that the real mommy might appear. In any case, it seems to me that this hesitation (2) is what spurred the discussion of real mommies (2–12).

1969), and produce behavior consistent with their conception of status expectations associated with this position in role play.

However, the developmental process is more complex than imitation theories as outlined by Bandura (1969) would have us believe. It seems that interaction between actors occupying various social positions may be filtered through the children's developing conceptions of status and role, and their repertoire of linguistic skills for realizing them.[11] In this sense, there is a distortion (or confusion) of the adult (superordinate) model in that the children organize cross-status role play around the strict control of subordinates.

But how different is the adult model from the children's role play enactments? Although I do not have comparative data on adult–child interaction in the homes of the children under study here, I do have adult–child data involving other children from similar socioeconomic backgrounds. These data (Corsaro, 1977, 1979b), as well as other studies of adult linguistic input to young children (Broen, 1972; Cross, 1977; Holzman, 1972; Newport, Gleitman, and Gleitman, 1977) show that much of adult communicative input is not related to discipline, and, when there are attempts to control their children, the adults often relied on indirect communicative strategies—most often specific variants of the interrogative.[12]

Although this interpretation stresses the limitations of social learning approaches to the development of social knowledge, it is consistent with recent work by cognitive-developmental theorists. Damon (1977), for example, has outlined a 6-level model of children's knowledge of authority, based on several studies involving clinical interviewing. Damon argues that children's conception of authority undergoes dramatic change between infancy and adolescence, and that that change is due not to modeling or reinforcement but to the child's cognitive structuring and restructuring of his own experiences. At the third level of Damon's model, "authority is legitimized by attributes which enable the authority figure to enforce his commands (physical strength, social

---

[11] I wish to thank an anonymous reviewer for this suggestion regarding features of the developmental process.

[12] Regarding sentence type, the adult–child data from these reports show that the adults (all middle-class mothers) used approximately (average all data) 13% imperatives, 41% questions, and 30% declaratives. In this study the children who occupied superordinate positions used 60.4% imperatives, 15.4% questions, and 23.2% declaratives while talking to subordinates in role play.

or physical power)" and at this level "power is invested with an aura of omnipotence and omniscience" (1977:178). At later levels, the child comes to see the need to legitimize authority in regard to special talents or abilities of those in power.

The role play behavior of the children in this study is consistent with Damon's third level. The children display knowledge of status as power, but do not exhibit a notion of legitimacy. The interpretation that interactive input from adult models is filtered through the children's developing conceptions of status is also in line with the cognitive-developmental position which focuses on the child's active structuring and restructuring of social experience.

The cognitive-developmental model outlined by Damon does not, however, tell us a great deal about children's development of the communicative skills necessary to articulate their knowledge of authority with features of interactive scenes (cf. Cicourel, 1972). Although the children produce a wide variety of linguistic forms, they most frequently relied on simple, what adults might term crude, sociolinguistic devices for the manifestation of status in role play. This pattern is consistent with Ervin-Tripp's argument that children produce a diversity of linguistic structures and social features, but fail to produce "systematic, regular, unmarked requests, which do not refer to what the speaker wants" (1977:188). The development of more indirect communicative strategies for marking status and exercising authority, as well as correlative rules regarding variation in status expectations across social settings, may occur much later in the developmental process.

A final implication regarding children's knowledge of status concerns the possible structuring or organizing functions of misbehaving and the resulting exertion of authority in role play episodes. The fact that the children in subordinate positions purposely misbehaved indicates a shared agreement among the children that role play involves discipline and showing deference to authority.[13] Misbehavior and verbal warnings against potential

---

[13] I feel the children in subordinate positions do not misbehave because they like being ordered around, but rather because that is what role play is all about from the children's perspective. A total of 40 children participated in the 36 videotaped role play episodes. Of this number, 6 children enacted only the superordinate position and 3 children enacted only the subordinate position, while 31 children enacted both superordinate and subordinate positions. Of the 6 children who only enacted superordinate positions, 4 participated only in fireman role play where the superordinate/subordinate distinction was not clearly marked.

rule violation may be cues which lead to the emergence of "discipline scripts" (cf. Schank and Abelson, 1977).

One way to evaluate this interpretation is to specify the frequency of "discipline scripts" in cross-status interaction, and to compare the length of cross-status and same-status role play episodes. Of the 18 episodes involving *only* cross-status interaction, 13 (72.2%) contained discipline scripts, while 7 of the 10 episodes involving *both* cross-status and same-status interaction contained discipline scripts. Clearly misbehavior and exertion of authority occur consistently in cross-status role play. The average length of episodes involving only cross-status interaction was 22.8 minutes and 32.6 conversational turns, while the average length of episodes involving *only* same-status interaction was 12.5 minutes and 18.7 conversational turns. The average length of episodes involving *both* cross-status and same-status interaction was 18.1 minutes and 39.2 conversational turns. In addition, episodes involving only cross-status interaction which contained discipline scripts were longer than those which did not (20.1 minutes and 34.9 conversational turns as compared to 15.4 minutes and 32.8 conversational turns).

Although length of episode seems to support the interpretation that discipline scripts serve organizing functions in role play, there are features of the data which limit the certainty of this inference. The role play episodes vary not only in terms of status alignments, but also regarding number of participants, type of role play, and occasions of teacher or peer intrusion into ongoing activity. To precisely test the possible structuring functions of discipline scripts in role play, it would be necessary to have much more control over context, participants, and type of role play. In fact, experimental studies of elicited role play may be the best method for empirical evaluation of this hypothesis. Despite these limitations, the present data do, however, demonstrate the importance of examining the functions of various language styles and scripted activity for the generation of social order in peer interactive contexts.

Children's Conception of Role

A second component of social positions in children's role play pertains to role expectations—the children's awareness of what they are "to do" (duties) when occupying a certain position (i.e., a husband with wife, a sister with brother, etc.) The best data for estimating children's knowledge of role expectations is role play involving participants of similar status. Earlier, when I noted the variations in speech styles across interaction with various status alignments, we saw that same-status role play was characterized by the children's use of informative statements and questions. The following sequence, drawn from the role play data summarized in Table 3.4, illustrates the children's use of this speech style to link role expectations (what husbands and wives "do") to contextual features of the interactive scene. The sequence begins immediately after the kitties (Charles and Denny) have been chased from the upstairs playhouse by the husband and wife (Bill and Rita).

Example 3.5 Family Role Play (Husband, Wife, and Pets)

Transcription			*Description*
(44)	H–W:	Let's clean the place. Let's—	H picks up a table while W is holding doll and singing.
(45)	H–W:	Be careful, I'm gonna move our table.	H puts down the table and pushes the stove to head of the stairs.
(46)	W–H:	Good, Bill. You're a handy man. Handy man.	W sings words "Handy man."
(47)	H–W:	Next.	H now pushes table behind the stove.
(48)	W–H:	Bill? Bill?	
(49)	H–W:	What?	
(50)	W–H:	You're a strong man.	
(51)	H–W:	I know it. I just moved this.	Referring to table.
(52)	W–H:	Yeah.	H and W move to head of stairs.
(53)	W–H:	Scraped the floor. Oh!	Points to vacant area where table had been.
(54)	H–W:	Yeah, that's new. Very new. That's—	Referring to floor.

Transcription, cont'd		*Description, cont'd*
(55) W–H:	That's—that needs mopping, right?	Referring to floor.
(56) H–W:	Yeah.	
(57) H–K1,K2:	Hey down kitties!	K1 and K2 now move back upstairs.
(58) W–K1,K2:	Ra! Ra! Scat! Scat!	H moves to block their entry.

With the departure of the kitties, the tone of the conversation switches. The children immediately see the need to engage in activity which is in line with their role expectations of the social position, husband and wife. The husband introduces the activity of furniture moving and cleaning as a joint activity for the husband and wife, with each performing duties embodied in sex role distinctions (i.e., husband moves the furniture and wife cleans). Note how the children arrive at a shared understanding of what they are doing. First H offers a suggestion (1), then simply goes about moving the furniture as he describes (informative statements) what he is doing. The wife shows she understands and falls into proper role play with her own use of declaratives (46), noting that her husband is a "handy man to have around." The wife has responded to H's shift of the conversational tone, switching from the imperative to the declarative with accompanying shifts in intonation patterns (heavy stress to normal). A new conversational rhythm has been established and remains intact until the kitties arrive. Whereupon we see a shift back to the imperative and heavy stress intonational patterns.

What is of sociological importance here is that the shift in conversational style depends on the awareness of sociological knowledge of dimensions of social positions. In this sequence, we see the shift from authority to task orientation and back to authority. Again we see the dominance of status in an unfolding interactive event. Later in the interaction, confusion arises concerning role expectations with a proposal to shift social positions by one of the children.

Transcription		*Description*
(84) H–K1,K2:	Come on, kitties, get out! Get out! Scat! Scat!	H shooing the kitties toward the stairs in upstairs playhouse.

Transcription, cont'd			*Description, cont'd*
(85)	W–K1,K2:	Come on, scat. Scat!	K1 begins to crawl down stairs while K2 stands up and walks toward W and H.
(86)	K2–HW:	I'm not—I'm not a kitty anymore.	
(87)	H–K2:	You're a husband?	
(88)	K2–H:	Yeah.	
(89)	H–K2:	Good.	
(90)	H–K2:	We need two husbands.	
(91)	H–W:	Hey, two husbands.	H walks near W.
(92)	W–H,K2:	I can't catch two husbands cause I have a grandma.	H points to K2 as she says "grandma."
(93)	K2–W:	Well, I—then I'm the husband.	
(94)	H–K2,W:	Yeah, husbands! Husbands!	
(95)	K2–HW:	Husbands! Husbands!	K2 and H dance around playhouse.
(96)	W–H:	Hold it, Bill. I can't have two husbands.	W holds up two fingers and shakes head.
(97)	W–H:	Not two. Not two.	Walks down stairs shaking head.
(98)	H–K2:	Two husbands. Two husbands.	Dancing around in upstairs playhouse.
. . . .			
(103)	W–H,K2:	I can't marry 'em, two husbands. I can't marry two husbands because I love them.	W is alone at head of stairs in front of downstairs playhouse. H and K2 move down behind her.
(104)	H–W:	Yeah, we do.	

Transcription, cont'd

(105) H–K2:   We gonna mar-
                 ry ourselves,
                 right?
(106) K2–H: Right?

In this sequence, one of the kitties (Denny) had decided to switch roles and verbally marks this decision (86). The husband immediately offers an alternative social position, a second husband. This sequence is interesting, because the wife is conscious of the violation of role expectations (i.e., she can't have, marry, or love two husbands; 92, 96, 103), but she finds it difficult to express this violation to the two boys. At first she tries to handle the problem by suggesting another social position to the kitty (grandma, 92), which he rejects. After repeated protests regarding the shift in social positions, the wife briefly leaves the scene and eventually gives up her position and becomes a kitty in the later phases of this episode.

This sequence, like the earlier data involving the big sister, indicates that young children's conceptions of same-status role alignments and expectations are underdeveloped when compared to adult knowledge. This inference is based on several aspects of the data, including (a) the switching to and dominance of cross-status speech styles once subordinates enter the interactive scene; (b) the children's limited view of the range of duties associated with certain social positions. The duties are often embodied in short "scripts" in the role play scenes (i.e., big sisters do whatever they want, husbands and wives address each other with terms of endearment, and husbands help wives with the more physical housecleaning chores, etc.); and (c) the children's confusion about role structure and the appropriateness of various alignments of social positions (i.e., the possibility of one wife and two husbands).

Overall, these data suggest that the children's knowledge of role expectations may be less developed than knowledge of status. Although the children consistently produce scripted behavior in line with the role expectations of various social positions, they were often confused about the structure of social institutions (i.e., family, workplace, etc.). The children understand institutions have positions that have to be distributed, but they are unsure about how positions are aligned and unaware of how various positions serve broader social functions.

Children's knowledge of role expectations may lag behind their knowledge of status, due to differences in social contextual features of early interactive experiences. While young children are direct participants in cross-status interaction (parent–child), they are most often observers of same-status interaction (mother–father and possibly sibling). As a result, their development of role expectations associated with same-status social positions may be delayed until they have more extensive interactive experience with peers. Peer interaction in the nursery school and informal play groups is important, because it brings the child directly into same-status interaction and provides experience which may often not be available within the family unit.

Role Play and Peer Culture

Although role play is important for the children's development and use of social information about the adult world, I want to reemphasize that it was also a central part of peer culture in the nursery school. As noted earlier, role play is not simply imitation of adult models, but is often an innovative expansion of the adult model (cf. Fortes, 1938; Raum, 1940; Schwartzman, 1978). In role play in the nursery school, there were numerous examples where structural features of the adult world (i.e., family role alignments and routines, occupational routines, etc.) were used by the children as general frames in which play themes were developed and enacted. However, the children would often spontaneously alter the play themes in ways which would bend but not radically distort the general frame.

An excellent example of this phenomenon is what I have termed "animal family" role play. In this type of play, which occurred only among the older group at the school (see Table 3.1), the children pretended to be animals and assigned family roles (usually mother and baby). This form of play contained many of the same features of human family role play, such as enacting family routines (fixing meals, shopping, cleaning, etc.) and an emphasis on authority and discipline. There were, however, important differences between human and animal family role play, as the following example demonstrates.

Example 3.6 Animal Family Role Play

Anita (A) and Brian (B) had been playing for about 15 minutes before videotaping began. Both children were "night lions,"[14] with Anita playing the mother and Brian the baby. The ground floor of the climbing house (see Figure 1.2) served as a home base for the night lions. Brian had just returned to the house when taping began, and he was "screeching" loudly to get Anita's attention. I (researcher, R) was sitting on the floor of the house with a microphone. Three other children (Antoinette, Ant; Alice, Al; and Mark, M) were playing near or in the playhouse when Brian returned. These children were not directly a part of the animal family play.

Transcription			Description
(1)	A–B:	You can go over ( ).	B is screeching loudly.
(2)	B–A:	Noo!	Screeches again.
(3)	A–B:	Then watch the program.	B still screeches.
(4)	A–B:	Watch the program!	
(5)	B–A:	I am.	B now sits on tire in house and looks straight ahead, pretending to watch TV.
(6)	B:	Da-da-da-da!	Screeches again as he watches.
(7)	A–B:	Watch the television!	A shouts at B from other side of house near R. A is pretending to cook a meal.
(8)	R–A:	He—the television?	R wanted to make sure B was pretending to watch TV.
(9)	A–R:	Yeah.	
(10)	B:	Da-da-da-da!	Continues screeching.
(11)	B–A:	It's over.	Referring to TV program.
(12)	A–B:	Oh, well, that was a short one.	A pretends to clean pretend TV.
(13)	B–A:	Didn't you like it?	"It" refers to the program.

---

[14]It was not totally clear to me what a "night lion" was or how it differed from regular lions. I observed these children and three others in the older age group playing "night lions" on other occasions. When I asked what "night lions" were, two of the children (Anita and Brian) said: "They are night lions, silly." When I asked if they were the same as regular lions, both children said: "No, they are *night* lions." I can only conclude that night lions are lions who play and prowl around at night.

Transcription, cont'd			*Description, cont'd*
(14)	A–B:	Yes, but the television is on channel 5 ( ), Ok?	
(15)	B–A:	Ok.	
(16)	A–B:	No-oo! In the important days of American (Sangas). Sangas? What are Sangas? There just a piece of bread. That's all they are.	B begins screeching again.
(17)	A–B:	Now the news is over. Do you wanna watch Lassie?	Pretends to turn off TV.
(18)	B–A:	Yeah. How long does it take?	
(19)	A–B:	Um-ah. A hundred minutes. Um-ah, three hundred minutes.	
(20)	B–A:	Ok.	
(21)	A–B:	There.	Pretends to turn on TV.
(22)	A:	Here I am. Ok, now let's fix dinner.	A moves to other end of house near R and another girl, Al. Ant and M are also playing near the house.
(23)	B:	This is an old—	Seems to be referring to TV program, but is cut-off by A.
(24)	A–R:	Here's your dinner.	Hands plate to R.
(25)	R–A:	Thanks.//	Takes plate from B.
(26)	B–A:	//These are arrows. Ok, there. Those are arrows.	Picks up something.
(27)	B–A:	Ok.	
(28)	Ant–R:	Bam!	Ant enters house and knocks R's plate out of his hand, and then runs off as A moves toward her.
(29)	R–A:	She spilled my dinner.	
(30)	A–Ant:	Don't!	Ant has now moved to outside of house.

Transcription, cont'd		*Description, cont'd*
(31)	B–A:	I'm gonna throw 'em at him.	B throws arrows (small pebbles) at R.
(32)	M:	And this is orange juice.	M has entered house and stands near R and points to a small can.
(33)	Ant–R:	Where's your food? Wa-wa!	Ant now moves back in house near R and M. R pretends to eat food by taking sand from plate and pretending to eat it.
(34)	A–R:	That's skabetti. And night lions don't eat with their hands!	Skabetti seems to be a variant of spaghetti. Volume increases during reprimand about how night lions eat.
(35)	R:	Oh.	R now bends head near plate and pretends to eat food.
(36)	A–R:	Yeah, they eat with their mouths.	
(37)	R–B:	Hey, Stop it.	B now comes over and pushes R's plate from his hands and hits R.
(38)	R–A:	Tell him to stop. Tell him to stop.	
(39)	M–R:	Here's some orange juice.	M tries to hand can to R, but R cannot take it because B is still hitting him.
(40)	B–R:	Ok. Then.	B now stops hitting and begins licking R. R laughs at this.
(41)	A–B:	Baby! Baby!	A now spanks B and tries to get him away from R.
(42)	R–B:	That's enough.	B is laughing as A pulls him off R and pushes him gently to the ground.
(43)	R–M:	Ok, I already got some.	M now pushes orange juice can toward R who declines the offer.
(44)	A–B:	Baby, stop it!	A continues spanking B.
(45)	B:	Wa-wa! Wa-wa!	B pretends to cry and then throws more pebbles (arrows) at R. A immediately gives him another spank for this mischief.
(46)	A:	Now get some orange juice. Now I need jelly.	A stops spanking B and begins working with dishes again. Ant and M have now moved out of house.

Transcription, cont'd			Description, cont'd
(47)	A–R:	Here's some—Oh, this is hot.	A gives plate to R while Ant and M return and play with B near sliding pole in house.
(48)	B–A:	Who are you talking to? Mommy?	
(49)	A–R:	Now eat that jelly.	
(50)	B–A:	Can I have one bite? I wanna get it.	B lifts spoon from plate and pretends to eat.
(51)	B–A:	Mommy, I'm going somewhere.	B gets on broomstick horse and gets ready to leave.
(52)	A–B:	Ok.	B now rides off on horses.

This sequence of interaction is typical of all observed instances of animal family role play, and it differs from human family role play in several respects. First, the children were more aggressive and mobile. Animal family role play always occurred outdoors, and, as was the case in this example, the climbing bars or house served as a home base, with the children moving throughout the entire outside yard area. This pattern of movement contrasts sharply with human family role play, which was almost always confined to the playhouse area with little movement to or from other locations during an interactive episode. In animal families, there was also a great deal of "screeching" and "growling" (mock aggression) among the family members and at children playing nearby. In this particular episode, both Anita and Brian "growled" and "scratched" at other children later in the episode, during their excursions from the home base.

A second difference in the children's enactment of animal and human families was the nature of the relationship between superordinates (mother, father, etc.) and subordinates (baby, pets, etc.). In both human and animal families, superordinates spent a great deal of time supervising and disciplining subordinates. However, in animal families the discipline was *more physical* but *less restrictive* than in human family role play. In Example 3.6, the mother night lion (Anita) first verbally reprimands her baby (Brian) (lines 1–7), then spanks him for further misbehavior (41, 42). Although the spanking is playful, there is actual physical contact, which contrasts with human family role play where subordinates were frequently verbally reprimanded and threatened but rarely punished physically even in a playful manner.[15] On the other hand, animal babies were granted much more freedom to move away from the home or den and play for lengthy periods of time without supervision. In Example 3.6, the baby night lion (Brian) informs (rather than asks) his mother about his leave-taking, and the mother shows no resistance (51–52). In this episode, the baby (Brian) was off at play for several minutes before being joined by the mother in another area of the school. They both then returned to the climbing house, but Brian left again shortly thereafter. The family role play theme remained intact until clean-up time at the end of the afternoon session. As we saw in Example 3.1, babies in human family role play had much less freedom of movement and were often not allowed to leave their cribs or beds, let alone the house.

A third difference between animal and human family role play is related to the overall nature or structure of the activity. Human family role play was characterized by a series of routines (cleaning, shopping, cooking, etc.) which were proposed and then enacted by family members (see Examples 3.1, 3.2, and 3.4). Animal family role play, on the other hand, was less structured, with family routines interspersed over long periods of unrelated activities which often involved interaction with other children who did not have precisely defined roles in the animal families. In Example 3.6, Brian (baby night lion) was joined by Mark (who had earlier been in the house but was not part of the family) and they rode on broomstick horses until Brian returned to the climbing house. Meanwhile, the mother night lion (Anita) also left the house and went riding her broomstick horse with Alice, who had observed but not participated in the family role play.

In specifying differences between the children's human and animal family role play, my point is not simply that children are learning and using knowledge about human and animal family structure and behavior. Clearly, this is true; animals are aggressive and the young of many species have more freedom of movement than human infants. As Example 3.6 demonstrates, however, animal family role play is a transformation of human family role play with some elements intact (authority relations, disciplines scripts, cooking, and TV viewing), some elements added (more aggres-

---

[15]There was only one occasion in human family role play where a subordinate was physically punished. In this instance, a pet ("kitty") was playfully spanked for pretending to urinate on a clean floor in the playhouse.

siveness and physical discipline, and less supervision of subordinates), and some elements intertwined (food eaten from plates but without utensils or one's hands).

My point here is that role play involves more than learning specific social knowledge; it also involves learning about the relationship between *context and behavior*. As Bateson (1956) argues, when the child plays a role he or she not only learns something about the specific social position but "also learns that there is such a thing as a role." According to Bateson, the child "acquires a new view, partly flexible and partly rigid" and learns "the fact of stylistic flexibility and the fact that choice of style or role is related to the frame or context of behavior" (Bateson, 1956, as quoted in Schwartzman, 1978:129). The children's mutual recognition of the "transformative power" of play is an important element of peer culture. In this sense, animal family role play is "playing at" human family role play, which in turn is "playing at" the adult model. This shared knowledge is part of peer culture because it is used by the children *to mutually construct a play context* which tranforms human family role play so that it includes personally valued behaviors like mobility and aggressiveness while at the same time preserving many of the human family texts and structures (i.e., authority relations, discipline scripts, and cleaning, cooking, and watching TV routines). As a result, in animal family role play the children are mobile and aggressive but still rely on shared social knowledge of human families, which is essential for the organization and maintenance of peer interaction.

The children's transformations of adult models in role play to develop mutually valued behavioral routines is aptly illustrated in the following sequence from the videotaped data involving three boys pretending to be hunters.

Example 3.7 The Hunters
As taping begins in this episode, Brian (B), Allen (A), and Mark (M) are moving toward the climbing bars with broomstick horses. B and A are carrying their broomsticks with the horses' reins around their necks, so that they have transformed the horse into a gun with a strap. M, however, is still riding his horse at this point. Two other children, Graham (G) and Lenny (L), are in the bars and are pretending to be firemen. When B and M reach the bars, they climb up a ladder and move into the bars while A stands below. I (researcher, R) am near the bars with a microphone, and a teaching assistant (TA) is also nearby.

Transcription			*Description*
(1)	A–BM:	Well, anyway, I'm going up here 'cause I'm a hunter.	
(2)	B–M:	Go. Go, for your guns. Aim right at them.	B and M are in bars holding broomsticks so stick end is pointing toward children ("them") over the fence in the adjoining school.
(3)	B–M:	( )	
(4)	B–M:	Hey look—that good guy.	B points gun over fence and then points with hand at a particular child in adjoining school when he says "good guy."
(5)	B–M:	Let's fire at them.	B pretends to shoot broomstick gun.
(6)	M–B:	I'm getting down—Spiderman.	M moves down from the bars; he refers to B as "Spiderman." B and M were playing Spiderman earlier in the day.
(7)	B–M:	Ok.	B also starts down.
(8)	B–M:	I havta stand on your head.	B playfully puts a foot near M's head as they move down. Both then reach bottom of bars, where A is waiting for them.
(9)	A–BM:	Hi, Hunters.	M pretends to shoot his gun in response to A's greeting.
(10)	B–A:	Hi.	
(11)	G–BMA:	No—Get off—the fire hydrant. You're on the fire hydrant.	B and A are standing near while M sits on a platform which G is pretending is a fire hydrant.
(12)	B–MA:	Pow! Go for your guns. Pow it again.	B now pretends to shoot gun, and A does likewise. B and M ignore G's warnings and move away from the bars while M remains on the platform. B and A move to the sandpile, where B finds a package of crackers. M now joins B and A.
(13)	B–R:	Here's something. Here's	B holds up crackers, asking the researcher what they are.

Transcription, cont'd		Description, cont'd
	something.	
	What's this?	
(14) R–B:	I just wanna look at it. It looks like crackers.	B pulls back crackers and puts them behind his back as R reaches for them.
(15) B–R:	I'll keep it.	The teaching assistant (TA) now moves toward B and reaches for the crackers.
(16) B–TA:	Well, I'll keep this though, Ok?	B pulls back crackers out of TA's reach.
(17) TA–B:	Oh, they–that's dirty. They threw it over. Did M throw it away?	TA is referring to children ("They") in adjoining school. But TA is not sure, and thinks M may have thrown them away.
(18) B–TA:	What is it?	
(19) TA–B:	I don't know, let me look.	
(20) B–TA:	Will you let me have it?	
(21) TA–B:	I'll look and give it back to you after I look.	B hands crackers to TA who looks at them.
(22) TA–B:	That used to be crackers, but they crumbled them all up so now they're not crackers anymore.	TA now returns crackers to B.
(23) B:	I will pretend they're bullets.	
(24) TA–B:	Why don't you put it on the ground, 'cause I bet the birds would like to eat it. Sprinkle them on the ground.	
(25) B:	No. I will pretend they're for us—for me.	

Transcription, cont'd		*Description, cont'd*
(26)	B: Our bullets.	B pretends to put bullets (crackers) in gun by sprinkling crushed crackers on the handle of his pretend gun.
(27)	A–B: One for everybody.	
(28)	B–A: Yeah.	B does not, however, give crackers to A.
(29)	M–B: Can I have some?	
(30)	A–B: Can I have some?	
(31)	B–AM: It's just a little bit of bullets.	B resists sharing crackers.
(32)	M–B: //I need some.	
(33)	A–B: //I need some.	
(34)	B–M: Ok, here.	B sprinkles some crackers on M's gun but holds onto package.
(35)	P–BM: What is it?	Another boy, Peter (P), now enters scene and asks about crackers.
(36)	B–P: Bullets.	
(37)	M–P: Bullets.	
(38)	TA: I hope you remember that— that we really don't like guns at school, 'cause they hurt people.	
(39)	A–TA: These aren't guns.	A quickly flips his broomstick horse so stick end is facing down and horse's head is up.
(40)	B–TA: These are just for pretending	
(41)	M–TA: Pretending.	
(42)	TA: Very pretend.	TA stresses the word "very" and begins to move away from the boys. The boys pretend to shoot guns, saying "Pow-Pow," as soon as TA is some distance away from them.
(43)	A–B: Can I have some?	A requests bullets when he sees B begin putting more crackers (bullets) on his gun.

Transcription, cont'd		Description, cont'd
(44)	M–B:	I need some more.	
(45)	A–B:	Can I have some?	B now gives a few bullets to A.
(46)	M–B:	I need some more.	
(47)	B–M:	No, you don't.	B puts bullets (crackers) in his pocket.
(48)	A–B:	I want some.	
(49)	B–AM:	No, it's just bullets. I found it and I don't have to—give—any— to you unless you—	
(50)	A–B:	Yes, you gave me a lot.	
(51)	B–A:	No—we can shoot.	B turns away from A and fires his gun.
(52)	B:	Cop'er!	B says this as he shoots gun. "Cop'er" seems to refer to policeman. M and A now also begin shooting. Another boy, Lenny (L), who had been watching B, A, and M from a distance, now runs up in front of them and pretends to shoot at them with his finger, saying: "Pow-Pow!". L then runs off.
(53)	B–AM:	Look at that bird, cop'er.	B is referring to a bird design on top of the climbing house. A and M then turn to look at the design. M now leaves with no verbal marking, and B and A do not notice his departure.
(54)	B–A:	You can never get dead, cop'er. Cop'er, I hit'em, cop'er. Pow-Pow!	B pretends to shoot at target (bird design).
(55)	B–A:	I'll read the sign, it says: "If you have guns that's	B now seems to be pretending that they are at a shooting gallery.

Transcription, cont'd		Description, cont'd
	the target; if you miss the target; you don't get a present; if you get the target, you win a present."	
(56) B–A:	Cop'er come. Cop'er let's try to shoot it. Pow! Shot it.	B pretends to shoot at target.
(57) B–A:	Bad shot. Good shot. Good shot, I mean.	B now puts more bullets (crackers) on his gun.
(58) A–B:	What about me?	A also wants crackers.
(59) B–A:	Nope, you don't get any.	
(60) R–A:	What about me?	Researcher (R) had been nearby with microphone throughout this interaction. Here he was trying to see if B would share bullets with him.
(61) B–R:	Nope, you don't get any.	
(62) A–B:	Where's M? He ran away. Where did he go?	A now notices that M is no longer playing with them.
(63) B–A:	Pow! Pow!	B shoots gun and moves toward the climbing house.
(64) B–A:	Away! There he is!	B sees M near the climbing house and moves toward him with A following. The episode continues for several more minutes until clean up time.

The nursery school teachers disapproved of play which involved pretend guns or shooting and role play like cowboys or army. However, during the beginning of the school term, many of the boys (especially in the older age group) frequently engaged in play with guns until discouraged by the teachers. Most of the children in the school soon became aware of the teachers' views regarding these activities and, as a result, I observed few sustained instances of play involving guns and shooting. The sequence in Example 3.7 is interesting because it reflects the boys' desires to engage in the restricted behavior, and their techniques for creating a context (role play activity) in which the activity was both more legitimate and more discreet than in cowboy or army role play. In this sense, the hunters role play episode reveals a behavioral routine valued by a subset (mainly older boys) of the children, and specific techniques they employed to evade adult restrictions of the behavior. Both the behavioral routine itself (guns and shooting) and the techniques for evading adult rules can be seen as features of peer culture.[16]

In this particular episode, the boys are pretending to be hunters. Hunters, like cowboys and soldiers, shoot guns; but, unlike cowboys and soldiers, they do not shoot guns at each other. The hunters episode was similar to two others (campers and fishermen) recorded in field notes where boys transformed objects (fishing poles and shovels) into guns during role play. In the hunters episode, the boys' transformation of broomstick horses into guns served a dual function. First, the horses served not only as guns, but also fit into the role play theme when used as horses. Some hunters may indeed ride horses, and the boys used the horses for riding to various areas during the role play. Second, since the broomstick horses were familiar objects in the school, they could be transformed into guns with a good chance of escaping the attention of the teachers, as long as the boys avoided shooting at each other. The role play theme of hunters is, therefore, a reflection of the children's desires to play "guns" and not attract adult attention.

As often occurs in much of children's play, however, there were some unexpected developments which resulted in a teaching assistant's discovery of the transformation of the broomstick horses to guns. These developments are also related to peer culture and, therefore, a close examination of the three main phases of the hunters role play is in order.

In the first phase of the hunters episode (1–8), the three boys

---

[16]Features of peer culture include values, norms, behavioral routines, and the children's strategies for evading adult rules. These features are discussed at length in Chapter 5. The notion of peer culture I am using in the monograph is in line with the recent conceptualization of "subculture" presented by Fine and Kleinman (1979).

move to the climbing bars and Brian and Mark climb into the bars while Allen waits below. Once in the bars, Brian and Mark turn their broomstick horses so that the stick end points away and the horses' heads are held against their chests, transforming them into guns. Brian then instructs Mark to "go for your guns" and to aim and shoot at children over the fence in the adjoining school (2–5). The decision to shoot at these children, rather than peers in their own school, may have been totally spontaneous, since the boys noticed the children when they got to a certain height in the bars. But another interpretation is possible. On numerous occasions, I observed these boys and other children in both age groups first climb high in the bars and then comment that they could see children in the adjoining school.[17] Therefore, Brian and Mark were not surprised at seeing the children. The decision to shoot at the children, then, may have been at least partially influenced by the fact that they could not be a part of the play and, therefore, would not shoot back. As a result, the probability of attracting the attention of one of the teachers to the gun play was relatively low. It is important to note in this regard that the boys were not pretending the children in the adjoining school were "animals," which would be in line with the hunters theme. Instead Brian's reference to "good guy" (4) indicates that he seemed to be arbitrarily labelling some of the children "good guys" and implying that the rest were "bad guys" who could be shot. In this respect, the hunters role play takes on characteristics of cowboys, soldiers, or police.

In the second phase of the sequence (9–53), Brian and Mark leave the bars and are greeted by Allen as hunters (9–10). Shortly thereafter, Brian discovers the crackers (13), and it is at this point that the unexpected developments begin. When he first finds the crackers, Brian has a good notion of what they are, but he is not sure about how they got in the outside yard. He first asks me about them (13) and is careful about not giving them up. In this situation, I am trusted more than a teacher (i.e., Brian does not hesitate to ask me about the crackers), but he still fears I may not return the crackers if he gives them to me. At this point, the teaching assistant (TA) notices the crackers and Brian responds

---

[17]In fact, a major attraction of the climbing bars was the ability to see outside the school when one climbed high up. See the discussion of the children's ritual involving "greeting the garbage man" from the top of the bars in Chapter 5.

to her recognition even before she attempts to get them from him (16). In line 17, the TA first tries to explain that the children from the adjoining school must have thrown the crackers over the fence. However, she is not sure about this and asks if Mark carried them from the juice room and then threw them away. The TA was concerned that Brian might eat the crackers, so she talks him into letting her look at them, but has to promise to return them to him (20–21). It seems that all this discussion is heightening the children's interest in the crackers.

Once Brian gets the crackers back, he transforms them into bullets and thereby fits them into the hunters theme. This action creates two unexpected problems for Brian. First, once the crackers become bullets, he has to contend with the attempts of the other hunters to get him to share (27, 29–34).[18] At the continual insistence of Allen and Mark, Brian first sprinkles a few crackers on Mark's gun (34) and later gives some to Allen (45). Brian resists sharing at first and is given a short reprieve, but only long enough to deal with a second unexpected problem.

In transforming the crackers to bullets, Brian has inadvertently drawn the attention of the TA to the guns (38–42). In handling this situation, the TA first asks the children to reflect back and recall the rule against guns, and she then goes on to justify the rule (i.e., " 'cause they hurt people"). Although attracting the teacher's attention to the guns was inadvertent, all three boys have a response ready. Allen immediately flips his broomstick horse right-side-up and denies even having a gun. Brian contradicts Allen and admits having guns, but says they are "just for pretending" (40), and Mark reiterates this claim (41). The children's reference to pretending is a logical argument, since it counters the TA's justification that guns hurt people. After all, you cannot really hurt anyone with a pretend gun. The TA realizes she has a problem here, so emphasizes the guns must be "very pretend." Although this statement may imply an implicit request that the boys not shoot the pretend guns, we see they do just that when she leaves the area.

At this point in the episode, the three boys shoot their guns at another child in the school for the first and only time. However, this occurs when the child (Lenny) first watches them for some

---

[18] Children's norms regarding sharing in peer interaction are discussed at length in Chapter 5.

time and then jumps in front of them and pretends to shoot the hunters with his finger. The hunters respond with return fire and Lenny runs off.

In the third phase of the sequence (53–64), Brian attempts to contextualize the gun play more closely into the hunters theme by pretending to shoot at a target (53–57). The fact that the target was a bird design on the climbing house supports this interpretation. However, even here Brian continues to use the phrase "cop'er," and his utterance (54) implies that he and Allen are police shooting at criminals. Finally, Brian shifts the play again and maintains that they are shooting at a target to win a present. This behavior seems to be more in line with going to a carnival or a fair, but is still not totally outside the hunters theme (i.e., hunters do take target practice).

Overall, the hunters episode and animal family role play are clear examples of the children's peer culture. There were also segments in many of the other role play episodes involving similar transformations. These data show how the children transform role play based on specific adult models to role play with several interwoven frames or themes (i.e., human and animal families; hunters, cowboys, police, and soldiers) and less rigid boundaries. *As a result, behaviors and activities the children regard as important (physical aggressiveness, mobility, play with guns, etc.) become part of peer interactive events*. In this sense, role play is not only important for the children's development and use of social knowledge, but is also a part of peer culture.

CHAPTER 4

Friendship and Social Integration in Peer Culture

The discovery of friendship is a major step in children's acquisition of social knowledge. Before children make friends, social bonds are primarily between the child and parents or other adult caretakers. This is not to say that children do not influence caretakers or do not actively construct concepts of social relations within the family by participating in interactive events. However, within the family children have relatively little opportunity for negotiation; they must recognize, accept, and adapt to their relationships with parents and siblings. When children first move outside the family unit, they discover a range of options in the selection of interactive partners. Through interaction with peers, children learn that they can regulate social bonds on the basis of criteria that emerge from their personal needs and social contextual demands. They also learn that their peers will not always accept them immediately; often a child must convince others of his merits as a playmate, and sometimes he must anticipate and accept exclusion.

Interest in children's friendships has increased dramatically in recent years, resulting in a growing number of research studies (see Asher and Gottman, 1981; Damon, 1977; Lewis and Rosenblum, 1975; Rubin, 1980, for examples and reviews of recent work) and several developmental theories of friendship (Damon, 1977; Selman, 1976, 1980; Youniss, 1975). However, much of the work to date has focused on school age children, and few studies have involved direct observations of children's use of developing conceptions of friendship in everyday peer activities. For the children in the present study, conceptions of friendship were directly tied to organizational features of peer culture. In examining this relationship, I will first discuss patterns in field notes and the video data, and then relate these findings to the recent work on children's friendships.

Social Participation, the Protection of Interactive Space, and Friendship

As stated in Chapter 1, the goal of this micro-ethnography is to discover (a) the basic features of the nursery school as a peer environment, and (b) consistent strategies of communication that the children employed to produce and sustain peer activities. Given the emphasis on peer culture, I felt it essential to identify what *mattered most* to the children in their everyday activities with peers and teachers.

When I examined field notes from the first 3 months of participant observation, I found that the children shared two major, interrelated concerns. These concerns involved social participation and the protection of interactive space, both of which were directly related to the children's conception and use of friendship in peer interaction. First, regarding social participation, the children rarely engaged in solitary play; children who found themselves alone[1] consistently attempted to gain entry into one of the ongoing peer episodes. As a result, the children developed a broad and complex

---

[1]In field notes, 10 episodes (1.6% of the total peer episodes) included solitary play. The 146 videotaped peer episodes included three (2.1%) instances of solitary play. Other researchers (Parten, 1932; Rubin, Maioni, and Hornung, 1976) have found higher rates of solitary play. It is difficult to compare the findings in these studies with the present research, because of the important differences in data collection techniques. In the other studies, the researchers worked with more structured sampling strategies in which they observed each child for "1" minute for a set number of times. I have previously discussed the advantages of using the interactive episode as the sampling or collection unit. Sampling by interactive episodes *insures* the contextual richness of naturalistic data. Although the issue cannot be pursued at length here, it is my belief regarding solitary play that time-sampling of sequences of behavior of short duration (1 to 5 minutes) may, in part, affect the level of solitary play recorded. This effect seems most apparent regarding what Parten (1932) has termed "onlooker/unoccupied" behavior, which is a type of solitary play. An observational study of adults at a cocktail party, using 1-minute time sampling techniques, would probably reveal a high level of such behavior, and would fail to capture, as it does with children in the nursery school, the functions of such behavior for access attempts into ongoing activities (Corsaro, 1979c).

set of access strategies (cf. Corsaro, 1979c), some of which were directly related to friendship. Consider the following example from field notes.

Example 4.1
Date: November 21
Morning Episode 3
Scene: Outside Sandbox
Participants: Jenny (J), Betty (B), Debbie (D), Researcher (R)

Jenny and Betty are playing around a sandbox in the outside yard of the school. I am sitting on the ground near the sandbox, watching. The girls are putting sand in pots, cupcake pans, bottles, and teapots. Occasionally one of the girls would bring me a pan of sand (cake) to eat. Another girl, Debbie, approaches and stands near me, observing the other two girls. Neither J nor B acknowledges her presence. D does not speak to me nor to the other two girls, and no one speaks to her. After watching for some time (5 minutes or so), she circles the sandbox three times and stops and stands next to me. After a few more minutes of watching, D moves to the sandbox and reaches for a teapot in the sand. J takes the pot away from D and mumbles "No." D backs away and again stands near me, observing the activity of J and B. She then walks over next to B, who is filling the cupcake pan with sand. D watches B for just a few seconds, then says:

(1)   D–B: We're friends, right? We're friends, right B?

B, not looking up at D and while continuing to place sand in the pan, says:

(2)   B–D: Right.
D now moves alongside B and takes a pot and spoon and begins putting sand in the pot.

(3)   D–B: I'm making coffee.
(4)   B–D: I'm making cupcakes.
(5)   B–J: We're mothers, right, J?
(6)   J–B: Right.

This now triadic episode continues for 20 minutes until the teachers announce "clean-up" time.

Debbie employed a variety of access strategies in this sequence. She first placed herself in the area of interaction, a strategy I have termed "nonverbal entry." She then "encircled" the area and eventually produced a behavior in line with the ongoing activity (she picks up a teapot). When this attempt was rebuffed, she used the verbal strategy "reference to affiliation" ("We're friends, right?") which received a positive response from Betty, and shortly thereafter Debbie was allowed to become a part of the playgroup.

Example 4.1 demonstrates that references to friendship can be used *as a device* for gaining entry and social participation. But just as friendship can be used to achieve access to play groups, it can also be used as a basis for exclusion. For example:

Example 4.2
Date: December 3
Morning Episode 3
Scene: Inside Block Area
Participants: Barbara (B), Betty (Be), Linda (L), Researcher (R), Teaching Assistant (TA)

I entered the block area after having watched Barbara (B) and Betty (Be) leave the juice room together, move to the block area, and begin to gather blocks and toy animals. As I sat on the floor a short distance from them, B said to me (R):

(1) B–R: Look, Bill, we're making a zoo.
(2) R–B: That's nice. You have lots of animals.
(3) Be–RB: Yeah, we're zookeepers, right, B?
(4) B–Be: Right.

The two girls played for about 10 minutes, building small enclosures with the blocks, placing the animals inside, and talking to each other. At one point, Be set some animals and blocks near me and said they were for me. I also built a small house and placed some animals inside. Then I noticed that Linda (L) was watching us from a distance. After a few minutes, L entered the block area, sat next to B, and picked up one of the animals.

(5)   B–L: You can't play.
(6)   L–B: Yes, I can. I can have some animals too.
(7)   B–L: No, you can't. We don't like you today.
(8)   Be–L: You're not our friend.
(9)   L–BBe: I can play here, too.
(10) B–Be: No, her can't—her can't play, right Be?
(11) Be–B: Right.
(12) L–R: Can I have some animals, Bill?
(13) R–L: You can have some of these. (R offers L some of his animals)

(14)	B–R:	She can't play, Bill, 'cause she's not our friend.
(15)	R–B:	Why not? You guys played with her yesterday.
(16)	Be–R:	Well, we hate her today.
(17)	L–All:	Well, I'll tell teacher. (L now leaves but then returns with a teaching assistant)
(18)	TA–BBe:	Girls, can L play with you?
(19)	B–TA:	No! She's not our friend.
(20)	TA–B:	Why can't you *all* be friends?
(21)	B–TA:	No!
(22)	Be–B:	Let's go outside, B.
(23)	B–Be:	Okay.
		(B and Be leave. L remains and plays with animals near R for a few minutes and then leaves and goes to juice room)

In this example, as was the case in most instances of resistance, the children were not so much attempting to maintain control over objects (play materials) or territory, but rather were *protecting interactive space* (i.e., the ecological area in which the interactive episodes were unfolding). Resistance to access attempts occurred frequently in the nursery school (see below), and in many instances they contained references to the denial of friendship.

The two patterns, desire for social participation and the tendency to protect interactive space, were the source of recurrent conflict, as demonstrated in Example 4.2. The patterns reveal a great deal about the structure of peer culture, solidarity among peers, and the children's developing conceptions of friendship. In pursuing the relationship among access attempts, protection of interactive space, and friendship, I first present data from field notes which specify how often access attempts were resisted, and the range of types of resistance. I will then examine the video data regarding the frequency of types of resistance, and present a microsociolinguistic analysis of an access–resistance sequence to capture the processual, negotiated features of this component of peer culture.

Patterns in Field Notes

Table 4.1 contains data on the frequency of initial resistance and acceptance of access attempts for both the morning and afternoon

Table 4.1   Initial Response to Attempts to Gain Access
(October 15–January 30)

Time Period	Morning Group		Afternoon Group	
	Accept	Resist	Accept	Resist
October 15–30	7	9	17	10
November 1–27	6	17	20	22
December 2–5				
January 6–30	3	7	6	4
TOTAL				
N	16	33	43	36
%	32.7	67.3	54.4	45.6

Source: Field Notes
Note: During these 3 months, for the morning group, the notes reported 213 total episodes, of which 49 (23.0%) contained attempts to gain access. For the afternoon group, the notes included 179 episodes, of which 79 (44.1%) contained attempts to gain access.

groups. For the younger children, 33 (67.3%) of the 49 episodes involving access attempts contained initial resistance. The percentage is lower for the older children, but even in this group more than 45% of the episodes involving access attempts included initial resistance.

In addition to the fact that access attempts were often resisted, several other features of peer interaction contribute to the concerns of gaining entry and protecting interactive space. First, most of the episodes were of relatively short duration. In field notes, 51.4% of all peer episodes lasted less than 5 minutes, and 32.5% lasted less than 10 minutes. Since peer episodes normally lasted less than 10 minutes during the 2-hour free play period in both the morning and afternoon sessions, the children were often confronted with the need to enter a new play group. Furthermore, the children had to be prepared for the breakdown of interaction at any time, because playmates often simply left a play area and terminated the activity without a formal, verbal marker (see Corsaro, 1979c). As a result, peer interaction was fragile in that termination could occur without warning at any time, and the predominant mode of leave-taking (simple physical movement from a play area) most often precluded any possible negotiation to continue the activity. Therefore, the children often found themselves with playmates one minute and alone the next; in which case they could choose from a range of options that included solitary play, entry into teacher-directed activity,[2] or attempts to gain access to an ongoing peer episode. If they tried to gain access to a peer episode, they frequently encountered initial resistance.

One important question regarding initial resistance to access attempts is whether it occurred for all children who attempted access. There is, for example, an established literature on peer relations which documents the existence of dominance hierarchies in children's play groups (cf. Hartup, 1970; Omark, Omark, and Edelman, 1975; Schwartzman, 1978; Sluckin and Smith, 1977; Strayer and Strayer, 1976). I did not find any clear dominance hierarchy in either age group at the school. Furthermore, there were no instances in which certain children were consistently either accepted or excluded.[3] Only four children were initially accepted or resisted more than three times. For each of these children, the frequencies of initial acceptance and resistance were nearly identical.[4] There was one pattern regarding sexual makeup of groups, sex of the child attempting access, and rate of resistance. While the rate of resistance was approximately 50% for access attempts by boys and girls to all girl groups and mixed groups, and for boys' access attempts to all boy groups, the rate of resistance was 75% for girls' access attempts to all boy groups.[5]

[2] Unfortunately, I recorded only a few episodes (5 in field notes and 17 on videotape) of teacher-directed activities. The behavior of the children who participated in these episodes followed no consistent pattern, but the sample was small and it is not possible to draw any conclusions about the children's use of this option.

[3] I should point out that dominance hierarchies and the ability of certain children to consistently gain access may be related to size of the school, both in terms of physical space and number of children (cf. Connolly and Smith, 1978). In the present research, the school was rather large in terms of physical dimensions, with each group made up of around 25 children.

[4] For the four children involved, the difference between initial acceptance and resistance were as follows: Debbie, 4 cases of initial acceptance and 3 of initial resistance; Denny, 2 cases of initial acceptance and 4 of initial resistance; Tommy, 5 cases of initial acceptance and 6 of initial resistance; and Brian, 5 cases of initial acceptance and 3 of initial resistance.

[5] The raw data regarding sexual makeup of groups and the percentage of cases of resistance to children attempting access is as follows: boy(s) attempting access to all boy groups, 46.4% resistance in 28 attempts; girl(s) attempting access to all girls groups, 58.8% resistance in 17 attempts; boy(s) attempting access to all girl groups, 53.3% resistance in 15 attempts; *girl(s) attempting access to all boy groups, 75.0% resistance in 24 attempts;* boy(s) attempting access to a mixed sex group, 45% resistance in 20 attempts; and for girl(s) attempting access to a mixed sex group, 52.2% resistance in 23 attempts.

To this point, I have used the term "initial resistance" because attempts to gain access did not always result in permanent exclusion. Of the 69 cases of initial resistance in field notes for both groups, 35 (50.7%) led to permanent exclusion. Given the frequency of initial resistance and the fact that it is overcome nearly 50% of the time, the children encounter an ambiguous interactive situation. There is no clear choice here regarding either strategies for gaining entry or protecting interactive space. The expectation of initial resistance is tempered by the knowledge that the resistance can be overcome. This ambiguity or uncertainty regarding access to ongoing episodes in turn leads to conflict and to a central concern on the part of the children, not only to resist intrusion, but also to seek access to ongoing events when they are uninvolved.

To this point, we have focused on the frequency of initial resistance. I will now turn to a discussion of features of the children's resistance strategies and justifications for exclusion. An analysis of all episodes recorded during the first 3 months of participant observation revealed five types of resistance. The first type, *verbal resistance with no justification*, occurred only as the first reaction to an attempt at access. When a child persisted in trying to gain access, this strategy was dropped in favor of one of the four described below. The following example shows this type of resistance:

Example 4.3
Date: November 27
Afternoon Episode 2
Laura (L), Daniel (D), and Lenny (Le) are playing house in the climbing bars. Jonathan (J) approaches:

J–D: I'll be the daddy.
D–J: Okay.
L–J: No, you won't! No! N-O spells No! No!
Le–J: No! Get out of here!

J leaves and is followed by D, while L and Le continue playing.

A second type of resistance is *reference to arbitrary rules* which involve justification of exclusion on the basis of arbitrary rules. The rules generally were related to either the excluder's own immediate needs and desires or observable characteristics of the intruder (e.g., sex, size, dress, etc.). Examples 4.4 and 4.5 show this type of resistance.

Example 4.4

Date: November 7

Morning Episode 1

Linda (L) and Jack (J) have lined up wooden boxes to make a train. Bill (B) and Denny (D) approach. B and D are barefoot:

B–L: What is this? Is it a city? Is this your train?

L–B: You can't play with bare feet!

J–B: Yeah, go away!

B–D: It's a train.

B and D leave the area and run towards the climbing bars.

Example 4.5

Date: November 4

Afternoon Episode 4

Graham (G) and Peter (P) are pulling dumptrucks in wagons. Tommy (T) approaches and tries to get in one of the wagons:

P–T: No. These wagons are for dumptrucks only!

G–T: For dumptrucks only!

T–PG: No, they are for people.

P and G move away, and T throws sand at them as they go.

A third type of resistance was *specific claims of ownership of objects or areas of play.* These justifications for resistance were not arbitrary, but were based on temporal aspects of possession ("I had that first"), school rules, or social rules of role play. Examples 4.6 and 4.7 show this type of response.

Example 4.6

Date: January 8

Morning Episode 1

Ellen (E) and Leah (L) are involved in role play. E is the mother and L is a baby. After some time, Denny (D) enters and approaches L, who is pretending to sleep:

E–D: No! Baby must sleep.

D–E: But . . . I just want to love her.

D kisses L.

E–D: No. Her must sleep. Get out of here. Go!

D runs off and does not return.

Example 4.7

Date: November 14

Afternoon Episode 3

Denise (D) and Eva (E) are playing in the climbing bars. Brian (B) approaches. B is pretending to be a wild animal and has a tail stuck in the back of his pants:

B–DE: That's my house.

E–B: We were living here first.

B–D: Well, remember I was up there before.

D climbs down behind B and pulls his tail.

D–B: You're bad.

B now chases D around the yard; then he moves inside the school and D returns to the bars and joins E.

    In a fourth type of resistance, which I term *justification with reference(s) to space or number of people*, the children's justifications for exclusion demonstrated a recognition that interaction can break down when a play area becomes overcrowded. This type differs from claims of ownership in that children go beyond claims to justify exclusion on the basis of ecological constraints of the school. Use of this type of resistance shows children's awareness of, and sensitivity to, the social organizational features of peer culture in this setting. In the following example, two children are allowed to enter an ongoing episode before one child, Laura, discovers the negative effects on stability of interaction of the large number of playmates. This discovery then serves as a basis for an attempt to exclude; the result is conflict and the eventual breakdown of the activity.

Example 4.8

Date: October 22

Afternoon Episode 8

Laura (L) and Sue (S) are playing in the upstairs playhouse. They are pretending to prepare a meal. Antoinette (A) moves up the stairs and S goes to the head of the stairs to block her entry:

L–S: She can come in.

S lets A enter and all three children continue to prepare the meal. Now Alice (Al) comes upstairs.

Al: Can I play?
L–Al: No!
Al–A: A, A can I play?
A–Al: Okay.

Al enters and stands next to A.

L–Al: This is only for girls.
Al–L: Okay.
Al–A: Can I be a little baby?
A–Al: Yeah, you can be a little baby.
L–A: No, she can't. We can only have one baby.

Al and A now play near a table, while L and S continue cooking. Then L walks over to the table.

L–AAl: Now what are you guys messing around for?

At this point, Allen enters.

L: Oh, we're having so many people!

L–Allen: Get out of my house! Get out of my house!
Allen–L: No, it's my house!
L–Allen: No!

At this point, a teacher intervened and told the children to clean up the house and come downstairs.

A final type of resistance involved the *denial of friendship*. Example 4.2 showed that children use friendship to differentiate defenders from intruders. Although the denial of friendship and accompanying expressions of dislike may seem cruel to adults, they are often qualified temporally (e.g., "We don't like you *today*"). This type of resistance must be evaluated in terms of the children's conceptualization of friendship at this age (Damon, 1977; Selman, 1976; Youniss, 1975), and the demands of the interactive setting. Consider the following example:

Example 4.9
Date: December 7
Morning Episode 2
Denny (D) and Leah (L) are running and pretending to be lions. Joseph (J) watches from a distance. Glen (G), who had been playing with D earlier, approaches D and L. J follows closely behind G.

D–G: Grr-Grr. We don't like you.
L–G: Grr-Grr.

G–D: You were my friend a minute ago.
D–G: Yeah.
G–D: Well, if you keep going "grr," you can't be my friend anymore.
J–D: Yeah.
D–G: Well, then I'm not your friend.
L–GJ: Yeah, Grr-Grr.

L and D now run off toward the climbing bars. G moves into the sand-pile with J and they begin digging.

In this example, when Glen encountered initial resistance, he reminded Denny that only a short time ago they were friends. Denny agreed, but continued to resist and was not dissuaded by Glen's threat to end the friendship. In fact, Denny decided that, at least at this point in time, he was no longer Glen's friend. In this sequence, the references to friendship are bound to the particular interactive situation. Denny used the denial of friendship as a device to protect the interactive space and ongoing episode (i.e., playing lion with Leah). In contrast, Glen used the threat of denial of friendship as a strategy to attempt to overcome Denny's resistance.

According to cognitive-developmental theory, the source of development of social concepts is the child's activities in dealing with objects and events in his environment. Example 4.9 demonstrates the complexity of contextual features of peer culture in which children *must actively construct and at the same time connect these concepts with specific interactive demands.* In example 4.9, the children were not only learning about the concept of friendship, but were also attempting to use the developing notion as a device to both justify and overcome exclusion.

Protection of Interactive Space in the Video Data

The video data were collected over the last 4 months of the school term (see Chapter 1). A total of 146 episodes were videotaped, of which 70 included attempts to gain access. Of these 70 episodes, 39 occurred in the morning group and 31 in the afternoon group. For the morning group, 20 of the 39 episodes (51.3%) contained initial resistance to access attempts, while 14 of the 31 episodes (45.2%) in the afternoon group included initial resistance. The percentage of initial resistance is similar in the field notes and video data for the afternoon group, while there is a 16% decrease for the morning group. These data suggest that resistance levels

Table 4.2   Frequency of Types of Initial Resistance to
Attempts to Gain Access

Type of Resistance	N	%
Verbal without justification	7	14.9
Reference to arbitrary rules	4	8.5
Claim of ownership of object or play area	22	46.8
Reference to overcrowding	8	17.0
Denial of friendship	6	12.8
Total N	47	100.0

off to around 50% of the access attempts after the children have
spent a few months in the school, and may remain near that level
during their second year in this setting.[6] As was the case for the
field notes, there was no evidence of dominance hierarchies in
peer interaction for either group in the video data, and there was
no pattern where particular children were consistently either accepted or excluded.

Since there were no significant differences across the two
groups regarding use of different types of resistance in the video
data, I have collapsed the data across the two groups for purposes
of this analysis. Table 4.2 shows the frequency of types of initial
resistance in the video data for both groups.

We can see in Table 4.2 that references to ownership and overcrowding were the two most frequent types of resistance (46.8%
and 17%, respectively). This finding suggests that the children
have gained knowledge of the organizational features and rules
of the school. The use of these types of justifications (especially
references to overcrowding) also suggests that the children are
aware of specific features of peer culture in this setting, such as
the tenuous nature of peer interaction and the disruptive effects
of allowing additional playmates to join a peer episode once it is
underway.

Finally, there were also several instances (12.8% of the total)
where the denial of friendship was used as a basis for exclusion.
Although the percentage is relatively small, it is in line with the
pattern in field notes regarding the relationship between protection
of interactive space and conceptions of friendship.

The videotaping of instances of access–resistance sequences

---

[6]This interpretation is based only on the pattern in these data. I have no data
on the children in the afternoon group during their previous year at the school.

in peer interaction allowed for the micro-sociolinguistic analysis of the children's use of access rituals (see Corsaro, 1979c) and of their strategies for the protection of interactive space. As I noted in Chapter 1, micro-sociolinguistic analysis allows the researcher to go beyond static frequency distributions of certain types of behavior (e.g., types of access attempts and initial resistance) to capture the dynamic, negotiated features of social interactive processes. The access and resistance strategies children carry into interactive episodes are, in Cook-Gumperz and Gumperz's (1976) terms, just a few of the multiple informational cues which the children use in the contextualization process. In short, micro-sociolinguistic analysis goes beyond the identification of developing social concepts and other contextual information (or cues), and focuses on *how the information is used in the interactive process*.

In videotaped episodes, I found that the children's acceptance of peers into ongoing episodes often followed a four stage process: (a) an attempt at access, (b) initial resistance, (c) repeated access attempts followed by further resistance with the eventual agreement among defenders of an area to let others enter, and (d) the assignment of positions (e.g., policeman, mother, baby, or friend) to the new members. In the following example, I present a micro-sociolinguistic analysis of a sequence of behavior which contained all four stages of the access–resistance process. The analysis demonstrates that acceptance of others into a play group is a negotiated process involving the use of a wide range of contextual information. Following the micro-sociolinguistic analysis, I present a description of my use of "indefinite triangulation" (Cicourel, 1975) with two of the participants (Jonathan and Graham) as a way of estimating the validity of my interpretation of this access–resistance sequence.

Example 4.10
Date: March 3
Afternoon Tape 12 Episode 4
Steven (S) and Jonathan (J) are on the climbing bars when Graham (G) approaches the bars and attempts to enter. S and J had been playing "police" for some time before G's attempt to gain access.

Transcription	Description
(1) S–G: No, you can't get in! You can't get in! You can't get in!	S is in bars, and moves near where G is trying to enter and shouts down. Volume increases

Transcription, cont'd	*Description, cont'd*
You can't get in!	with each repetition. G begins climbing up board, which is slant-ed against bars.
(2) G–S: Yes, we can.	
(3) S–G: It's only for police! It's only for police-men!	
(4) S–JG: He's gonna have it, policeman. He's gonna have it.	S climbs down bars toward G. S is referring to J with the title "police-man."
(5) J–G: You're gonna have it, dum-dum!	S is now standing on ground next to G. As he says "dum-dum," J jumps down and pushes G down. The push is just hard enough to knock G off his feet.
(6) G–J: You are!	G gets up and moves toward J, who backs off. S then moves in front of G and they exchange threatening karate chops, but there is no physical contact. Tommy (T) now enters area and stands near G.
(7) G–T: T, get them! Grab them! Grab them, T.	G moves behind T, pushing him forward toward J and S.
(8) T–G: Kick 'em?	
(9) G–T: No, grab them. Grab them, quick!	T moves toward J and S, who are now climbing back onto the bars.
. . . .	
(13) J–G: I'll *really*—	G begins to move into bars and is confronted by J. J stresses the word "really."
(14) G–J: You're gonna *really* get it though.	G backs away from J a step and then holds ground. G stresses the word "really" as J did in his pre-vious utterance.
(15) T–J: Oh, yeah.	T now moves up to support G.
(16) G–T: Yeah, they *really* are.	G again stresses "really."
(17) T–G: Come on, let's go.	T turns and moves away from bars.

Transcription, cont'd	*Description, cont'd*
(18) G–T: Yeah.	G follows T away from bars.
(19) J–S: Good! We got the run of *our* police-house.	J moves higher in bars near S. J stresses the word "our."

S's first utterance to G was a direct warning for him to stay out. S used several types of contextual information here (physical movement, the second person pronoun, repetition, heavy stress, and increasing volume) to make his utterance a clear defense of the play area. G not only realized that his attempt at access was being resisted, but that S was very serious about his intent to defend the area. In line 3, S offered a justification for excluding G based on arbitrary rules. There was no way G could be a policeman; he could only have been a policeman *if* he had been playing from the start of the episode. The first three utterances also demonstrate how access attempts and resistance get strung together in an initiation–response sequence. G's initial strategy was just to move into the area. This attempt was resisted by S with no justification. G persisted and, in turn, S offered a justification for exclusion based on arbitrary rules. This pattern of "stringing together" types of resistance by the defender of an area occurred in all cases where there were persistent access attempts. In this case, there was a movement from a simple type of resistance (i.e., resistance with no justification) to a more complex type (justification based upon arbitrary rules) as the negotiation process progressed.[7]

S's utterance (4) marked an important shift in the interaction, in that it was a strategy to involve his fellow "policeman," J, in the protection of interactive space and also to symbolize or mark solidarity in the dyad. Instead of calling J by name (or assuming J heard his threats to G), S used a different contextualization cue (the title "policeman") to threaten B through speech directed to J. As a result, S's one utterance performed multiple functions. J took up the threat to G (5) and jumped down from the bars to push G to the ground. G then enlisted help from T, and the dispute

[7]In the video data, 10 of the 34 episodes which contained resistance to access included multiple resistance. Of these 10 episodes, 9 fit the pattern of movement toward a more complex type of justification for resistance (e.g., a movement from either resistance without justification or resistance with justification, based on arbitrary rules, to one of the other three types of resistance).

continued until T recommended leaving and G agreed (18). At this point, the children had moved through the first two stages of an attempt at access and initial resistance.

However, the dispute did not end at (19), because G returned shortly thereafter to renew his attempt to gain access. Upon his return, G first enlisted aid from a girl (Antoinette) and then they together asked a teaching assistant for help. In negotiation with G, A, and the teaching assistant, S and J first used resistance based on ownership, claiming that they had been on the bars first. The teaching assistant, however, invoked a higher-order rule, that the bars were a public place which had to be shared. As a result, G and A were able to move onto the bars. We will now pick up Example 4.10 shortly after G and A have moved into the bars. In this sequence of the episode, we see that J and S now begin to negotiate with each other regarding whether or not G and A should be allowed to stay in the bars.

Transcription			*Description*
(113)	A–S:	I already got in.	A is standing behind S and informs him she has entered the bars.
(114)	S–A:	Well you—well—then—then get out!	S turns to look at A standing above him in the bars.
(115)	A–S:	No, I won't!	
(116)	S–A:	Out, out, out!	
(117)	J–S:	Go on—it's your lunch time. Go on—go—go on out. It's your lunch time. I'll get her out.	J has now moved to stand next to S. J points to a platform in front of bars when he says "go on out." After this utterance, S moves down on the platform and pretends to eat his lunch. J moves next to A.
(118)	A–J:	J, how old are you?	
(119)	A–J:	I'm 4 1/2.	
(120)	J–A:	Do you have a big brother?	
(121)	A–J:	I'm fast and I have a big brother and I have a big brother and he's 10—no—no 11.	
(122)	A–JS:	You can't catch me.	S now moves back up in bars toward A.

Transcription, cont'd		*Description, cont'd*
(123)	J–S: You get out—back to your lunch.	
(124)	S–J: O.K.	S moves back to platform and pretends to eat.
(125)	J–S: You go on and I'll talk to A—oh—	
(126)	A–J: You can't even catch me.	
(127)	J–A: Hold it. (A, come here).	
(128)	S–J: I had my lunch, police officer.	
(129)	A–J: You didn't even catch me.	
(130)	J–A: You really can come in.	J is standing next to A and leans close to her and almost whispers this utterance.
(131)	S–A: I'll catch you. You snot!	S moves up in bars toward A.
(132)	A–S: No, you won't.	A moves away from S down bars to the ground. J now moves down from bars next to A and whispers in her ear. A then moves back into bars and climbs high toward G, who has been high in the bars for some time.
(133)	S–A: Oh, no, you won't! Oh, no—	S moves toward A. J moves into bars, cutting off S.
(134)	J–S: Get down and have your lunch. Steven (last name), get down and have your lunch— ( ) and have your lunch.	
(135)	S–J: I already had my lunch.	
(136)	S–J: (something that's).	

Transcription, cont'd			*Description, cont'd*
(137)	S–J:	I just had my lunch already, chief. So what?	A now moves in bars near S.
(138)	S–A:	Oh, no!	
(139)	J–S:	Oh, S, I said she could come in.	J pronounces each word in a slow, rhythmic cadence.
(140)	S–J:	But I don't want her to come in.	S repeats J's rhythmic cadence.

In this sequence, the children move to the third stage of the access–resistance process. After repeated attempts involving a series of access strategies, Graham and Antoinette have physically entered the climbing bars. They have not, however, been accepted into the ongoing play activity (i.e., ''police'') by Steven and Jonathan. However, we can see at this point that Jonathan is attempting to separate Antoinette from Steven. His goal is to inform Antoinette that she and Graham can play without being overheard by Steven. Jonathan's plan is impressive in that he ties it into the theme of playing ''police.'' Jonathan does this by telling Steven to go to lunch while he (the ''chief'') takes care of Antoinette (117). Jonathan's plan is deceptive, because he has no intention of ''getting Antoinette out'' (117), but rather eventually tells her that ''she really can come in'' (130). Indeed, as I discuss in detail below, Jonathan told me he had a plan to trick Steven. For now, it is clear that Jonathan's plan to inform Antoinette that she and Graham could play was successful. Once that plan was accomplished, Jonathan directly confronted Steven's continued resistance of Antoinette's presence in the bars (140). Steven did not give up easily, but, with continued pressure from Jonathan, an agreement was reached. How that agreement came about is illustrated in (195–201) of the episode.

Transcription			*Description*
(195)	J–S:	We want to talk about it, so—ah—let's—let—S, why don't we cooperate and why don't you agree to be a nice policeman?	J is standing in the bars next to S. G and A are also in the bars just above S and J.

Transcription, cont'd	Description, cont'd
(196) S–J: O—o—ok.	S stretches out "Ok" and seems unhappy but resigned to the agreement.
(197) J–S: Here, shake hands.	J reaches over bar and extends his hand to S. S and J shake hands while A and G watch from higher in the bars.
(198) J–S: Hey! I shook it from over this bar!	
(199) S–J: We have to get those robbers—	S points to A and G.
(200) A–G: Come on. We— come on, let's go, G.	G and A climb higher in the bars, while S moves toward them.
(201) S–J: We have to get the robbers who stole the jewels.	

With J's request to "talk about it," it is clear that the sequence has moved to the direct negotiation between the defenders regarding the possibility of allowing the other children to enter the activity. This stage is often marked, as it was here, by a shift from communication between defenders and intruders to communication between defenders. In this example, the end of the negotiation phase was marked by an extralinguistic cue (the handshake) between the defenders (S and J). Once agreement was reached, there was direct movement to the last phase, which involved the integration of the new members into the ongoing activity (i.e., S's utterances at 199 and 201).

In chapter 1, I noted that, even with the advantages of prior ethnography, participant observation, and videotape recording, it is often necessary for the field researcher to estimate the validity of his interpretation of the data by way of indefinite triangulation (Cicourel, 1975). Indefinite triangulation is a procedure in which the researcher creates circumstances so that respondents can react to information obtained on a previous occasion. In using the procedure in this instance, I first transcribed and analyzed the episode from which the sequences in Example 4.10 were drawn; I then explicitly wrote out my interpretations of the access–

resistance behavior. Later, approximately 2 1/2 months after the episode occurred, I carried out indefinite triangulation sessions with two of the children (Graham and Jonathan) who participated in the videotaped episode. In the sessions, which were audiotaped, I used an elicitation procedure similar to the one outlined by Gumperz (1976). I first played back short sequences of the videotaped event for the children, then asked a series of probing questions. In my initial questioning, I generally asked the children for subjective evaluations of what was happening (e.g., "What were you doing?"), while my later questions were more specific and were often based upon the children's previous responses.

The transcripts of these indefinite triangulation sessions appear in the Appendix. It is clear from the transcripts that use of indefinite triangulation with children of this age is a difficult process. Young children seldom reflect on past activities in this fashion, and when asked to do so they often find the task tedious and uninteresting. In fact, Graham and Jonathan both informed me that the event I was asking them about happened "a long, long time ago," and both children found objects in my office much more interesting than seeing themselves on TV or answering my questions. Nevertheless, the children did make several comments which in some instances confirmed my original interpretations and in other cases led to the refinement and expansion of my initial views. I will proceed by moving through each of the indefinite triangulation interviews, focusing on the children's responses which were most relevant to the four phases of the access–resistance process, those phases being: (a) the access attempt (including strategies and purpose), (b) initial resistance (including justifications and strategies), (c) negotiation and eventual acceptance, and (d) integration of new members into the ongoing activity.

My indefinite triangulation session with Jonathan was much more productive than with Graham. This difference may have been due to the fact that Jonathan is nearly a year older than Graham, or because Jonathan remembered the event more clearly than Graham, since he was one of the defenders of interactive space and had a more active and complex role in the episode. In any event, I had a difficult time getting Graham to respond to my initial questions.

Indefinite Triangulation Session with Graham

Date: May 23

B = Researcher (Bill)

G = Graham

(1) B: Now, I want you to watch this and see if you remember. See, what happens is that I was watching this and I couldn't figure out what was happening. And I want you to watch and see if you can remember what was happening and tell me what was wrong, Ok?

(2) G: Ok.

(3) B: Ok. Here we go. Now watch. (Plays tape)

(4) B: See yourself?

(5) G: Nope.

(6) B: Who's that right there?

(7) B: Who are those people?

(8) B: Who's this guy? (G smiles, signifying his recognition of himself on the tape)

(9) G: (You know what) happening?

(10) B: Do you remember this?

(11) G: There's Bill. There's you.

(12) B: Um-hum. There I am.

(13) G: I'm *tired*.

(14) B: Let's watch it for a little bit, Ok? Cause I don—I want you to tell me something.

(15) G: Is Peter in this?

(16) B: I don't think so.

(17) G: (   ).

(18) G: This is a long, long time ago.

(19) B: Yeah. What's going on? Why did the—why did they knock you down? What's happening? Huh?

(20) G: I don't know.

(21) B: You don't know what's happening?

(22) G: Nope. (Tape continued to play)

Although Graham has yet to respond substantively to my questions, he does recognize himself and the researcher in the tape playback. Also his observation (18) that "this is a long, long time ago" is a cue that he does, if somewhat vaguely, remember the activity. Later in the session I was able to get Graham to confirm that he was attempting to gain access to the bars.

(28) B: Did you want to go in the bars?
(29) G: Yeah.
(30) B: And what did you want to do in the bars?
(31) G: Climb.
(32) B: Climb? And how come—and they wouldn't let you in?
(33) B: Is that what was happening? (Pause)
(34) B: Is that why they were pushing you? (Pause)
(35) B: Why didn't you just go away then? (Pause)
(36) B: When they pushed you, why didn't you go away?
(37) G: I don't know.
(38) G: I wanna go.
(39) B: Well, just watch a little more, Ok? (Plays tape again)

Although Graham confirms his access attempt and notes that he wanted to climb, he does not offer an explanation for the resistance of Steven and Jonathan, or for his own persistence in trying to overcome that resistance. However, later in the session I switched from asking Graham about Steven and Jonathan's motives to asking him if he had ever resisted the access of other children when he was playing. The following sequence resulted:

(47) B: Do you ever do that to anybody? Tell them they can't come in when you're playing?
(48) G: No.
(49) B: You always say: "Come on right in and play." Or do you say: "No, we're playing here first."?
(50) G: No.
(51) B: What do you do?
(52) G: Peter says it. Sometimes—I do *at school.*
(53) B: Um-hum.
(54) B: If you and Peter are playing and somebody else comes over, do you sometimes rather they wouldn't play with you? So you could play with Peter by yourself?
(55) G: If Peter—if they wanna—if—if Peter wants to play with them and play with them. And Peter—don't want 'em to.
(56) B: If Peter don't want 'em to, then you tell 'em not to come and play?
(57) G: Yeah.

This sequence is interesting because G answers my question at (51) by referring to his frequent playmate, Peter. In fact, as we shall see in the next section of the chapter, Graham and Peter were one of the closest dyads in the afternoon group. What is of most interest here is that Graham's description of what he and Peter would do in resisting the access of other children is quite similar to what Steven and Jonathan did in the initial phases of Example 4.10. Let's look at one more sequence from the session with Graham which is relevant to the occurrence of negotiations between defenders of an area regarding the access attempts of other children.

(58) B: Wonder if you want 'em to and Peter doesn't? What do you do then?
(59) G: I don't want 'em to and Peter (does)?
(60) B: Yeah, if you don't want 'em to, but Peter does, what do you do then?
(61) G: I let 'em play. (Let 'em) play. But if he changes his mind and he don't want 'em to play—I don't want 'em to play—instead—(of) play, they have a fight.
(62) B: They have a fight? Who does?
(63) G: The people who wanted to play.
(64) B: And Peter don't want 'em to, so they have a fight?
(65) G: Yeah.

In this sequence, Graham implies he is always willing to go along with Peter in the protection of interactive space. However, I have observed activity in which Graham was not always so accommodating. In truth, Graham and Peter often negotiated and at times disagreed over whether other children could play or be their friends (e.g., Example 4.14 below). However, what is most important here is Graham's connection of my question regarding what he would do in response to access attempts to his play with Peter and their experiences in dealing with the access attempts of other children.

Although the data from the indefinite triangulation session with Graham are limited, they are generally in line with my conclusions regarding the importance of negotiation between defenders in the protection of interactive space. The data also suggest that Graham was not surprised by, and even identified with, the resistance of Steven and Jonathan to his attempts to gain access to their area of play.

As I noted earlier, my indefinite triangulation session with Jonathan was more productive than the one with Graham. Jonathan immediately identified the activity he saw on the tape as "playing police" and he was responsive to my initial questions, as the following sequence from the session indicates.

Indefinite Triangulation Session with Jonathan
Date: May 23
B = Researcher (Bill)
J = Jonathan

(1) B: I want you to tell me what's going on. All right?
(2) J: Ok.
(3) B: Here we go. See if you remember when this was happening. (Plays tape)
(4) J: That's me and Steven.
(5) B: Uh-huh.
(6) J: And that's you. You funny guy.
(7) B: Yeah, that's me.
(8) J: You silly koo-koo nut!
(9) J: That was a long, long time ago.
(10) B: Yeah.
(11) J: And that was you. You silly koo-koo nut.
(12) B: Who's this?
(13) J: I don't know—Graham.
(14) B: Um-hum.
(15) J: And that's me.
(16) B: Yeah.
(17) J: Only I had a green shirt on then. Those are my police (clothes).
(18) B: Now what's happening there? Why—why'ya doing that?
(19) J: *Cause*—we want to play police with nobody else in that, except for when we put the people in jail.

It is clear that Jonathan remembers the activity, but like Graham he notes that it happened "a long, long time ago" (9). Jonathan also readily notes the cause for his resistance of Graham's access attempt (19), and his response is in line with my interpretation regarding the children's desire to protect interactive space. Later in the interview, Jonathan is more specific about the seriousness of his and Steven's initial resistance of Graham.

(27) B: So you were already in the house. And they tried to come in? Was that it? And you were already playing police?

(28) J: Yeah. We—we meant it that time.

(29) B: You meant it? What do you mean, you meant it that time?

(30) J: Cause when they—when—(Pause)

(31) B: Sometimes when people come in, you really don't mean it. When you say: "You can't come in"?

(32) J: (un-huh). I mean, I *really* do mean it!

. . . .

(58) B: Now what are you telling Tommy?

(59) J: I told him (the Jungle Jim is taken right now) (   ).

(60) B: Were you really gonna hit 'em?

(61) J: Yes. (I was).

(62) B: Or were you just trying to scare 'em?

(63) J: I was trying to scare 'em.

(64) J: I didn't want them to get in.

These two sequences illustrate that Jonathan is aware of his use of contextual cues which signal the seriousness of his resistance of Graham and Tommy's access attempt. Jonathan notes in (28) that he meant it (i.e., his resistance of Graham) that time, and, later, he uses the term "really" to emphasize his determination (32). Although I used the term "really" in my question to Jonathan (31), the stress pattern of his pronunciation of "really" in (32) was different from mine, but it was exactly the same as his and Graham's pronunciations (13, 14, and 16) in Example 4.10. It is clear that the children's use of "really" in these instances was a cue to the seriousness of their intent in both access and resistance. In the second sequence (58–64), Jonathan first says he was going to hit Tommy, but then, in response to my question, he agrees that he was trying to scare Tommy and Graham with his threats. These two sequences illustrate that Jonathan was aware that the seriousness of his resistance of other children's access attempts must be signaled via specific communicative cues. Later in the indefinite triangulation session, I asked Jonathan about his negotiations with Steven once he had decided that it was all right for Antoinette and Graham to join the ongoing play. The following sequences are drawn from that discussion.

(89) B: Yeah, this is you. (Points to J on tape) You said—you said: "You go on and have your lunch, and I'll talk to Antoi-

> nette." Remember when you said that? What did you tell
> Antoinette when you talked to her? I think you were gon-
> na—

(90) J: I—I forgot. That was a long, long, long, long time ago!

. . . .

(98) B: Now what—see here. Jonathan, look. Now, Jonathan—now,
Steven said they couldn't come in. Were you changing your
mind?

(99) J: Yes.

(100) B: You were saying they could come in? How come you
changed your mind?

(101) J: Cause they wanted to come in.

(102) B: Un-huh. But they wanted to come in *at first* too. When Graham did, and you didn't change your mind then.

(103) J: Because I thought they wanted and needed to come in, so I
let them in.

In (90), Jonathan says he forgot what he was whispering to
Antoinette. However, a short time later (99), Jonathan agrees that
he had changed his mind and told Antoinette that she and Graham
could play. Jonathan notes (103) that he changed his mind because
they (A and G) "wanted and needed to come in." One interpretation of his response here is that persistent access attempts may
be successful because they signify to defenders of an area that
the children seeking access are serious and have a genuine "need"
to enter.

Once Jonathan had decided to allow Antoinette and Graham
into the play area, he began negotiations with Steven.

(119) B: So now you changed your mind, and you said she could
come in? How could you convince Steven that it's OK?

(120) J: Well, I'd say—well, I had a plan, I'd say: "Steven, well they
can't come in." And then I'd whisper in their ears: "But you
could come in." I was tricking Steven.

(121) B: Um-hum—what would you—then you thought, once they
got in, then Steven might change his mind?

(122) J: Yeah.

(135) B: ———. Why did you shake hands with—with, ah—Steven—with Steven (last name), and not Graham and Antoinette?

(136) J: What did I do when I shake their hands?

148 • *Friendship and Peer Culture in the Early Years*

(137) B: See, you said—you asked Steven to be a nice policeman
and let them come in. And then he said: "Ok." And then
you said: "Let's shake on it." Why didn't you shake hands
with Graham and Antoinette and say: "You can come in
now."?

(138) J: Cause I gave my agreement with him.

(139) B: And they already were agreeing with you, so you didn't
have to shake their hands?

(140) J: Yeah.

(141) B: How did they know it was all right for them to come in?

(142) J: Cause (I shaked) hands with Steven.

(143) B: I see.

Jonathan describes his plan for negotiating with Steven in (120),
and his description of "tricking" Steven is in line with my interpretation of the sequence which was presented earlier. When I
asked Jonathan about the significance of the handshake with Steven, he noted that it was necessary because he "gave his agreement with him" (138). Jonathan then suggests (142) that Antoinette
and Graham would interpret the handshake as a sign that Steven
had agreed with the plan and that it was now all right for them
to stay in the bars.

After we had covered initial resistance and the negotiation and
agreement with Steven, I then turned to questions which had a
bearing on the last phase of the access–resistance process; that
being the integration of the children into the play activity.

(144) B: Now that they're in there, wh—what—wa—ah—are they
gonna be able to play with you guys? And what do they
have to do?

(145) J: Be policemen if they lived here. Or—

(146) B: What else could they be?

(147) J: Or they could be the guards.

(148) B: The guards?

(149) B: How 'bout robbers?

(150) J: No. They don't like to be the robbers.

(151) B: Why not?

(152) J: Cause they just don't.

(153) B: Um-hum.

Jonathan does not agree with my suggestion that Antoinette
and Graham could be robbers, even though they actually took

that role in the videotaped episode. Jonathan's response that they "wouldn't like to be robbers" (150) may have been how he remembered the episode. In the episode, only Steven clearly designated Antoinette and Graham as robbers. Jonathan did, however, join Steven in chasing Antoinette and Graham around the yard and taking them back to jail after apprehension. So Jonathan's response at 150 is somewhat difficult to interpret. In any case, Jonathan's statement that Antoinette and Graham could be policemen (145) or guards (148) is in line with my interpretations that, once intruders are accepted, they are then assigned a role in the ongoing peer play.

Although I have presented a lengthy discussion of Example 4.10, I still have focused on only a few of the many contextual cues involved in the peer interactive event. The purpose of the discussion was to demonstrate the importance of micro-sociolinguistic analysis and indefinite triangulation for studying peer culture. Micro-sociolinguistic analyses capture processes (such as the nature of access–resistance sequences and stages in the process of accepting peers into ongoing episodes) that are difficult if not impossible to detect when one relies only on frequency distributions of coding schemes. Even sequential analyses of codes are often insufficient for identifying processual features, because no coding system is sensitive enough to capture all of the contextual information social actors routinely employ in communicative processes. Finally, the micro-sociolinguistic analyses and indefinite triangulation demonstrate the importance of access–resistance experiences for the children's developing awareness of competition, cooperation, and solidarity in peer interaction; all of which are important elements in the children's acquisition of stable conceptions of friendship.

Summary

In this section, I have used field notes from the first 3 months of the school term to identify the children's basic concerns and to isolate social organizational features of peer culture in the nursery school setting. I then went on to explore further the patterns in field notes by examining access–resistance sequences in the video data.

The analysis of field notes revealed that the nursery school has definite organizational features which affect the children's concerns and behavior. The school is what Goffman (1961b) has called a "multi-focused" setting. In such a setting, the "persons immediately present to each other can be parceled out into different encounters" (Goffman, 1961b:18), with the cocktail party being an excellent adult example. In addition to the multi-focused nature of the setting, the children are also faced with the knowledge that interactive episodes can be terminated at any moment without formal marking or opportunity for negotiation. Furthermore, once an episode ends, the children then must deal with the very real threat of resistance to their attempts to gain access to other ongoing peer episodes.

Given these features of peer culture in the nursery school, the children develop two conflicting concerns: (a) to gain access to ongoing episodes when uninvolved, and (b) to protect interactive space from the intrusion of others when participating in ongoing episodes. These concerns are manifested most clearly in the children's strategies for gaining access and the nature and frequency of resistance to access attempts. Patterns in access–resistance sequences in the videotaped episodes suggest that the children *are aware of the fact that peer interaction is fragile, that acceptance into ongoing episodes is often difficult, and that entry of others into ongoing episodes is potentially disruptive.*

Finally, the children also, at times, used the denial of friendship as a basis for exclusion. The use of this type of resistance to access attempts suggests that the children's developing conceptions of friendship are tied to the organizational features of peer culture in this setting (i.e., friendship is used as a device for protecting interactive space from potential disruptions which occur routinely in peer interaction in this setting). I will pursue these working hypotheses in the next two sections of the chapter, where I focus on the structure of social contacts in the video data and on the children's spontaneous references to friendship in peer interaction.

The Structure of Social Contacts

If, as the data reported on in the last section suggest, the children are aware of the fragility of peer interaction, the difficulty of gaining access to play groups, and the potentially disruptive effects of the entry of peers into ongoing episodes, then the structure of their social contacts should reflect this awareness. Specifically, if the children are aware of these contextual demands, then they

will try to distribute their social contacts in such a way as to maximize their options for dealing with the demands. For example,
by playing with several (4 to 7) peers regularly, as opposed to
concentrating social contacts around one or two playmates, a child
increases his or her chances of successful access to play groups.
Thus, an examination of the structure of social contacts in the
two groups is necessary.

In previous studies of peer relations and friendships among
preschool children (Challman, 1932; Green, 1933; Koch, 1933;
Marshall and McCandless, 1957; Parten, 1932), friendship has been
defined in terms of frequency of contact or ranking of sociometric
choices. If recent work on early conceptual levels of friendship
is correct (Damon, 1977; Selman, 1976; Youniss, 1975), then an
association may indeed exist between conceptions of friendship
and frequency of contact. However, there is some question about
the nature of such a relationship.

Young children probably do view frequent playmates as friends,
but, contrary to what earlier researchers have claimed, young
children may not perceive frequent playmates as "best friends."
The notion of best friends, or of degrees of friendship, implies a
recognition of personal qualities upon which the concept is based.
Best friends, according to this line of argument, are differentiated
from other friends because they possess these qualities. However,
a recognition of personal qualities may not be part of most preschool children's conceptions of friendship (Damon, 1977; Selman,
1976). Instead of concentrating only on degrees of friendship with
children of this age, it may be more fruitful to focus on the overall
structure of play contacts in the analysis process. Such analyses
may provide support for recent theories about conceptual levels
of friendship, and also serve as a basis to further investigate
hyoptheses about the influence of social context on children's peer
relations which were discussed earlier.

Procedure

I selected videotaped episodes for the analysis of the structure of
social contacts because (a) the quality of the data allowed for repeated micro-sociolinguistic analysis in making decisions regarding
whether or not a social contact had occurred, and (b) the data
had been collected during the last four months of the school term,
when interactive patterns had stabilized. Of the 146 videotaped
episodes, 17 involved teacher-directed activities and were not in-

cluded in the analysis. For the remaining 129 episodes, I coded instances of social contacts for all the children in each group.

I coded as a social contact an instance in which the children involved engaged in *associative play* at some point during the course of an episode. Following Parten (1932), I defined associative play as instances when the children were engaged in and *mutually aware of common activity and interest.*[8] In this coding procedure, no child could have more than one social contact with any other particular participant in a given episode.[9] Prior ethnography, as well as the advantage of multiple viewings of the video data, greatly enhanced coding decisions. Although the coding decisions may seem simple (i.e., associative play or no associative play), there were numerous instances in peer interaction where both multiple viewings and background knowledge of participants were necessary, to determine if all the children participating in a given episode were really playing together.

The sequence of peer interaction in the following example demonstrates features of the coding process. This sequence began with two children, Ellen and Leah, playing alone in one corner of a playhouse in the school. A third child, Glen, entered shortly thereafter. There had been no prior interaction between Glen and the two girls on this day. Although all but one of Ellen's reactions to Glen's behavior are negative, I coded both Ellen and Leah as involved in associative play with Glen.

Example 4.11

Date: February 5

Morning Tape 1 Episode #5

Glen (G), Ellen (E), Leah (L), and Barbara (B) are in the downstairs playhouse with other children. E is the master of L, who is pretending to be a baby kitty. G moves around the house, pretending to eat everything in sight. B is outside the playhouse, and is mainly involved with other children who

---

[8]If all but one child left an area, and the one remained in solitary play, then I sampled this behavior as a new episode.

[9]This fact is due to the decision to code social contacts *by episode*. For example, if three children (A, B, and C) are involved in associative play, and B leaves, but the episode continues with A and C involved in play, then, should B return during the course of the same episode and begin playing with A and C again, the renewal of play would not be recorded as an additional social contact. In this coding decision, B's leaving is seen as a temporary withdrawal from the earlier play, and his return is not a new contact.

are pretending to be her kitties, but she often enters the activity in the playhouse with G, E, and L.

Transcription		Description
(1)	E–G: That's my kitty's!	L crawls into corner, followed by E. G comes over and pretends to eat pans.
(2)	E–G: You're in my kitty's little bed and she hates you.	G continues to pretend to eat pans.
(3)	L: Yucky!	
(4)	E–G: Yucky. Go away!	G gets another pan.
(5)	E–G: Go away.	E hits at G with pan lid. G takes lid from E and pretends to eat it.
(6)	E–G: Go away. We don't want you.	G moves from corner to table in center of playhouse.
(7)	L–E: He's messing up my room!	
(8)	E–L: He ate your food. Oh, too bad.	E says this with very high pitch and endearing intonation similar to adult baby talk. G now takes plate from table, pretends to eat it, and then drops it to the floor. E moves over near the table and picks up the plate. G moves toward the bed at far end of the playhouse, away from corner where L still sits.
(9)	E–G: Go away!	E comes up behind G, taps him with the plate, and then runs back to the corner with L. G then pursues her to the corner.
(10)	E–G: Don't eat this food!	G grabs a hat off rack in the corner and begins eating it. E takes the hat away from G.
(11)	E–G: No! That's hers.	E means that the hat belongs to L. E places the hat back on the rack while G grabs and pretends to eat a plate, which E then takes away from him.
(12)	E–G: G, we don't need you.	G now moves toward telephone, which is near the front of the playhouse.

Transcription, cont'd	*Description, cont'd*
(13) E–L: I washed my hair, baby.	G meanwhile pretends to eat the telephone. E, seeing G, comes over and takes the phone away, and then pretends to make a call while G moves back toward the corner.
(14) E–G: We don't need you, get out of our house.	E grabs hat before G can get it from rack. B now enters and attempts to take tinker toy G has been carrying. G pulls away from B and now grabs and pretends to eat coat rack. After finishing rack, G licks his lips.
(15) E: Ha! Ha! A piece of candy!	E is laughing and seems to be referring to G's apparent enjoyment of the coat rack. G and B now struggle over the tinker toy G has in his hand. A teacher intervenes, and B moves outside the house to tend to her pet kitties. G now wanders out of house briefly, then returns to corner.
(16) E–G: Go away.	G now eats a wig he finds on the floor, and then moves to center of playhouse and attempts to eat the table. E now begins to gather all things in corner away from G. But G moves to corner and grabs a belt and eats it.
(17) E–L: We don't need him.	E says this as she pushes G away. G now moves back toward phone and eats it again.
(18) E: Go away out of our house! I don't need G.	G moves back toward corner but is distracted by B's asking researcher about microphone.
(19) E–L: (I don't know where) he went. I'll see.	G now leaves and goes to upstairs playhouse. E and L are in corner; G is upstairs eating things as another child, Nancy, watches from a distance. E now comes upstairs

Transcription, cont'd	Description, cont'd
	and takes blanket near where G is sitting. G grabs blanket from E, eats it, and gives it back. E then moves downstairs and G follows, and eating routine continues until episode ends with clean-up time.

As I noted earlier, I coded both Ellen and Leah as involved in associative play with Glen in this sequence. I coded no social contacts between Barbara and Glen, Ellen, or Leah. My decision to code associative play was first anticipated around utterance (9), when Ellen seemed to lure Glen back to the corner. It was all but settled by (15), where she genuinely appreciated his enjoyment in eating the coat rack as if it were candy; and the decision was finalized when Ellen followed Glen upstairs on the pretense of needing a blanket. It was necessary to observe the entire development of this spontaneous peer event to see that *rejection itself ("We don't want you") had become a game that these children were playing together.*[10]

The use of the episode as the sampling unit, the multiple viewing of the videotape, and prior ethnography of these children in the school were all important factors in making these decisions regarding associative play. If, for example, I had relied on time-sampling of sequences of one minute or so, I could not have captured the contextual richness of this event. In fact, even when using the episode as a sampling unit, the final decision was based on multiple viewings where both verbal and nonverbal information, as well as temporal features of the unfolding event, were examined carefully. Prior ethnography was also important, in that I had witnessed Glen pretending to be a monster on two previous occasions. I was also skeptical of Ellen's intentions to be rid of him in this sequence, because she had been a participant (frightened child) in one of the earlier instances.

---

[10]Although Glen (or any of the other children) did not refer to his behavior as similar to that of "Cookie Monster" on the children's television show "Sesame Street," this sequence may indeed be based upon shared knowledge about this character. I have consistently found that it is not always necessary for the children to overtly connect emerging activities with underlying shared knowledge and expectations in childhood culture (cf. Cook-Gumperz and Corsaro, 1977).

After I coded the entire sample of peer episodes for associative play, I selected a subsample of 42 episodes which were then coded independently by a research assistant.[11] There was over 92% agreement between myself and the assistant for the coding of associative play in these episodes.

After the reliability coding, I tabulated the number of playmates and the total number of social contacts for each child in both groups. Because I was concerned with the overall structure of social contacts for each child, rather than with just the identification of the most frequent playmates, I also computed the mean number of contacts, the standard deviation of contacts (SD), and the coefficient of variation (V) for each child. The SD is a way of estimating how widely each child spreads his or her contacts across the number of possible playmates. A low standard deviation indicates that social contacts are spread out over many playmates, while a high SD means that contacts are clustered around a few, specific playmates. The coefficient of variation (V) (Freund, 1952; Muellar, Schuessler, and Costner, 1977) controls for the number of contacts and is computed by $V = SD/\overline{X}$ (100). A V score of around 90 or above indicated clustering of social contacts around a limited number of playmates; a score of near 50 or below indicated little or no clustering. A V score between 51 and 89 indicated clustering around several playmates. Figure 4.1 depicts the distribution of V scores for children in the two groups.

Findings

Tables 4.3 and 4.4 contain data on social contacts for children in the morning and afternoon groups. The mean V score for the morning group was 70.2 (SD = 19.6), while the mean V score for the afternoon group was 66.6 (SD = 19.9). The difference was not significant, $t(46) = .62$.[12]

In the morning group (Table 4.3), the V scores for most of the children fell within the range from 51 to 89. Only four children had V scores of 90 or more; and only three children had V scores

---

[11]This subsample included all transcribed episodes, and was not random. The episodes were representative in terms of the children involved, activities, areas of the school, and over time.

[12]One child in each group was not included in the analysis because the children discontinued attendance during the fifth month of the school term.

Key:
Morning = _____
Afternoon: = ...

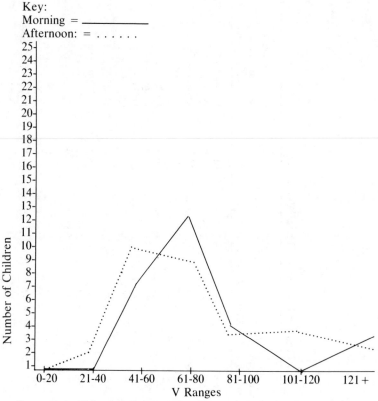

Figure 4.1 V Scores, Representing Patterns of Social Contact, for Morning and Afternoon Groups

of less than 51. There were no significant differences by sex or age. For boys, the mean *V* score was 67.8 (SD = 12.8), while the mean *V* score for girls was 71.8 (SD = 24.1), *t* (21) = .48. For children who ranged in age from 2 years, 11 months to 3 years, 4 months, the mean V score was 64.6 (SD = 14.0), while the mean *V* score for children from 3 years, 5 months to 3 years, 11 months was 75.7 (SD = 27.1), *t*(21) = 1.16. It is clear, however, that the four children with high *V* scores are two same-sex dyads (Martin and Denny, and Betty and Jenny). I will return to talk about the significance of the relationship between Betty and Jenny in the next section of this chapter.

In the afternoon group, the pattern of distribution of *V* scores was similar to that of the morning group (Table 4.4). Only three

Table 4.3 Structure of Play Contacts in Morning Group (Video Data)

Name	Age	Number of Playmates	Total Social Contacts	$\overline{X}$ Contacts	SD	V[a]	Most Frequent Playmate
Martin	2.11	20	69	3.45	3.14	91.0	Denny—15
Barbara	3.0	16	51	3.19	2.26	70.8	Debbie—8
Dwight	3.1	11	26	2.36	1.29	54.7	Joseph—5
Jimmy	3.1	12	20	1.67	0.99	59.0	Michelle—4
Nancy	3.1	16	37	2.31	1.58	68.4	Barbara—7
Michelle	3.1	6	11	1.83	1.17	63.9	Jimmy—4
Joseph	3.2	18	67	3.72	2.67	71.8	Denny—11
Leah	3.2	11	35	3.18	1.47	46.2	Charles—6
Concetta	3.3	13	22	1.69	0.86	50.6	3 children—3
Ellen	3.4	15	32	2.13	1.19	55.9	3 children—4
Denny	3.5	19	74	3.89	3.62	93.1	Martin—15
Rita	3.5	16	49	3.06	1.53	50.0	Barbara—6
Charles	3.7	20	59	2.95	1.64	55.6	Joseph, Liah—6
Betty	3.7	18	45	2.50	2.47	98.8	Jenny—11
Linda	3.8	12	20	1.67	1.23	73.7	Nancy, Charles—4
Jack	3.8	17	36	2.12	1.50	70.8	Denny—6

Jenny	3.8	10	23	2.30	3.13	136.1	Betty—11
Roger	3.8	13	30	2.31	1.55	67.1	Charles, Joseph—5
Cindy	3.9	15	18	1.20	0.78	64.6	Leah—4
Glen	3.9	19	53	2.79	1.69	60.6	Joseph—8
Debbie	3.9	20	52	2.60	2.16	83.1	Barbara—8
Bill	3.10	14	29	2.07	1.38	66.7	Rita—5
Richard	3.11	9	18	2.00	1.22	55.6	Joseph, Leah—4
Total		340	876	56.99		70.2	
$\overline{X}$		14.78	38.09	2.48	1.76	6.96	

Note: One child was not included in the analysis, because she left school during the fourth month. In the far right hand column, the number is the number of times the child in the far left column (e.g., Martin) played with the child in the far right column (e.g., Denny).

[a]$V = \dfrac{SD}{X}\,(100)$

159

Table 4.4 Structure of Play Contacts in Afternoon Group (Video Data)

Name	Age	Number of Playmates	Total Social Contacts	$\bar{X}$ Contacts	SD	V[a]	Most Frequent Playmate
Allen	3.9	15	26	1.73	0.96	55.5	Daniel—4
Lenny	3.9	20	31	1.55	0.89	57.4	Peter—4
Mark	3.10	22	71	3.23	3.29	101.9	Peter—13
Graham	3.11	24	67	2.79	3.29	116.1	Peter—16
Sue	3.11	13	17	1.31	0.86	65.3	Lisa—4
Denise	4.1	22	44	2.00	1.31	65.5	Shelia, Lisa—5
Antoinette	4.1	19	41	2.16	1.21	56.0	4 Children—2
Laura	4.1	16	19	1.19	0.40	33.6	3 Children—2
Christopher	4.1	11	14	1.27	0.47	37.0	3 Children—2
Beth	4.3	14	18	1.29	0.61	47.4	Brian—3
Tommy	4.3	9	14	1.56	0.88	56.5	Daniel, Peter—3
Brian	4.4	22	58	2.64	2.22	84.1	Mark—11
Sheila	4.4	8	14	1.75	1.49	85.1	Denise—5
Daniel	4.4	18	32	1.78	0.94	52.8	Allen—4
Peter	4.6	20	75	3.75	4.04	107.7	Graham—16
Anita	4.6	18	44	2.44	2.09	85.7	Brian—6

Lisa	4.6	21	48	2.29	1.19	52.0	Denise—5
Eva	4.7	16	25	1.56	0.96	61.5	Denise—4
Dominic	4.7	16	38	2.38	1.75	73.5	Peter—7
Larry	4.7	11	16	1.45	0.82	56.6	Lisa—3
Vickie	4.9	12	17	1.42	0.79	55.6	Anita, Sheila—3
Lanny	4.9	13	26	2.00	1.29	64.5	Peter—5
Frank	4.9	12	19	1.58	0.99	63.0	Lanny—4
Jonathan	4.9	17	34	2.00	1.22	61.0	Steven—5
Steven	4.10	12	29	2.40	1.68	70.0	Jonathan—5
Total		401	837	49.22			
$\overline{X}$		16.04	33.48	1.97	1.42	66.6	5.72

Note: Two children were not included in the analysis, because they left school during the fifth month. For explanation of number in far right column, see note to Table 3.

[a] $V = \dfrac{SD}{\overline{X}}(100)$

161

children had V scores of 90 or more, while three other children had scores of less than 51. Again there were no significant differences by sex or age. The mean V score was 70.5 (SD = 19.4) for boys, and 60.8 (SD = 15.7) for girls, $t(23) = 1.28$. The mean V score for children ranging in age from 3 years, 9 months to 4 years, 3 months was 62.9 (SD = 24.0), while it was 69.5 (SD = 15.3) for children 4 years, 4 months to 4 years, 10 months, $t(23)$ = .76. The one consistent cluster was a same-sex triad, made up of three boys (Peter, Graham and Mark). I will return to discuss this triad in the next section when I look closely at the functions of children's references to friendship in peer interaction.

In addition to computing V scores, I also compared each child's distribution of social contacts in both the morning and afternoon groups with a random distribution using the Kolmogorov-Smirnov test (Hays and Winkler, 1971). For both groups, each of the children's observed distributions differed from their random distributions at less than the .01 level, except for one child in each group. For these two children, the observed distributions differed significantly from the random distributions at less than the .05 level.

Overall, these findings show that most of the children in each group play more often with some children than with others, but do not concentrate their social contacts around one or two playmates. This pattern is in line with earlier findings regarding the children's awareness of organizational features of peer culture in the nursery school, and suggests the following hypothesis. Because interaction is fragile and acceptance into ongoing episodes is often difficult, the children may develop stable relations with several playmates as a way to maximize the probability of successful access.

To this point, I have investigated the relationship between social organizational features of peer culture and patterns in peer interaction. In the final section, I will demonstrate the linkage between this relationship and the children's conceptions of friendship by examining the children's spontaneous references to friendship in peer interaction.

Functions of Spontaneous References to Friendship

Hartup (1975) has argued that "a differentiated analysis of the functions of language in the ontogeny of friendship is a high priority need'' (p. 23). Thus far, I have presented data which show that the children mention friendship when they protect interactive space from intruders. However, the children also referred verbally to friendship in other interactive situations. Examination of the 51 spontaneous references to friendship in field notes and video data resulted in the identification of six categories of talk about friendship.

Of the 51 references to friendship, 23 occurred in situations involving attempts at access or exclusion. Example 4.1 demonstrated how a child used a reference to friendship to gain access, while Example 4.2 showed an instance in which friendship was tied to exclusion. The following example shows an instance in which a child refers to friendship following a successful attempt to gain access.

Example 4.12
Date: May 20 Morning
Tape 23 Episode 2
Martin (M) and Dwight (Dw) are playing in the climbing box. Denny (D) runs by and Martin yells:

M–D: Denny!
D–M: Martin!
Denny climbs in box next to Martin.
M–D: Dwight is here.
D–M: Can I come?
M–D: Yeah, you can come.
D–M: Yeah, 'cause I'm your
       friend, right?
M–D: 'Cause I'm your friend.

Twelve references to friendship occurred within the course of ongoing events, and often signified that the children were *now friends because they were playing together*. For example:

Example 4.13
Date: February 20 Morning
Tape 7 Episode 1
Richard (R) and Barbara (B) are building with blocks, while Nancy (N) sits nearby.

R–B: We're playing here by our-
       selves.

B–R: Just—ah—we friends,
       right?
R–B: Right.

The children's references to friendship as demonstrated in Example 4.13 are in line with Selman's (1976, 1980) findings on early conceptions of friendship. According to Selman, at the earliest level the relation is based on physical–geographical space or bonds formed by temporary action. At this level, friends often are people with whom you happen to be playing. Regarding the notion of temporality in peer relations, we saw in earlier examples that the children did, at times, qualify the denial of friendship temporally (e.g., "you're not our friend today.").

A third type of verbal reference to friendship, which occurred on three occasions in the data, *marked competition within*, and possible segmentation of, play groups. The following example shows this type of reference.

Example 4.14
Date: May 5 Afternoon
Tape 22 Episode 3
Five children are playing with water in the outside sandbox. Each child has an individual hose. The children are Peter (P), Graham (G), Frank (F), Lanny (L), and Antoinette (A).

L: Hey, we made the best waterfall, see?
E–L: Yeah.
P–L: That's not a waterfall.
L–P: Yes, it is—
P: L's can't. L's isn't.
L–F: I did the—a waterfall, right, F?
F–L: Yeah.
A: F's is.
F–L: Don't L. L!
L–F: Yes. Mine is, isn't it, F?
F–L: It's mine.
L–F: It's both of ours, right?
F–L: Right, and we made it ourselves.
L–F: Right.
P–G: G, we're not gonna be F's and L's friend, right?
G–P: I am.
F–P: I'm gonna throw water on you if you don't stop it. And tell the
       teachers.

On four occasions (two in each group), the children used references to friendship as *an attempt at social control.*

Example 4.15
Date: May 5 Afternoon
Tape 22 Episode 3
Peter (P) tries to get Graham (G) to move over and play next to him while they are playing with other children around the sandbox.

P–G: Graham—if you play over here where I am, I'll be your friend.
G–P: I wanna play over here.
P–G: Then I'm not gonna be your friend.
G–P: I'm not—I'm not gonna let—I'm gonna tell my mom to not let you—
P–G: All *right,* I'll come over here.

The previous two examples are interesting because, in both instances, the main participants (Peter and Graham) were two of the three children in the afternoon group who confined most of their social contacts to each other and one other boy (see Table 4.4). We also know from the indefinite triangulation session with Graham that he and Peter tended to protect their activities from the intrusion of other children. Examples 4.14 and 4.15 demonstrate that Peter may be trying to protect his relationship with Graham as they participate in a larger group.

A fifth category of references to friendship, which occurred five times, involved the children's specification of *personal characteristics* of friends or nonfriends. In one example, Barbara told her playmate (Rita) "I'm not your friend" after Rita had taken a doll Barbara had been playing with. Barbara then told me that Rita was "a naughty girl." In all five cases, the references (positive or negative) were tied to preceding actions of playmates and did not imply enduring characteristics.

On four occasions, the children referred to friendship in the course of *expressing concern for the welfare of playmates.* All but one of these references were tied to the recognition of a child's absence from school. For example:

Example 4.16
Date: January 6 Afternoon
Field Notes Episode 1
Anita (A) and Vickie (V) were frequent playmates and had referred to each

other as friends on several previous occasions. Today, Vickie is absent from school and Anita is sitting on a box near the sandpile. Mark (M) approaches.

M–A: Are you playing with Brian, A?
A–M: No, I'm waiting for Vickie.

Vickie was absent from school for the second day in a row.

M–A: Oh.
A–M: But I don't think she's coming here.
M–A: Maybe she's sick.
A–M: Yeah, maybe.
A–M: Or maybe she quit—
M–A: Well, maybe she has a babysitter.
A–M: Well, anyway, I'm busy.

A now goes to have juice, and M runs to climbing bars and joins Brian.

Finally, on one occasion recorded in the video data, two children showed a *mutual concern* and referred to each other as *best friends*.

Example 4.17
Date: May 27 Morning
Tape 25 Episode 6
Jenny (J) and Betty (B) are climbing in a large wooden box. B has just returned to play with J after being away for some time, playing with another child, earlier this morning. Ellen (E) approaches J and B, and offers pieces of paper.

E: Do you guys want—do you guys—want a ticket?
J–E: No, we don't!

E now moves to the other end of the box.

B–J: I do like you. J, my (   ). I do.
J–B: I know it.
B–J: Yeah. But I just ran away from you. You know why?
J–B: Why?
B–J: Because I (   )—
J–B: You wanted to play with Linda?
B–J: Yeah.
J–B: I ranned away *with* you. Wasn't that funny?
B–J: Yes.
J–B: Cause I wanted to know what happened.
B–J: I know you wanted—all the time—you wanna know because you're my best friend.
J–B: Right.

These two children not only use the term "best friend," but discuss friendship at a fairly abstract level. From the discussion, it is apparent that the children feel they are best friends because they care about each other. They show an awareness of how their actions affect the "feelings" of the other; this awareness is most clear in Betty's explanation of why she ran away, and Jenny's expression of her need to know what happened to Betty. In Damon's (1977) synthesis of work by Selman and Youniss on developmental progressions in children's conceptions of friendship, he argues that, at the most advanced level, "friends are persons who understand one another, sharing with each other their innermost thoughts, feelings and other secrets; therefore friends are in a special position to help each other with psychological problems (loneliness, sadness, loss, fear, and so on) and must, in turn, avoid giving psychological pain or discomfort to each other" (pp. 161–62). This level of friendship was found only among older children (11-years-old and older) in Damon's (1977) and Selman's (1976) research, which was based on clinical interviews. Betty and Jenny are, of course, considerably younger, both being younger than 4-years-old. However, in Example 4.17, Betty and Jenny are displaying a spontaneous awareness of elements of friendship which is tied to specific events that they have recently experienced (i.e., Jenny's concern for Betty while she was playing with Linda). This type of awareness is different from children's responses to what are usually hypothetical questions during clinical interviewing. Finally, Betty and Jenny had a closer relationship than most of the other children in the nursery school and consistently played together over the entire school term. This finding suggests that children who develop intensive, long-term peer relations may acquire abstract conceptions of friendship at an early age.

Summary and Conclusions

In this chapter, I have emphasized the important effects of social organizational features of peer culture in the nursery school on the children's social relations and conceptions of friendship. Field notes from the first 3 months of participant observation revealed important organizational features of peer culture. The field notes and later video data showed that the children rarely engaged in solitary play, and that, when they found themselves alone, they consistently tried to gain entry into ongoing peer activities. However, because of their recognition of the fragility of peer interaction and the multiple sources of disruption in the nursery school, children who were participating in peer activities often protected the interaction by resisting children who were attempting to gain access. These two patterns led to recurrent conflict. In these conflict situations, the children occasionally used claims of friendship in attempts to gain access, and the denial of friendship as a basis for exclusion. The patterns in field notes and the video data suggested two hypotheses: (a) *The children construct concepts of friendship, while, at the same time, linking these concepts to specific organizational features of peer culture in the nursery school setting;* and (b) *the children's developing knowledge of friendship is closely tied to the social contextual demands of this peer environment.*

Analyses of the overall structure of social contacts in the video data showed that most of the children in both age groups played more often with some children than with others, but did not concentrate their social contacts around one or two playmates. This pattern was in line with the earlier findings and hypotheses and suggested the following hypothesis: (c) *Through peer interactive experience in the nursery school, the children come to realize that interaction is fragile and acceptance into ongoing activities is often difficult, and, therefore, develop stable relations with several playmates as a way to maximize the probability of successful entry.*

These three hypotheses were further supported by the examination of access attempts and the protection of interactive space in peer episodes which were videotaped during the second half of the school term. We saw, for example, the children's justifications for exclusion reflected an awareness of the organizational features and rules of the nursery school. In addition, micro-sociolinguistic analyses of the videotaped episodes demonstrated the complexity of the negotiation process in the children's development of social knowledge and communicative skills. The negotiation process often led to the increased solidarity of small (dyadic and triadic) play groups, and provided the children with experience in accommodating to the social needs and rights of others who wish to join the group.

Although examination of children's spontaneous references to friendship resulted in the identification of six categories of "talk about friendship," the majority of the references (35 of 51) fell into two categories. In support of the earlier hypotheses, the children often referred to friendship as a basis for both inclusion and exclusion from play groups. In addition, many of the children's references to friendship occurred in the course of ongoing events, and signified that the children were now friends because they were playing together. In the nursery school, references to friendship in this context signaled growing solidarity within the play group and were often followed by plans to protect the emerging, shared activities. When children refer to friendship during access attempts or during the course of ongoing episodes, the relation between the social contextual demands of peer culture and the conception and use of friendship is apparent. These findings suggest a fourth hypothesis: (d) *For these children, friendship often serves specific integrative functions (such as gaining access to, building solidarity and mutual trust in, and protecting the interactive space of play groups) in the nursery school, and is seldom based on the children's recognition of enduring personal characteristics of playmates.*

When generating hypotheses, the researcher must be concerned with how well they are grounded in the data. Although there is seldom a perfect fit between data and hypotheses, any exceptions to general patterns in the data should not contradict major claims of the hypotheses. In the present data, several of the children's spontaneous references to friendship displayed personal concern for the welfare of playmates, and in the case of one dyad a mutual intimacy approaching "best friends" was evident. However, these children were also exceptions regarding the overall structure of their social contacts. Unlike the majority of the children in the school, these children concentrated their social contacts on one or two playmates. In short, there were exceptions to specific hypotheses, but the exceptions were in line with the general emphasis of the set of hypotheses on the relation between contextual demands of peer culture in the nursery school and the development and use of social knowledge.

This analysis is exploratory, but the hypothesis regarding features of the children's conceptions of friendship is generally in line with recent research on children's development of social knowledge (Damon, 1977; Selman, 1980; Youniss, 1975) and may be extended generally to preschool children. Selman (1980), for example found that preschool children's conceptions of friendship (which were elicited in clinical interviews) generally were based on thinking which focuses upon propinquity, and that, for young children, a close friend is someone who lives nearby and with whom one is playing with at the moment.

The primary goal of Selman's work is to build and validate general developmental models of social knowledge. What ethnographic studies of children's social worlds add to the work of cognitive developmental theorists (such as Selman) is insight into (a) the importance of social context in the development of social concepts, and (b) how children use social concepts to meet social contextual demands in everyday activities.

Social knowledge is acquired and used in a variety of settings making up children's worlds. The present research provided and intensive examination of one such setting (a nursery school). There is a need for further ethnographic work across a range of social settings for children at different stages of development. The recent work of Gottman and Parkhurst (1978), on spontaneous play among best-friend dyads in the home setting, demonstrated the complexity of friendship processes among young children in these situations. Many more such studies are needed. We know little, for example, about the role played by parents and other adults in young children's exposure to social knowledge in the home setting.

If children construct social knowledge—including conceptions of friendship—by acting upon the environment, then we need to examine those actions *within their situational contexts*. The many practical problems associated with such research must be faced, but they should not dissuade us from discovering how children are exposed to, acquire, and use social knowledge in their life worlds.

CHAPTER **5**

Features of Peer Culture and Children's Conception of Adult Rules

Joseph and Roger are building with blocks at one of the worktables. I am sitting with them watching. It is early morning. The teaching assistants are still greeting late arrivals and readying various areas of the school for upcoming activities. I notice that Joseph's building is now getting very tall. A teaching assistant, Catherine, also notices, and comes over to the table. "Boy, what a tall building!" Catherine says to Joseph. "Yeah," says Joseph, "It's the Vampire State Building!" Catherine and I look at each other and laugh heartily. Catherine now moves away, and I look back at Joseph and Roger. They are not laughing. They continue to work on their buildings.

Earlier, I argued that the children in the nursery school constructed and shared a peer culture which includes a set of common activities or routines, artifacts, values, concerns, and attitudes. As the above example suggests, elements of peer culture may involve a mixture of information obtained from a variety of sources. Young children receive and process information about real objects (e.g., tall buildings), people, and events, and about myths, legends, and make-believe people (e.g., vampires), and events from parents, other adults, peers, and the media. Children's unique combinations or transformations of some of this information often seem inappropriate and thus humorous to adults. These transformations are, however, often appropriate and real to the children, and, therefore, can be seen as elements of peer culture.

171

However, analytic decisions regarding what can qualify as elements of peer culture are often difficult. Therefore, before I move to a detailed discussion of these elements, it is important to clarify further my use of the concept "peer culture."

First, I am not claiming that the elements of peer culture are part of a more general childhood culture shared by all children of this age group. The notion of childhood culture is attractive, but it is also conceptually problematic. Surely, it is incorrect to argue that a culture of childhood—shared by all children—exists alongside, but separate from, the adult world. Some elements of peer culture, such as children's games and lore, may indeed be acquired solely within children's groups and trasmitted from child to child beyond the influence of adults (see Opie and Opie, 1959, 1969). Nevertheless, the majority of elements of peer culture originate from children's perceptions of, and reactions to, the adult world.

Second, I do not claim that the children's shared activities, concerns, values, and attitudes in the nursery school are part of a more general children's subculture in American society. Such a subculture may exist. But its discovery must go beyond the identification of the shared values, ritual behaviors, and attitudes of a specific group. As Fine (1979) has argued, the study of subcultures should be based on the examination of interlocking groups networks through which cultural elements are diffused. The analysis of interlocking networks is essential for understanding both the origins and boundaries of subcultures.

Since I have limited data on interlocking networks, my claims are confined to those peer cultural elements shared by the children in this and similar nursery school settings. However, as I discuss elements of peer culture, I will assess the likelihood of their emergence from peer interaction within the school itself as opposed to their diffusion through interlocking networks with teachers in the school and with others (parents, peers, and the media) outside this setting.

Values and Concerns

Social Participation and the Protection of Interactive Space

In Chapter 4, I argued that the children were chiefly concerned with social participation in school activities, especially peer play. The children rarely engaged in solitary play. When they found themselves alone, the children consistently attempted to gain entry into one of many ongoing events. To get a better sense of the children's concern with social participation and the problems they encounter when they attempt to act on this concern, let us put ourselves in a child's place on a typical morning in the nursery school.

Let's assume we are Glen and that we have just arrived at school. We enter the school with the other children in our ride group and stop at our locker and hang up our coat. We then turn the corner and see several activities in progress. This morning there are four groups—each including two or more children and one teacher, teaching assistant (TA), or volunteer—inside the school, and two TAs and one child in the outside yard. Outside, the TAs are moving play equipment (mats, wooden, boxes and boards, shovels, balls, etc.) to various locations in the yard, while Denny tags along talking and laughing. We decide to stay inside for now and quickly assess what is going on in the four groups.

In the first, a TA, Catherine, is seated at a worktable with Nancy and Linda. The girls are placing red, green, blue, and yellow pegs into a peg board. Catherine talks to the children as they work. The talk is typical of teacher–child exchanges at this time of the morning. Catherine questions the children: "Are you awake yet?" "What did you have for breakfast?" "Who rode with you to school today?"; and the children respond: "Yeap," "Cereal and toast," "My dad drove, and Betty, Martin, and Mia rode with us." The second group is in the storybook and puzzle area just in front of the worktables (see Figure 1.2). Jimmy, Michelle, and Leah are looking at storybooks and talking with Penni (a volunteer aide) about pictures in the books.

We now talk over near a third group in the block area. Rita, Bill, and Joseph are playing with small toy animals. George (another volunteer) sits on the floor with the children and now and then asks about the animals. As was the case at the worktables, the children's answers are brief and they are seldom expanded by George. We now hear music coming from the juice room, so we walk near the open door. Inside, we see Barbara, Betty, Jenny, and Dwight, as well as the head teacher, Margaret. Margaret sits at a table with Dwight while the girls dance to the music. They are up on tip-toes like ballerinas. "Can you dance like that, Dwight?" asks Margaret. Dwight seems to shake his head no. Margaret gets up and takes Dwight's hand and leads him in a dance.

We do not feel like dancing, so we move away from the juice room. Having explored the range of activities, we make our choice. Returning to the worktables, we sit down next to Nancy and begin placing pegs in a board. "Well, good morning, Glen!" Catherine is now talking to us. Soon we hear ourselves say: "Pancakes with syrup."

While we work with the peg board, we continue to monitor other activities in the school. We notice several things of interest. First, George has left the block area and the three children are building block houses or cages for the animals. That might be fun to do. We also notice that Debbie and Charles are now in the playhouse. Debbie is upstairs and is talking on the phone to Charles, who is in the downstairs apartment. We could go over and play house. But we also see that Martin and Jack have now joined Denny outside, and the three boys are digging in the sandpile. It might be fun to go outside.

Still undecided, we leave the worktable and walk over near the block area and watch Rita, Bill, and Joseph playing with the toy animals. After watching for a few minutes, we leave this area and move outside. Once outside, we circle the sandpile and note that Jack is no longer digging with Martin and Denny. Jack's shovel is stuck upright in the sand. Is Jack gone for good?

We now stop just in front of the sandpile and watch Martin and Denny. "We're 'struction workers!" declares Martin. "Right, and we have to dig a deep hole," replies Denny. Neither child notices us as we slowly move into the sand and take the available shovel. We scoop up a shovelful of sand, fling the sand away, and scoop up a second load. "Hey, that's Jack's shovel!" yells Denny. "You can't play with us!" retorts Martin. "Well, I'll get my own shovel!" we answer, and we run toward the box where the shovels are stored. We pick up a shovel and head back to the sandpile. And that is when we see Betty swinging.

The second swing next to Betty is vacant. We quickly pitch the shovel into the sandpile and run and jump into the empty swing. After a few minutes of swinging, Betty says: "I can go higher than you." "No, I can go higher!" we reply. And the contest begins. We match Betty's height with every swing until she comes to a sudden halt by dragging her feet on the ground. She then jumps from the swing and runs straight ahead above five yards. Betty then turns and looks back at us with a big smile on her face. She starts running at full speed toward the vacant swing—"Whee-ee, whee-ee, whee-ee"—and lands on the swing belly-down. "Now it's my turn!" we exclaim and run from our swing and copy Betty's movements. "Now let's both do it," suggests Betty. We agree and the run-and-jump sequence is repeated several times. On the fifth repetition, we run from the swing, stop, turn, then head back. Halfway to the swing, we notice that Betty is not running with us We spin around and just catch a glimpse of Betty disappearing inside the school. Where is she going? To juice? To play inside? To the bathroom?

Now what do we do? It is again time to check out the activities occurring all around us. It is again time to gain access to an ongoing event.

Having spent a good part of a morning with Glen, we have seen that participation in peer activities in the nursery school is a matter of some complexity. As was the case with Glen, children often find themselves alone in the school with the desire to gain access into an ongoing event. In many respects, the nursery school is like adult *multi-focused parties* (Goffman, 1961b). At multi-focused gatherings, there are generally several clusters of adults (who usually know one another) dispersed in various areas of the setting. When party participants find themselves alone, they, much like the children in the nursery school, have a strong need to gain access into an ongoing conversation or activity.

Although the nursery school shares features with the adult multi-focused party, there are important differences. Interaction in the nursery school is fragile, and peer activities can break down with even minimal disruption. As a result, the children often protect interactive events by discouraging the access attempts of others (see Chapter 4). This need to protect interactive space is a concern shared by all the children. In fact, I repeatedly observed children deciding "not to let anyone else in" their interactive space while in the early stages of deciding exactly what it is they are doing. Note the following exchanges between two boys shortly after they arrive in a vacant area of play (the outside sandbox).

Example 5.1
Peter and Graham move to the sandbox and each picks up hoses in the sand. The teacher has just turned on the hoses so that water is flowing into the sandbox from each of several individual hoses.

P: Hey, the hoses are on!
G: Yeah, let's make a lake.
P: And nobody else can come in, right?
G: Right.

To adults, the protection of interactive space is often seen as selfish and uncooperative. The teacher often reacted to such behavior by referring to the importance of "sharing" play materials and areas of the school. But it is not that the children are resisting the idea of sharing. On the contrary, they wish to continue to share the interactive experience *with each other;* but they know from past experience that the acceptance of additional playmates often leads to the breakdown of interactive events.

The children's concern with the protection of interactive space is also expressed in verbal negotiations which occur prior to a participant's temporary leave-taking from an area of play. Temporary leave-taking is often necessary for a variety of reasons, including going to the bathroom, getting and bringing back materials (shovels, cups, chairs, etc.) to the play area, checking to see if there is a place at juice, and investigating activities occurring in other areas of the school.

In the following example, three boys who are playing with hoses and water around the outside sandbox have become interested in an activity occurring inside the school where two TAs are inflating a large beach ball, much to the delight of several children. As we see, the boys negotiate the "saving" of their hoses and places around the sandbox before leaving the area to get a closer look at what is happening inside the school.

Example 5.2
Tape 22 Episode 3
Peter (P), Frank (F), Lanny (L), and several other children are playing with hoses around the outside sandbox. The three boys hear several children loudly responding to two TA's attempts to inflate a large beach ball inside the school. Frank decides to go inside and get a closer look at what is going on.

F–L: Save my hose. Save it.
P–F: I will. (Reaches for hose)
L–P: Save mine too, ok?

(L hands his and then F's hose to P and then follows F inside. Both F and L return to the sandbox after a short absence)

F: It's a big boogie ball!
P–L: Save mine, Lanny. (Peter hands his hose to Lanny and runs inside to see the ball)

In all the instances of temporary leave taking involving the negotiation of protection of interactive space that I observed, the children were quick to accept the responsibility of "saving" or "guarding" another's place in play. In addition, the guardians were often challenged by intruders attempting to gain access to the vacated space. These challenges frequently involved disputes—some of which had to be settled by teachers—in which the guardians firmly defended the play space. In some instances, these defenses were purely symbolic, since the child who had originally requested the aid decided to make his or her leave-taking permanent instead of temporary.

Concern for the Physical Welfare of Playmates.

It was not until several weeks after I began participant observation that I discovered how deeply concerned the children were for the physical welfare of their playmates. The reason for the tardiness of this discovery was my tendency to be more of a participant than an observer when incidents involving a child's physical well-being occurred. Although none of the children were ever seriously injured in the school, there were a few minor scrapes and bruises now and then, and the momentary shedding of tears was quite common. When such incidents occurred, the teachers or TAs quickly arrived on the scene to comfort the child in distress. Since most injuries were more apparent than real, the comforting process was often ritualistic. The teacher or TA would hug the child, kiss the injured finger, hand, etc., or, in some cases, carry the child off to the kitchen area for the application of a band-aid.

After a few days in the school, I had witnessed this soothing ritual on several occasions and recorded its basic elements in field notes. What I failed to notice for several weeks were the reactions of the children to the distress and consolation of their playmates. During these injury–comfort dramas my attention, like that of all the children in the vicinity of the incidents, was on center stage rather than the periphery of the events.

What first pulled my attention from center stage were some comments one of the children, Betty, made to me while we watched a TA (Tony) console an injured child. Betty, Jimmy, Jenny, and I were in the outside yard, drawing squares and circles on the ground with colored chalk, when we suddenly heard Rita crying. I looked up and saw Rita sobbing and holding her knee while sitting near the door of the school. It seemed Rita had tripped as she was about to enter the school. Tony quickly arrived on the scene and began to soothe Rita with hugs while he gently rubbed her knee. Tony then lifted Rita in his arms and carried her into the school.

"She'll be all right. She just needs a band-aid," said Betty. I turned and saw that Betty, Jimmy, and Jenny were all watching the event. "Don't worry, Bill," said Betty, "I bumped my knee once and it just hurt for a minute." Somewhat surprised at Betty's comment, I nodded and mumbled "Yeah," and then the children and I resumed our drawing with the colored chalk.

After this incident, I was careful to watch for the children's reactions to the distress or injury of one of their playmates. I found that, in every instance, the children in the vicinity (i.e., within sight or hearing of the event) stopped their activities and closely monitored the activity until a teacher or TA arrived. Many of the children continued to pay careful attention until they were sure the injured child was all right. Some children would even move near the injured child and ask the teacher if their playmate was ok. At times, the children would talk to each other about the nature of the injury as they attended to the comforting process. Consider the following example.

Example 5.3
Tape 14 Episode 3
Morning
Roger (R), Joseph (J), and Concetta (C) are digging for buried treasure in the outside sandpile. They hear crying from near the climbing bars and see that Debbie is on the ground in front of the bars and is being comforted by a TA (Marie).

J: What is she crying about?
R: Maybe she jumped all the way down there. (R points to the ground in front of the climbing bars).

    J and C now leave the sandpile and join several other children who have gathered around the TA and Debbie. Debbie has now stopped crying. J and C return to the sandpile, where R has remained.

R: I did that one time and I didn't hurt much.
    I did that one time at my house.
    I did that one time, too.

It is clear from this example that the children are not only concerned about the physical welfare of their playmates, but also display empathy by recalling past injuries of their own which are seen as similar to those of their peers. What we have here is an important *interactive alignment* in that the children are observing, talking about, and reflecting upon the well being of a fellow peer and are in the process developing empathy skills in the course of peer play. Finally, the children's concern for the physical welfare of playmates is something that is communally shared and frequently displayed in the nursery school. It is clearly a feature of peer culture.

Concern with Physical Size: Being Bigger than Anybody Else

Preschool children are constantly looking up, up to adults and the adult world. Although many of the objects (tables, chairs, climbing bars, lockers, etc.) in the nursery school are scaled to the physical size of the children, the physical dimensions of the school building itself (room sizes, ceiling heights, the size of the wall around the outside yard) reflect the physical size of the adults who must also participate in everyday activities in this setting. In addition, adults are in control in the nursery school. They and the children know that "teachers" have the right to tell children what they can and can not do. In this sense, the nursery school is much like all other settings in the world of the preschool child. For young children, interactive settings are characterized by the children's looking up to those (adults) with power and authority (see Denzin, 1977a). As a result of the recurrent need to look up to the adult world, young children are deeply concerned with physical size. They come to value "growing up" and "getting bigger." In fact, for young children the primary distinguishing characteristic between themselves and adults is *that adults are bigger*. This difference in size was a fact that I could never overcome in participant observation, and it was the primary reason for my being labelled "Big Bill" by many of the children.

The best support for my claim that the children value "being bigger" is their attraction to, and their patterns of play in, certain areas of the school. Three of the most popular areas of play in the nursery school were the upstairs playhouse, the climbing house, and the climbing bars (see Figure 1.2).[1] These play areas share two common features. First, when playing in these areas, the children are, in a very sense, *bigger*. They are higher up and are able to look down on the rest of the school. They are even able to look down on adults. In short, the children's perspective of the adult world is reversed while in these areas of the school. As a result, the children feel more in control of their activities in these areas and are, at least temporarily, out of the reach of adult caretakers.

This fact brings us to a second feature of these areas of play. Since these areas are scaled to the size of the children, they are not easily entered by the adults. In fact, during my year at the school the teachers or TAs entered the upstairs playhouse on only two occasions, the climbing bars only once, and they never entered the top floor of the climbing house.[2] On the few occasions when adults did enter the bars or playhouse, it was verbally commented on as unusual by the children and the adults were assigned subordinate roles in the ongoing play (e.g., a baby sister, a guest at dinner).[3] Since it is both the children's attraction to these areas and the nature of play in them that is essential for illustrating the children's concern for "being bigger," it is necessary to examine each of the three play areas in some detail.

---

[1]Since my intent in this study was not to verify empirically the frequency of use of various play materials or areas of the school, I did not gather data which would allow me to claim that the children's preference for the upstairs playhouse, the climbing bars, and the climbing house over other areas of the school was statistically significant. I did, however, carefully record frequency of use of areas in the inside of the school and the outside yard for the first 2 weeks of observations behind the one-way screen (see Chapter 1). For that period, the upstairs playhouse was the most frequently selected area inside the school, and the climbing bars, followed by the climbing house, were the most frequently occupied in the outside yard. As a result, I made sure to record a representative sample in these settings in field notes during participant observation, and on videotape, in the last several months of the study.

[2]These areas of play were as difficult for me to enter as they were for the teachers. When recording interactive episodes in field notes or on videotape, I stationed myself in or near the upstairs playhouse (most often on the floor at the bottom of the steps—see Figure 5.1), on the ground floor of the climbing house (see Figure 5.3), and on the ground near the climbing bars (see Figure 5.2)

[3]Being a guest at dinner can be seen as subordinate from the children's perspective, because the host is in charge and directs and carries out most of the activity (meal preparation, clean up, etc.). The guest primarily sits at the table and waits for and watches the host carry out the main activities.

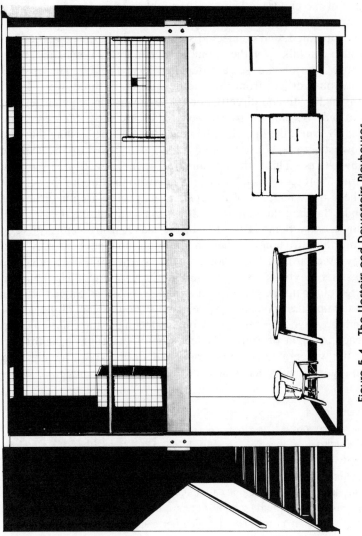

Figure 5.1   The Upstairs and Downstairs Playhouses

The upstairs playhouse. There is an upstairs and a downstairs playhouse in the nursery school (see Figure 1.2). The playhouses are designed to resemble small apartments, and are scaled to the size of the children. They contain tables, chairs, dressers, beds, mirrors, stoves, dishes, and telephones. The telephones are battery-operated, and connected so that a child in the upstairs playhouse can talk over the phone to a child in the downstairs playhouse. The playhouses are depicted in Figure 5.1. The upstairs playhouse differs from the one downstairs in three ways. First, it is higher up and directly above the downstairs playhouse, and can only be entered by way of a staircase at its far right hand end. Second, the upstairs playhouse has a higher ceiling than the downstairs playhouse (around 6 feet, as opposed to 5 feet in the downstairs). Third, the upstairs apartment is enclosed by a wire grate to protect the children from falling to the floor of the school. These three features of the upstairs playhouse are important for understanding the children's attraction to this area of play. The single entry point at the top of the stairs insures more privacy from the intrusion of other children into ongoing peer play than any other area in the school. The most attractive feature of the upstairs playhouse is its height and the wire grate. The children often climb up the grate to get as high as possible. Since the floor of the upstairs playhouse is 5 feet above ground level of the school and the playhouse ceiling is around 6 feet high, the children often reach a height of around 11 feet when they, climb near the top of the wire grate. When climbing high on the grate, the children do indeed feel bigger. Consider the following example.

Example 5.4
Tape 4 Episode 1
Morning
Cindy (C) and Leah (L) are in the upstairs playhouse. Shortly after arriving upstairs, C goes to the telephone and pretends to call the police and report a robbery. During the phone call, L stands nearby, watching other children and adults below in the school. At times, L sticks out her tongue, but none of the children in the school notice her. After the phone call, L and C pretend to eat dinner. Then L tries to open a suitcase as C sticks her head over the staircase and looks to see if anyone is coming up to the playhouse.

Transcription	*Description*
(27) C: Don't come in here!	C is leaning over stairway and ad-
Don't come in here!	dressing the apparent warning to

Transcription, cont'd	*Description, cont'd*
Don't come in here! Don't come in here! Don't come in here! We don't want anybody to come in!	children who are playing nearby. Since they are no children at- tempting access or even near the stairway, the repetition of this phrase is probably not a warning but more of an invitation for someone to try to enter.
(28) C: We want to stay here alone. We have two of us. Two. We have such a lot of stairs. We need guests. Look at our house. We have such a lot of furniture.	C has moved in front of a table and stands looking through grate. C is bilingual and speaks English with a German accent, which may be related to her use of phrases like "such a lot of."
(29) C: Now I'm big! Now I'm really big! Now I'm big and bending! Dum-de- den! Dum-di-den! Now I'm looking very big!	C now climbs grate so that her head is near the ceiling of the playhouse. C then steps two notches down and bends to look down.
(30) C: My foot's coming out. Here is my foot. We have no shoes on! We are going out, but we have no shoes on!	C sticks her foot through the grate. Then climbs higher.
(31) C: Whoops! What was that? What this?	C slips and falls to floor, but is un- injured. She then moves over by L, who is trying to open a suit- case.
. . . . . .	
(41) L: Hey, want to do that letter thing?	L has now opened the suitcase. She then looks downstairs and sees children tracing letters at the worktables. L starts downstairs.
(42) L: Come down. Let's go downstairs.	L is on the stairway and moves down into the school toward the worktables. C follows.

Cindy's repeated warnings (27) can be interpreted as "calling
for the attention" of children playing below in the school. In a
sense, she is not warning, but rather inviting one or more of the
children to attempt to gain access to the playhouse. In fact, after

first saying they want to be alone, Cindy goes on to note that they need guests (28).

After receiving no response from the children downstairs, Cindy begins climbing the grating of the playhouse. With every step higher, Cindy announces that she is getting bigger and bigger. These announcements stop when Cindy reaches the top of the grating. She then steps down a bit and bends forward, looking down into the school. As she does so, Cindy notes that she is "now looking very big" (29). In fact, Cindy is looking down the same way that big people (grown-ups) do when they address young children. In this instance of play, Cindy actually feels like an adult because of the change in her physical perspective (i.e., looking down at children in the school rather than looking up at adults).

Cindy's minor accident is what the teachers always fear might happen when children climb on the grating. For this reason, the teachers always tell the children to climb down. In this instance, however, the teacher had not yet noticed Cindy climbing on the grating. Ironically, the grating, which is there to protect the children, is a source of possible injury. The children often resisted the teachers admonishments regarding climbing, not because they simply wanted to climb, but because they wanted to be bigger.

The climbing bars. The climbing bars are located in the far right-hand corner of the outside yard (see Figure 1.2). The bars are depicted in Figure 5.2. There are two sets of bars joined together, with set A slightly taller than set B. Set A has six levels and stands around 7 ½ feet tall, while set B has five levels and stands nearly 7 feet tall. The fourth level of both sets is slightly higher than the wall which encloses the outside yard. When standing at this level or above, the children can see over the wall into a nearby street and into the outside yard of the adjoining nursery school (the city cooperative school; see Chapter 1). Given these features, the children can, when on the bars, overcome many of the physical boundaries of the school. In fact, a recurrent peer ritual ("Garbage Man," discussed below) took place in the bars in response to activity which regularly occurred in the street just beyond the wall of the outside yard.

In addition to climbing, the children used the bars as a jail when playing police, as a burning house when playing firemen, as a restaurant, as a site for a circus, and as a home or den when pretending to be wild animals. However, as was the case for the

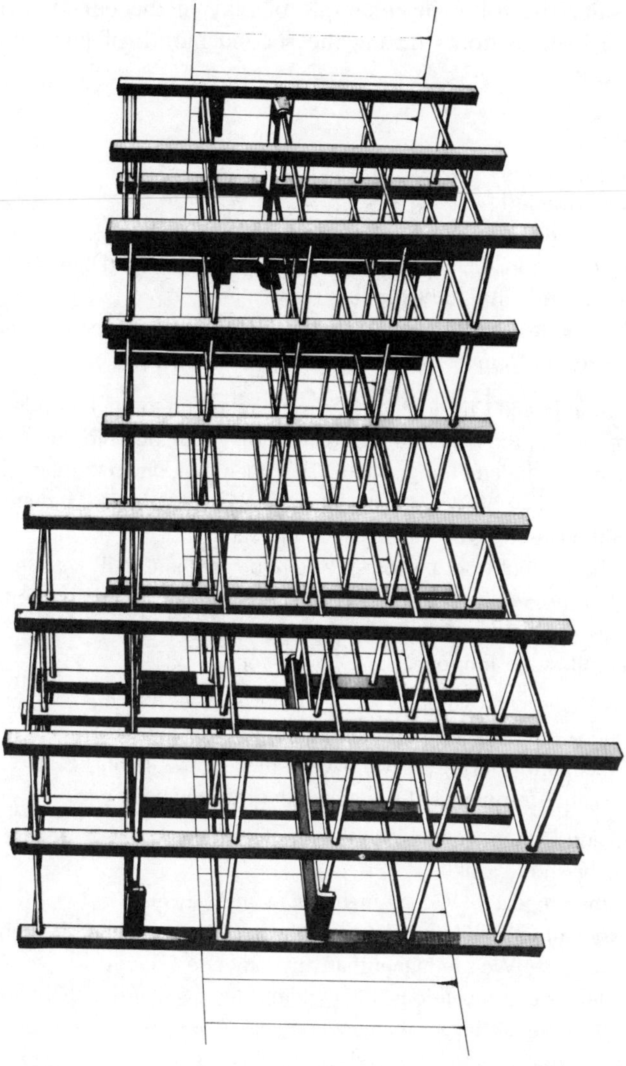

Figure 5.2   The Climbing Bars

upstairs playhouse, the children most liked the bars because they were high up when they played in this area, allowing them to look down on their peers and teachers.

Consider the following example of play in the bars which I recorded in field notes during the second month of participant observation.

Example 5.5

December 4

Afternoon Episode 1

Scene: Outside, Climbing Bars

Participants: Laura (L), Christopher (C), Vickie (V), Daniel (D), Steven (S), Jonathan (J), Brian (B), and Larry (L)

FN = Field Notes; MN = Methodological Note; PN = Personal Note; TN = Theoretical Note

FN: Laura (L) and Christopher (C) have climbed up to the fourth level of set B of the bars (see Figure 5.2). They look out into the street and into the adjoining school. They then look down at other children in the outside yard. L yells to Vickie (V), who is standing with Daniel (D) near the base of the bars

When V looks up, L shouts: "We're bigger than you!"

"Oh, no, you're not!" retorts V, and she begins to climb into the bars.

D follows V and repeats: "Oh, no, you're not!"

As V and D move up to the fourth level of set B of the bars, L and C move over and up to the fifth level of set A.

Once at this level, C says; "We're higher now, right, L?"

"Yeah," responds L. "We are higher than anybode else!"

V and D then climb up on the fifth level, and V says: "We are higher now, too!"

L then repeats: "We are higher than anybody else!"

Now all four children chant in unison: "We are higher than anybody else! We are higher than anybody else!

After several repetitions, the children slightly alter the chant and yell: "We are bigger than anybody else!"

This phrase is also repeated several times.

The children then recycle and chant: "We are higher than anybody else" 10 more times.

Meanwhile, the chanting has attracted a group of eight children who are standing at the base of the bars looking up at L, C, V, and D.

Six additional children are also now attending to the chanting at various places in the outside yard.
After listening for awhile longer, four boys (Steven, Jonathan, Brian, and Larry) climb into the bars.
They quickly climb up and join the other children at the top level.
Once at this height, the boys also take up the chant: "We are higher than anybody else!"
There are numerous repetitions of the chant (at least 20) before all of the children except L and C gradually leave the bars and begin playing in other areas of the school.
After several minutes of additional chanting, L begins climbing down and C follows close behind.
"We were the highest, right, L?" asks C.
"Yeah," says L. "Highest of anybody else."

L and C now reach the bottom of the bars, hop to the ground, and run across the yard and into the school, while all the time chanting: "We were highest than anybody else!"

PN: I was somewhat surprised by how a form of competitive play eventually turned into group chanting and then back to references to competitiveness.
I was also impressed by the shared enjoyment the children displayed with the repeated chanting.
It was as if the form of expressing (chanting in rhythm) became as important as the claim of being higher and bigger.

MN: Once I begin videotaping, I should try to capture group events of this type.
One strategy would be to watch for the reactions of children who are at first noninvolved.
It would be important to document their movement from noninvolvement to attraction to access and participation.

TN: Group events of this type which develop spontaneously are good example of peer culture.
In this episode, the children are displaying both a value of "being bigger" and their appreciation of group production.

The climbing house. The climbing house is located in the left-hand corner of the outside yard. The name for this area was used consistently by both the children and the teachers. However, it is somewhat of a misnomer, since the structure does not physically resemble a house. The area is depicted in Figures 5.3 and 5.4. As

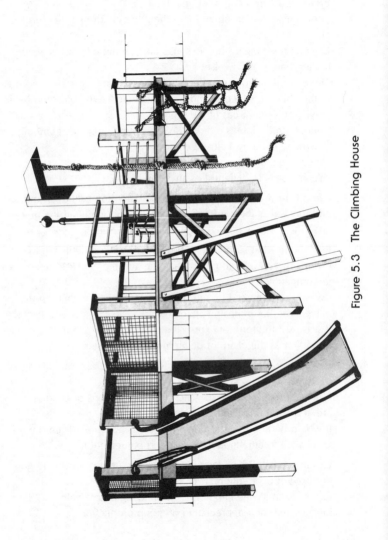

Figure 5.3 The Climbing House

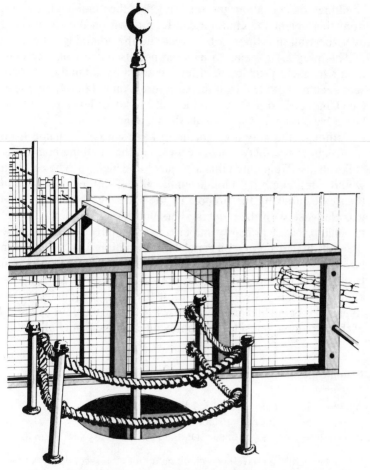

Figure 5.4   A View from the Top of the Climbing House

we can see from Figure 5.3 (a ground level view of the area), the structure is two-tiered. Entry to the second tier can be accomplished by climbing a sturdy wooden ladder or a not-so-sturdy and often swaying rope ladder, or a single strand rope with equidistant knots. The floor of the upstairs level is approximately 5 ½ feet high. When on the second level, the children's eye-view is around 7 ½ feet above ground level. From Figure 5.4, we can see that the children can look down across the outside sandpile and sandbox to the inside of the school. The second level of the climbing house is about the same level of the climbing bars, and from this height the children can look down on the swings and over the wall into the nearby street and the adjoining school.

This play area seems to have earned its name from the children's frequent production of human and animal family role play sequence on both levels of the structure. Animal family role play (see Chapter 3) often involved use of the lower level as a den or home base for the wild animals (lions, alligators, etc.).

Although the play area seems to have earned its name from the frequent role play which occurred in the climbing house, the children also frequented this area just to be high up. The children would often climb up, look around, call out to those below, and then exit either by the firepole or the slide (see Figure 5.3). As was the case with the climbing bars and the upstairs playhouse, the children were primarily attracted to the climbing house because they felt higher up or "bigger." This attraction was displayed in two ways. First, the children consistently called to peers and teachers in the outside yard when on the second level of the climbing house. As was the case for the bars, the children often referred to being higher and bigger when they gained the attention of those below. Consider the following example from field notes.

Example 5.6
November 3
Afternoon Episode 8
Scene: Outside, Climbing House
Participants: Eva (E), Dominic (D), Beth (B), Allen (A), and Brian (B)

FN: Five children have been climbing up into the second level of the house and and then sliding back down.

At one point, Dominic (D) yells out to a teaching assistant: "Willy! Willy!" Willy looks up and waves to D.

Then Eva (E) and Allen (A) yell out: "Willy! Willy! Hi, Willy!" Willy again waves and then begins to move away toward the inside of the school.

Now Beth (E) and Brian (Br), who have been climbing up while the other children called out, reach the top and call out: "Willy! Willy!" Willy turns, looks up, and laughs.

Now all five children yell in unison: "Willy! Willy! Willy!" This chanting continues for several repetitions.

Willy seems slightly embarrassed be all the shouting. He laughs,

shakes his head, and moves inside the school. The children, however, continue to chant: "Willy! Willy!" several more times. Then the chant is slightly altered and they yell: "Willy! Willy! We are bigger than you!"
The new version is repeated four times.
Then Allen breaks from the group and goes down the slide.
The other four children follow one at a time.
On their trips down the slide, Beth and Brian repeat the phrase: "We are bigger than you!"

PN: I had been standing near the slide during this incident and felt a great deal of sympathy for Willy.
On occasions of this type, adults are not really sure how to respond, and often feel uneasy about the children's chanting. In fact, the teachers seem to feel a bit out of control and often will withdraw as Willy did in this instance.

MN: I felt somewhat uneasy that the children might begin to taunt me after Willy went inside.
As a result, I moved slightly away from the climbing house and sat down on the ground to the left of the slide.
The children seemed not to pay much attention to me after Willy left. It is clear, however, that since I can not enter the top level of the climbing house I am somewhat more obtrusive when observing in this area. My being an adult seems more apparent to the children and it makes it difficult for me to participate even in my peripheral way.

TN: It is clear that the children felt in control during this incident. By the end of the encounter, they were almost taunting or challenging Willy to respond to their claim of being bigger.
In this instance, the children really may have felt bigger and they shared the enjoyment of challenging an adult.

A second way the children felt "bigger" or more "grown up" in the climbing house was the result of their ability to exit the top level on the firepole. Almost all the children in the school went down the firepole at some point over the course of the year. Children in the afternoon group often descended on the pole with little hesitation. However, they still often called attention to their feat by shouting to teachers or peers: "Watch, I'm going down the firepole!" Many children in the morning group were quite a bit more timid about going down the pole. Consider the following short exchange drawn from field notes:

Barbara grabs hold of the pole tightly and sticks out and then withdraws her foot.

Nancy is watching at a distance and says: "Go ahead, Barbara."

"You want to go first?" Barbara asks.

"No," says Nancy, "I'm not ready to go down."

Barbara then again grabs the pole, sticks out her left leg and wraps it around, but still stands with one leg on the floor.

Very slowly dropping her foot, Barbara begins to descend.

Finally, she moves her right leg to the pole and descends slowly, holding on tight all the way down.

At the bottom, Barbara shouts to Nancy and all others standing nearby: "I went down the firepole! I went down the firepole!"

Nancy now comes over near the pole and peers down into the hole in the floor of the climbing house.

Barbara looks up at her and says: "Come on, Nancy!" Nancy hesitates, then sticks out her left leg.

"Come on, Nancy, don't be scaredy. Don't be scaredy!" shouts Barbara.

"I'm not scaredy!" says Nancy, "I'm big!"

Nancy then grabs hold of the pole, leans forward, wraps her legs around, and descends.

At the bottom, Nancy says: "See, I told you I'm big. I went down the pole too!"

"Want to go down again?" asks Barbara.

"Not now," answers Nancy.

"Me neither," says Barbara. "Let's go inside."

The two girls run off toward the entrance to the school.

Themes in Spontaneous Fantasy

So far in describing peer values and concerns, I have focused on behavioral evidence. For example, we saw that the children's strategies for gaining and resisting access to play groups were indicative of their concerns regarding the protection of interactive space. In addition, both behavioral patterns (e.g., preferences for certain play areas) and verbal proclamations (e.g., "we are bigger than anybody else") were seen as evidence of the shared values of "being bigger." In this section, I examine how underlying *themes* of the children's spontaneous fantasy play reflect shared concerns in peer culture. This evidence is also based on behavioral patterns, but is more indirect and subtle than the support offered previously.

Peer play in the building-block area and around the inside and outside sandboxes in the school often took the form of spontaneous fantasy (see Cook-Gumperz and Corsaro, 1977). In this type of play, children became animals, monsters, race car drivers, and construction workers. During spontaneous fantasy play, themes emerged in the process of verbal negotiation, and these themes were rarely tied directly to specific plans of action (i.e., shared knowledge of social scripts).

By "themes" I am referring to the general underlying plot structures of spontaneous fantasy episodes (see Garvey and Brendt, 1975; Schwartz, 1983). Themes should not be seen as mere descriptions of play (e.g. "playing with toy animals"), but rather refer to underlying schemata (Rumelhart, 1975) the children introduce and use to frame ongoing and subsequent play. A careful analysis of several videotaped episodes of spontaneous fantasy led to the discovery of three recurrent themes. All three themes shared a basic structure involving the generation and the resolution of tension.

In a general sense, the tension generation and reduction sequence can be seen as a central schema, and spontaneous fantasy episodes can be analyzed in line with work on story grammars (see Rumelhart, 1977a, 1977b). However, my purpose here is not to analyze how spontaneous fantasy events are produced (but see Cook-Gumperz and Corsaro, 1977; Corsaro, 1983; Corsaro and Tomlinson, 1980), but rather to demonstrate how the nature and content of themes in spontaneous fantasy reflect peer concerns and values. Therefore, it is necessary to examine examples of spontaneous fantasy play which are representative of three recurrent themes in the videotaped data: (a) lost–found, (b) danger–rescue, and (c) death–rebirth.

Lost–found theme. The lost–found theme occurred frequently during spontaneous fantasy and was often repeated several times within the same interactive episode. There are two basic variants of the lost–found theme. The first involves the loss (either purposeful or accidental) of a possession which is followed by a search for and discovery of the lost object. Consider the following example.

Example 5.7
Tape 14 Episode 3
Morning
Scene: Outside Sandbox
Participants: Joseph, Roger, Concetta, Denny
Joseph (J), Roger (R), and Denny (D) have been playing in the sandpile for around 10 minutes. When they first began play, they buried a toy boat deep in the sand. They then built a large pile of sand and took turns jumping on it. The jumping continued for several minutes until the children fell on their knees and began to tap the top of the sandpile.

		Transcription	Description
(83)	D–R:	Now let's pat it, ok?	D and R pat top of sandpile.
(84)	R–D:	Ok.	
(85)	R–D:	Pat it on the top.	J now joins the other two boys.
(86)	R–D:	Wait! I know how to pat it.	R motions for D and J to stop and then takes a shovel and scoops sand off the top.
(87)	D–R:	Let's dig it again.	
(88)	R–D:	Ok.	R puts down his shovel.
(89)	D–RJ:	Let's dig it like this so we can have a cake.	All three dig with their hands.
(90)	J–DR:	Yeah. Cake!	
(91)	R–JD:	A cake—	
(92)	D–RJ:	We can see a boat—a boat!	D now discovers the boat they earlier buried in the sand.
(93)	J–RD:	A boat! This is our treasure!	
(94)	D–RJ:	Our treasure! Our treasure!	
(95)	J–RD:	Our treasure!	
(96)	D–RJ:	I feeled the boat!	R now pulls the boat from the sand.
(97)	J–RD:	We got the treasure!	
(98)	R–JD:	Now cover it up—bury it up.	R puts the boat back in the sand and all three begin covering it up.
(99)	D–RJ:	Now let's—	
(100)	R–JD:	Build a castle.	

Transcription, cont'd	Description, cont'd
(101) D–RJ: No, make the cake. The cake!	D pushes down sand on top of the pile and R hits the sand with his shovel.
(102) R–DJ: Cake—I have to flatten it.	

Prior to this sequence, the boys hid or purposely lost the boat as a way of initiating play. While covering the boat with sand, a new game developed (i.e., building and patting a sandpile), and the boat seemed to be temporarily forgotten. In this sequence, the boys began to dig again and then find the boat. They are quite excited by the discovery (92–97) and say that the boat is their treasure. They then decide to bury the boat again (98), and the lost–found theme is initiated anew. In fact, once the boat was buried, the children first made a cake on top of the pile and then took up Roger's suggestion (100) to build a castle. The boys worked on the castle for some time, and Denny left the area before the castle was finished. Roger and Joseph were joined by Concetta and they continued to work on the castle. When it was completed, Roger and Joseph invited Denny to return and help them "jump on the castle." After much jumping and laughing in the sand, the following sequence occurred.

Transcription	Description
(160) R–JD: Now find the boat.	D starts to dig in the sand looking for the boat.
(161) R–JD: We can't find the boat.	
(162) R–DJ: Come on, let's keep on fighting.	R and D wrestle in the sand.
(163) D–R: The—boat!	D notices the boat in the sand.
(164) R–DJ: I found it! I found it!	
(165) R–DJ: It's heavy—Oh!	R and S pull the boat from the sand, pretending that it is heavy.
(166) R–DJ: Now put it back there. Put it back.	

Later, the boat was rediscovered with renewed excitement. Soon after this third discovery, the children left the area and the spontaneous play activity was terminated.

Regarding shared peer values, it is important to note the *genuine excitement* the children display in finding the buried object. Although the repeated concealment and rediscovery of the toy boat may not arouse much excitement in older children or adults, it must be remembered that the nursery school children have recently moved from Piaget's sensory motor stage to the preoperational stage of cognitive development. Object constancy is a recent acquisition for these children. Repeated reenactments of play episodes involving hiding and discovering objects have both magical and self-autonomous features for the children. The children are simultaneously excited about their *mastery of the still somewhat magical behavioral routines in which objects are made to disappear and reappear.*

As we can see it Example 5.7, the children expand upon the basic lost–found theme to create a complex and organized fantasy episode. The elaboration and appreciation of the lost–found theme are elements of peer culture. However, the source of the children's knowledge of the theme is most likely the children's earlier involvement in mother–infant play and games. As Bruner and his associates (Bruner, 1975; Bruner and Sherwood, 1976; Ratner and Bruner, 1978) have demonstrated, mother–infant disappearance–reappearance games (e.g., peekaboo) have important consequences for children's language development. It is also clear that play of this type is important for children's acquisition of object constancy. In addition, there is some empirical support (see Ratner and Bruner, 1978) that young children recreate the basic elements of mother–infant disappearance–reappearance games in solitary play. Therefore, a highly likely developmental pattern is that the lost–found theme first *emerges* in mother–infant games, is *practiced* and *solidified* (along with object-constancy in solitary play), and then is *used* as a basic schema in peer play.

The second variant of the lost–found theme involves *personally* "becoming or being lost." Like the lost object variant, the being lost theme involves a great deal of excitement upon discovery. However, the initial, tension-building phase of the the theme is much more intense and anxiety-provoking. Consider the following example.

Example 5.8
Tape 9 Episode 6
Scene: Inside Sandbox
Participants: Rita, Charles, Leah
In this episode, the children are playing with toy animals in the sandbox. They are pretending to be the animals as they move them about in the sand. Several themes are interwoven (Lost–Found, Danger–Rescue, and Death–Rebirth); and enacted and repeated several times during the fantasy play. The first lost–found sequence follows an earlier danger–rescue sequence involving a rain storm. The lost–found sequence is initiated by Rita, who calls for help. Prior to the initiation of the following sequence, the children had reached a shared understanding that it was cold outside, but warm inside, their hideout (a large pile of sand).

Transcription			*Description*
(91)	R–CL:	Help! Help! I'm off in the forest!	R has three horses and moves them at the end of the sandbox some distance from L and C, who have placed their animals in the sandpile (hideout). R moves one horse up and down as she calls for help.
(92)	C–R:	Come in here.	C is referring to the hideout.
(93)	L–R:	In here.	
(94)	C–R:	Come in here! Come here!	
(95)	R–C:	I can't!	
(96)	C–R:	Come in this—	
(97)	R–C:	I'm lost!	
(98)	C–R:	Ok.	C reaches over and takes R's horse from her hand and puts it in the sandpile.
(99)	R–CL:	My friends, they'll get burnt.	
(100)	R–CL:	I'm cold! Freezing!	R now moves her horse up and down near the sandpile.
(101)	C–R:	Stay in here.	C takes R's horse and puts it in the hideout.
(102)	R–C:	I'm freezing too! I'm freezing too!	R picks up the third horse.

Transcription, cont'd			*Description, cont'd*
(103)	C–R:	Get in here!	C takes third horse from R and places it in the sandpile.
(104)	R–C:	Let me ( ).	
(105)	C–R:	Get in here.	All animals are now in the hideout. C taps the top of the pile.
(106)	R–CL:	Warm!	R pats top of the sandpile.
(107)	L–RC:	It's starting to rain. O—O—O—Oh!	L sprinkles sand on top of the pile.

There are two aspects of the personal lost–found theme that are important for understanding peer culture. First, the children's pretending to become lost in spontaneous fantasy play often *serves as a basis for the initiation of interpersonal cooperative exchanges among peers*. Note in Example 5.8 that Rita (91) initiates the lost–found theme by simply calling for help. Since it was not clear why help was needed, Charles and Leah advise Rita to leave the forest and come into the hideout (92–94). Once Rita says that she, in the role of one of the horses, is lost (97), Charles promptly takes action and places Rita (her horse) in the hideout. Once she is safe, Rita immediately shows concern for the other horses (99). Rita then pretends to be each of the other horses who are rescued one at a time by Charles (100–105). Rita finally displays relief and thanks to Charles (106), where she shouts "Warm!". With the tension of Rita's being lost now relieved, Leah introduces a new sequence of play which involves a rainstorm.

As we see, the enactment of the personal lost–found theme often generates interpersonal exchanges among peers. Thus, fantasy play of this type results in the development of interpersonal skills plus a shared sense of trust and gratitude among peers.

A second, more abstract, aspect of the personal lost–found theme is that it is a *manifestation of and an attempt to cope with an underyling fear*. This is the young child's fear of being lost and alone. Many preschool children have directly experienced, even if only briefly, the amorphous and almost overwhelming anxiety that accompanies being lost. If they have not experienced this anxiety first hand, most preschool children have been warned by parents of the danger of getting lost, or have shared the experience vicariously as a result of being told stories or fairy tales.

In spontaneous fantasy play, children often enact lost–found themes and as a result share this very real fear of "being lost."

In fact, by enacting lost–found themes in spontaneous play, the children are able *to share* both the anxiety of being lost and the relief and joy of being found. In this sense, the children are able to directly confront and attempt to cope with this anxiety in peer play without experiencing the actual risks and dangers of being lost in the real world.

Danger–rescue themes. Danger–rescue themes occurred even more frequently in spontaneous fantasy play than lost–found themes. Danger–rescue themes differ from personal lost–found themes in that the threat or danger is more specific. The children's ability to think up or create danger seemed almost limitless. There were rainstorms, fires, tidal waves, snowstorms, lightning, falls from cliffs, threatening animals, earthquakes, and poison, just to name a few. Consider the following sequence from the spontaneous fantasy episode described in Example 5.8, which aptly illustrates the danger–rescue theme.

Example 5.9

Transcription		*Description*
(10) C–LR:	This is our b-i-g home! And I—I'm a freezing squirrel.	C moves his rabbit up and down and then begins burying it in the sand, while L gets another animal and buries it.
(11) R–CL:	And this got out. And I'm freezing. Whoop-whoop-whoop-whoop!	R takes her horse out of the sand and holds it up. She then moves her horse up and down. Down with each whoop.
(12) L–R:	Get in the house!	L smoothes the sand so the pile or house is higher.
(13) R–CL:	Oh—wow—get in the house!	R puts her horse in the sandpile and buries it.
(14) R–CL:	Oh, look, it's raining. Gonna rain.	R now picks up a handful of sand and sprinkles it onto the pile.
(15) C–RL:	Rain! It's gonna be a rainstorm!	C takes his rabbit out of the sand.
(16) R–C:	Yeah.	
(17) C–RL:	And lightning. Help!	

Transcription, cont'd			*Description, cont'd*
(18)	C–RL:	But I won't be hit though—cause lightning only hits a biggest—big-ger—will hit our house cause it's the biggest thing.	C now moves his rabbit away from the sand to the other side of the sandbox.
(19)	C–RL:	Cause our house is made of—	
(20)	L–CR:	Going—going—	L and R now move their animals from the sandpile.
(21)	C–RL:	But our house is made of steel. So the lightning just fall to the ground.	C now returns his rabbit to the sandpile.
(22)	R–C:	Yeah.	R and L return their animals to the sand.
(23)	R–CL:	Won't get horsie.	R is referring to the lightning, which won't get her horsie, which is now in the sand.
(24)	C–RL:	I'm going on the big part.	C moves his rabbit from the sand to the top of the pile and then covers it. R and L help in covering it.
(25)	C–RL:	Hey creature! Don't go in the house. That's a snake. That's the snake—that want-ed to go into the house.	C pretends to pick up something from the pile and places it at the far end of the sandbox from the house.
(26)	C–R:	That's the horse.	C says this as he and R cover a horse with sand.
(27)	L–CR:	Hey! I'm cold. Cold. I'm cold.	L says this after she moves a cow from the sand and moves it up and down on the pile (house).
(28)	C–L:	Get into this pile!	C moves sand to cover L's cow.
(29)	R–CL:	Yeah!	R and L now help to cover the cow.

Transcription, cont'd			*Description, cont'd*
(30)	C–LR:	No! Don't get it off the top—sand off—our else our house will break down.	L moves back and C reaches for more sand.
(31)	R–CL:	Yeah!—Yeah, yeah! Get more! The faster we get, the faster we can get the sand away!	R now joins C and L, who are pushing or raking sand from around the box to the pile to rein- force the house.
(32)	C–RL:	Yes, the faster we push—the—the snow over, the faster we'll get the warm.	C says this in the exact rhythm of R's previous utterance, while he, R, and L continue to rake the sand to the pile.
(33)	R–CL:	The—the sun goes on. Whoopee! Whoopee!	R continues to rake the sand.
(34)	C–RL:	Hey! The rain- storm is over!	
(35)	R–CL:	Yea! Whoopee! Get out!	R reaches in and takes her horse from the sand and holds it high in the air. R is very excited and screechs, "Get out!"
(36)	L–CR:	Out!	L and R now reach into sandpile (house) to get out their animals.

The danger–rescue theme in this example (and in all the other spontaneous fantasy episodes in which it occurred) involved three basic steps. Each of these steps display a different feature of peer culture regarding the children's perceptions of danger. The first step entails the *recognition of danger*. What is most interesting about this step is the manner in which danger evolves. Although danger is expected in spontaneous fantasy, its arrival is always a surprise. One must be on the lookout! Danger can come from anywhere and out of nowhere.

Consider Example 5.9. The children first build a home to escape the cold (10–13). Then it, quite spontaneously, begins to rain (14). The rain becomes a storm (15). The storm is accompanied by lightning, and now there is a need for help (17), because the danger has emerged. Note that the children take no risks here. The danger which arises is not the result of reckless behavior. Rather, danger *is something that happens to the children.* The children share a concern for danger, and they see danger as something which can occur at any time.

Since danger often occurs without warning in spontaneous fantasy, the children are prepared to deal with it once it does emerge. The children's main tactic for coping with danger is not confrontation but *evasion,* and the second step in the danger–rescue theme is "to avert the danger." Let us again consider Example 5.9. Once the danger of lightning is recognized, Charles immediately takes evasive action. He moves his rabbit away from the house because "lightning only hits a biggest—bigger—will hit our house cause it's the biggest thing" (18). Once Charles moves his rabbit, he begins to rethink his strategy (19). Meanwhile, following Charles' lead, Rita and Leah move their animals from the house. However, Charles quickly decides that the house is safe after all, because it is made of steel and the lightning "will just fall to the ground" (21). Rita agrees and all three children place their animals back into the house so the lightning "won't get them" (23).

Note that averting danger is something the children do together. It involves communication and cooperation. In averting danger, one must be calm and careful and should not take unnecessary risks. In this sense, danger–rescue is somewhat a misnomer. The children do not rescue one another; rather, they *cooperatively escape the danger.*

The third step in the danger–rescue theme involves the recognition that the *danger has dissipated or gone away.* In this sense, the danger often departs as quickly as it arrived. And the departure of danger, like its arrival, is something that happens to the children. Danger comes, it is averted, and it disappears. The recognition of danger's disappearance brings about a *shared display of relief and joy.* Let us again return to Example 5.9. Once all the animals are safely inside the house (23), several limited lines of action are played out. A snake, a possible source of danger, is removed from the house (25). Although one might question why Charles introduced the snake, it would seem that its presence was not that unusual. The snake, like the other animals, wanted to get into the house to escape the storm. But since the snake had no animator, it was removed. After the snake is removed, the animals venture outside briefly, but they stay close to the house (26–29). The house is then reinforced (30–32). During this period of stabilization of the shelter, Rita (33) initiates the third step of recognizing the dissipation of the danger (i.e., the storm is ending because the ''sun goes on''). Charles quickly takes up on Rita's claim and announces that ''the rainstorm is over'' (34). All of the children then share in a celebration of danger's departure by removing their animals from the house amidst shouts and cheers (35–36).

Death–rebirth theme. The final theme in children's spontaneous play, death–rebirth, occurred less frequently than either the danger–rescue or lost–found themes. However, the death–rebirth theme did occur with some consistency in that it appeared at least once in 15 of the 20 videotaped episodes which involved spontaneous fantasy. Like the two other themes in spontaneous fantasy, the death–rebirth theme had a basic structure. The structure was composed of four steps or phases: (a) announcement(s) of dying or death, (b) reaction(s) to the announcements by peers, (c) responses or strategies to deal with the death by peers, and (d) rebirth.

On some occasions, the announcement of the death was ignored and the sequence was aborted, while in other instances the announcement was reacted to negatively (i.e., the death was challenged or not certified) and the sequence again stopped short of full enactment. Let us begin by looking at two examples from the spontaneous fantasy episode first described in Example 5.8 which demonstrates both abortive and complete sequences of the death–rebirth theme. After considering these examples, I will turn to a brief discussion of the implications of the death–rebirth theme regarding shared peer values and concerns.

Example 5.10
Tape 9 Episode 6
Morning
Scene: Inside Sandbox
Participants: Rita, Charles, Leah

Transcription		*Description*
(83)	C–RL:	Now they're sailing away.
(84)	R–CL:	Bit! Bit! Bit!

Transcription, cont'd	*Description, cont'd*
(85) R–CL: We're dead! Help we're dead!	R lays her animals on their sides.
(86) C–RL: (Water).	
(87) R–CL: We're dead! We're dead! Help!	
(88) C–RL: Water flattened it. //The have to go to ( ).	
(89) R–CL: //We're dead. We're dead! Help!	
(90) C–RL: We're gonna send them under water cause they're sailing away in a cave.	
(91) L–CR: My sheep are safe. My sheep are safe.	
(92) R–CL: We're all dead. Help!	R moves animals while on their sides in the sand.
(93) C–R: I can't—you can't talk—if they're dead.	
(94) R–CL: Oh, well, Leah's talked when she was dead. So mine have to talk when I'm dead. Help. Help. I'm dead. Help!	R's last utterance spoken very softly.
(95) R–CL: (Inaudible)	
(96) L–CR: Here's our chimney! Here's the chimeny!	L and C are placing animals in the sandpile.
(97) C–L: Our chimney. Have to go in chimney. Bye chimney ( ).	
(98) R–CL: Help! Help! I'm—a—lost in the forest. Help! I'm lost in the for—	R moves her horse to far end of sandbox.
(99) C–R: Come in here!	

Example 5.11
Tape 9 Episode 6
Morning
Scene: Inside Sandbox
Participants: Rita, Charles, Leah

Transcription			*Description*
(199)	C–RL:	Rabbit's dead.	C lays his rabbit on floor of sandbox near R's horse.
(200)	L–CR:	Rabbit's dead.	L lays her rabbit next to C's.
(201)	C–LR:	No, only my rabbit's de—dead.	C picks up L's rabbit and gives it back to her.
(202)	L–C:	What's a matter?	L says this with her rabbit in hand, and she is talking to C's rabbit.
(203)	C–L:	(Inaudible)	C moves his rabbit near L's rabbit.
(204)	R–CL:	Oh, my horse is dead.	R takes horse from the sandpile and lays it down on far side of the sandbox.
(205)	R–CL:	My horse is dead.	
(206)	C–RL:	Hop! Hop! Hop! If I bang on it. Bang! Bang! Bang! He'll be alive—	C hops over near A's horse and bangs rabbit on ground near A's horse.
(207)	L–CR:	Bang! Bang! Bang!	L bangs her rabbit on ground next to C.
(208)	C–R:	If I bang on it, it will be alive. Bang! Bang! Bang!	C again bangs his rabbit on ground while L returns her rabbit to the sandpile.
(209)	R–C:	You better—you bang on that bell on'em. He'll be alive and he'll open up.	R points off camera at a microphone hanging from the ceiling.
(210)	C–R:	Bang on what?	
(211)	R–C:	Bang on that bell. If you—if you wake'em up. Bang on that pretend bell.	R points off camera at microphone and both C and L turn to look.
(212)	C–R:	What bell?	
(213)	R–C:	That pretend bell. That—bell. That microphone.	R again points off camera at the microphone. R stands and looks for the bell.

Transcription, cont'd			*Description, cont'd*
(214)	C–R:	I don't see the bell.	C is still looking.
(215)	R–C:	That microphone.	R points directly at the microphone.
(216)	C–R:	Oh.	M sees the microphone.
(217)	R–C:	Not that. This. This horse.	R now picks up a large horse and holds it in the air while the smaller (dead) horse still lies on the ground.
(218)	C–R:	Bring! Bring! B—ring!	C now hits R's horse as he says this.
(219)	R–C:	Jump, horse. Whoa! Jump! Whoa! Jump! Whoa! Jump! Whoa! Jump! Whoa! Jump!	R now moves both her horses up and down. Smaller horse is now alive.
(220)	L–CR:	Help! Help! I'm lost!	L has her rabbit in hand. C immediately brings his rabbit next to L's and touches hers.
(221)	C–L:	Thank you, rabbit.	C and L put their rabbits in the sandpile. R also places her horse in the sandpile.

In Example 5.10, Charles and Rita are both talking at the same time in (88–89), and Charles is announcing the threat of the tidal wave while Rita is announcing the death of her horses. At (93), Charles momentarily stops his enactment of the danger–rescue theme he is engaged in with Leah, to react to Rita's "death" announcement (92). The reaction is negative, in that Charles tells Rita that her animals "can't talk" if they are dead (93). Rita, however, persists, informing Charles that Leah's animals talked when they were dead. Charles and Leah ignore Rita's contention and her attempt to enact a death–rebirth theme, and they continue to develop their own danger–rescue theme (96). At this point, Rita initiates a lost–found theme which is responded to by Charles and eventually enacted in subsequent discourse.

Although it may appear that Charles's negative reaction to Rita's announcement is abitrary, this is not the case. It is, of course, true that one could never announce one's own death if a rule of "no talking when you're dead" was strictly enforced. However, Rita's error was not her announcement of death, but rather her additional calls for help (85, 87, and 89). These additions prompt a reaction, but in the process violate the original claim that the animals were in fact dead. As a result, Charles reacted negatively to Rita's attempt to initiate a death–rebirth theme and, therefore, the sequence fails to develop fully.

Example 5.11 is interesting, because it contains both abortive and completed death–rebirth sequences. Charles first announces that his rabbit is dead (199). Leah then follows with her own announcement of death. Charles seems to react negatively to Leah's announcement because she failed to respond to his initial announcement, thereby delaying the possible enactment of the death–rebirth sequence. Charles seems to justify his negative reaction to Leah's announcement by offering an implicit rule (201) that his rabbit was dead first. Leah then reacts to Charles' initial announcement by asking "what's a matter" (202). At this point, Rita enters the discourse by announcing the death of her horse (204). She repeats her announcement again (205), and Charles reacts positively to Rita's announcement (206).

Although I cannot definitely infer the intentions of the children, it appears that Charles decides to "give up" on his animal being dead and move on with the sequence by responding to Rita's announcement. We should also note that, unlike her announcements in Example 5.10, Rita's announcements in Example 5.11 are just that. She does not go further to call for help.

Charles' positive reaction (206) is also a response to the problem of death, in that he offers a strategy for bringing Rita's dead horse back to life. Thus, the third stage of the death–rebirth theme is initiated. In this example, the third stage is fairly lengthy, because there is some debate about the elements of the strategy which are necessary to bring the horse back to life (209–217). Rita wants Charles to bang on her horse with a bell, and points to a microphone which could serve as a bell. It is worthy of mention here that Rita, as she did in Example 5.10, talks even though she (her horse) is supposedly dead. However, in this case, Rita's talking is not inappropriate as it was in Example 5.10, because in this instance Rita is no longer the animal but rather the animator of the animal (see Goffman, 1974). From this example, it appears that the children have the communicative abilities to shift from "play" to "talk about play" with relative ease.

Returning to the transcript, we see that Charles eventually sees the microphone (216), whereupon he offers (217) an alternative strategy of pretending a large horse is a bell. Having reached an agreement, Charles hits Rita's horses with the bell, and the sequence is completed with the occurrence of the final, rebirth, phase of the death–rebirth sequence. Once this sequence is complete, Leah immediately initiates a brief lost–found theme, and the end result is that all the animals end up safely in the sandpile.

Although these data demonstrate that children have knowledge of and talk about death, it is difficult to infer the degree of their concerns and anxieties about death. Surely, children think about death, and they are frequently exposed to information about death and dying by the media (especially television, movies, and fairy tales). In fact, the enactment of the death-rebirth sequence in Example 5.11 bears striking similarities to death–rebirth themes in fairy tales like *Sleeping Beauty* and *Snow White*.

It is clear that the children's enactments of death–rebirth themes allow them jointly to share any concerns or fears they have about death. In this sense, the death–rebirth theme is quite similar to both the personal lost–found and danger-rescue themes discussed earlier. However, it also seems that there is less tension in the death–rebirth theme than in the others. What seems to get *emphasized or foregrounded* in the death–rebirth sequences *is the strategy or tactics involved in bringing the dead back to life*. In this sense, the death–rebirth theme has a magical quality that children like first to enact and then later *to share* in the enjoyment of the magical outcome.

I have, of course, only briefly touched on the important implications of themes in children's fantasy play in this chapter. My purpose has been to focus on those aspects of spontaneous fantasy play which pertain most directly to the children's shared values and concerns. There is a need for further, in-depth studies of children's naturally occurring fantasy play to develop the full implications of these activities for our understanding of children's lifeworlds.

Behavioral Routines in Peer Culture

Thus far, in discussing peer culture, I have focused on children's shared values and concerns. In this section I move to a direct analysis of the children's behavioral routines. Routines can be seen as elements of peer culture because they involve *activities that the children consistently produce together.* Routines are, therefore, peer activities which are recurrent and predictable.

Although tempted to refer to the children's routines as rituals, I have resisted this impulse, because many of the routines do not seem to be symbolic in nature. Some routines do indeed signify specific events and shared understandings, but others seem only to approach symbolic ritual, and some routines are enacted primarily because the children are fascinated by their repetitive nature. Although I cannot undertake a description of all the behavioral routines which appeared over the course of the school term, I will examine several consistent types of peer routines. Near the end of this section, I turn to an analysis of an unusual and highly interesting routine which emerged spontaneously in the morning session for two successive years. This particular routine, which I call "Garbage Man," is totally a product of peer culture in this school.

Children's Humor: Group Glee, Jokes, and Riddles

Smiles, laughter, and general mirth are all very much a part of a typical day at the nursery school. In fact, laughter is often infectious among the children. Any number of things might set off a wave of laughter and giggles through a group of children at any time.

The eruption of spontaneous laughter is a frequent occurrence in the play activities of young children (see Garvey, 1977b:17–23). In fact, Sherman (1975) has carefully studied this phenomenon in nursery schools and has referred to it as "group glee." Sherman found that group glee, involving laughter, screams, giggles, and jumping up and down, often occurs during teacher-directed activities or meeting times. Group glee frequently occurred during meeting time in this nursery school, but also emerged in peer activities.

Although group glee can be seen as a form of humor, it has a very simple communicative structure and is basically imitative. On several occasions, the children also produced more complex forms of humor such as jokes and riddles. The jokes followed a simple setup–punch line structure (see Tomlinson, 1981) involving three steps. For example:

Dominic runs up to me in the outside yard of the school and says:
"Bill, say forty!"
"Forty," I repeat.
Dominic cocks his right hand while pointing his finger at me and says:
"Stick'em up, shorty!"
Dominic and Jonathan, who was standing behind him, now laugh up-
roariously. They both then turn and run toward their next victim.

This same joke was repeated more than a dozen times in the
school throughout the afternoon by Dominic, Jonathan, and several other children. In fact, the joke persisted for several days.
Although this joke seems quite simple, it was somewhat difficult
for the children to master. The joke has a two-step exchange, and
it demands some patience or waiting before the punchline can be
delivered. Jokes of this type only occurred in the afternoon group,
and even there they were not always successfully delivered.

Shortly after my encounter with Dominic, one of the younger
children in the afternoon group, Mark, came up to me and said:

"Bill."
"What?" I replied.
(5 second delay)
Mark then cocked his hand like a gun and said: "Stick 'em up, shorty!"
Mark laughed loudly and ran off.

On another occasion that same day, I witnessed the following
variant of the joke.

Tommy: Tell me to say Forty.
Eva: Say Forty!
Tommy: Forty!
(Pause)
Tommy: Now say, stick 'em up, shorty!
Eva: Stick 'em up, shorty!
Both Tommy and Eva laughed loudly and then ran off toward the swings
together.

In addition to jokes, some of the children in the afternoon group
produced several riddles. The riddles were of the form:

A: "How can———?"
B: Attempted answer, or "I don't know"
A: "The answer to the riddle."

McDowell (1979) referred to this form as an interrogative ludic routine. McDowell notes that there are two types of interrogative ludic routines: (a) descriptive routines, and (b) true riddles (1979:38–41). Descriptive routines are simply question/answer routines (e.g. what is———? a rose), where children ask and answer questions leading to a cooperative ethos among participants. True riddles, on the other hand, involve true tests of wit, and lead to a competitive ethos. In this concept, I am concerned with the few (four in all) true riddles that I recorded in my data. All occurred in the afternoon group. Consider the following example.

Mary, the head teacher in the afternoon group, is in the playhouse with several children pretending to have dinner. One of the children, Daniel, says:
"Mary, I want to tell you a riddle."
"Ok," replies Mary.
Daniel asks, "How can a man fall into the ocean and not get his hair wet?"
"I don't know," says Mary. "Maybe he had a hat on."
"No," yells Daniel. "He was bald-headed!"
All the children and Mary laugh at Daniel's riddle.
Daniel laughs the loudest and continually repeats the word "bald-headed."

Unlike the result of the joke-telling, there was no attempt to repeat the riddle by other children. However, Daniel and several of the children who heard the riddle went around the school later, calling out: "You're bald-headed!" to other children and some of the teachers. After calling someone "bald-headed," the children would laugh gleefully and then run off, find a new target and repeat the routine. Since most of the children labeled "bald-headed" had not heard the riddle, they either protested (e.g., "I am not!") or looked bewildered and said nothing, or laughed and ran off with Daniel and some of the other children to join in the name-calling. A similar episode occurred later in the school year, when Daniel told a riddle about man-eating sharks.

In summary, it is clear that the children are developing rudimentary conceptions of humor. However, the main feature of the children's humor was not the nature or structure of a joke or riddle, but rather the infectious and repetitious laughter and mirth which resulted from a performance. Further, this mirth or group glee (Sherman, 1975) often emerged time and time again, even in cases where the joke or riddle was improperly performed. It was almost as if attempts at humor could not fail when delivered within the peer group culture of the nursery school.

"Poo-Poo on You": Children's Threats and Insults

In her classic analysis of children's humor, Martha Wolfenstein (1978) noted that much of the humor of 3- to 6- year-olds contained simple references to excretion. Wolfenstein offered a psychoanalytic interpretation of children's preoccupation with excretory activities by tying this behavior to the anal stage, when young children are at odds with their parents regarding toilet-training. Wolfenstein (1978: also see McGhee, 1979) has noted that as children grow older they no longer see the mere mention of "poo-poo" or "pee-pee" as funny. In fact, school age children often react to such behavior as childish. References to excretion, however, do not disappear from children's humor. Rather, they often become incorporated into more advanced forms of humor like the dirty joke (see Wolfenstein, 1978: 168–170).

Whatever the source of preschool children's concern with bodily products, the younger children in the nursery school often could be heard talking and laughing about "poo-poo" and "pee-pee." Although the children felt any reference to "poo-poo" (or "poop" as it was sometimes called) was funny, they most often used the terms to tease, insult, or threaten one another. In many cases, the teasing involved simple references to poo-poo or pee-pee. For example, one child may say: "You got poo-poo on your head," and another child will retort: "Well, you got poo-poo on your face." In other cases, the teasing turned to threats and was accompanied by physical threats and gestures. Consider the following example:

Example 5.12
Tape 2 Episode 1
Morning
Scene: Stairway of Upstairs Playhouse
Participants: Richard, Denny, Joseph, Martin, Ellen, and Debbie

Richard and Denny have been playing on the staircase with a slinky toy. The boys have taken turns letting the slinky go down the stairs and then retrieving it. One child, Ellen, attempted to join the play earlier, but the boys chased her off. We will pick up the play when two other boys (Joseph and Martin) attempt to gain access.

		Transcription	Description
(98)	R–J:	Give us the slinky, please.	R has just let the slinky go down the stairs, and J, who has just entered the scene, picks up the slinky at the bottom of the steps. M now also enters and stands next to J. D and R are at the top of the steps.
(99)	D–JM:	You can't come up. You can't! No! You can't cause we're working the slinky, you'll get hit in the face with it.	J and M now move up the steps in the face of D's threat.
(100)	R–JM:	And don't come up here!	D moves down the steps and takes the slinky from J. J and M remain on the steps.
(101)	M–R:	I'm not.	M now starts back down the stairs.
(102)	R–J:	Move!	J holds his ground halfway up the stairs. D has returned to the top of the stairs with the slinky, and sits next to R.
(103)	R–D:	Can I have it?	R takes slinky from D.
(104)	D–J:	Get out! Bla! Bla!	J stays put. M is now standing at the bottom of the stairs.
(105)	D–J:	Go! Go!	
(106)	R–D:	We want them to go.	
(107)	D–R:	Yeah, we want them to go. Go away. La-la-la-la . . .	D sings as R plays with the slinky. They are refraining from throwing the slinky down the stairs until J and M leave.
(108)	R–D:	We're gonna wait until they leave.	

Transcription, cont'd		*Description, cont'd*
(109) D–JM:	Go!	M now runs off and D moves downstairs, passing J to see if M has really left.
(110) J–RD:	Now I'm gonna throw—	J throws a small hat he was holding to the bottom of the stairs.
(111) R–J:	Boom. Boom. Boom.	R starts down stairs and playfully bumps J, saying "boom" as he passes him. D now comes back up stairs and bumps into R.
(112) R–D:	Don't push me. Push him!	R points to J standing on the stairs. D then sticks out his foot and threatens to kick J. J responds by kicking at, but not actually touching, D.
(113) J–DR:	These are (big) shoes!	
(114) R–D:	I'll punch him in the eye.	R is referring to J in this indirect threat. R pulls slinky apart as if to snap it at J as he says this.
(115) J–R:	I'll punch you right in the nose.	
(116) D–RJ:	I will punch him with my foot.	D again holds out foot toward J.
(117) R–DJ:	I will punch him with my big fist.	R holds up his fist.
(118) J–RD:	I—I'll—I'll—	J seems to be grasping for something to say.
(119) R–DJ:	And he'll be bumpety, bumpety and punched out. All the way down the stairs.	
(120) J–R:	I—I—I'll—I could poke your eyes out with my gun. I have a gun.	
(121) D–J:	A gun! I'll—I— I—even if—I—	D leans toward J and seems to be uncertain of what he wants to say.
(122) R–J:	I have a gun, too.	

Transcription, cont'd		*Description, cont'd*
(123)	D–JR: And I have guns, too, and it's bigger than yours and it poo-poo down. That's (gun) poo-poo.	All three boys laugh loudly at D's reference to poo-poo.
(124)	R–J: Now leave.	
(125)	J–DR: Un-Huh. I gonna tell you (to put on—)—on the gun on your hair and the poop will come right out on his face.	J points his finger to top of his head, then to R's face.
(126)	D–J: Well—	
(127)	R–J: Slinky will snap right on your face too.	R holds slinky close to J's face. Debbie now comes to bottom of steps and looks up at the boys.
(128)	D–J: And my gun will snap right—	
(129)	Debbie–J: Batman.	All three boys turn to look down at Debbie.
(130)	Debbie–J: Hey, where's Robin?	
(131)	B–J: No.	
(132)	J–Debbie: I'm Batman.	
(133)	Debbie–J: Where's Robin?	
(134)	J–Debbie: I'm Robin.	
(135)	Debbie–J: No, I'm looking for a different Robin without a badge.	J is wearing a paper police badge on his shirt. Debbie leaves after saying this, and J follows after her. R and D remain at top of the stairs, but hesitate in playing with the slinky. D now climbs up on bannister and looks into the playhouse. R flips the slinky and it goes halfway down the stairs. D then goes down, picks up the slinky, and tosses it to the bottom of the stairs.

Transcription, cont'd			*Description, cont'd*
(136)	R–D:	My turn still. It's my turn Denny.	R slightly taps D on the shoulder
(137)	D–R:	What? Hit! Hit! Hit!	D turns around and taps R, and says, "hit" with each tap. R then moves up into playhouse, followed by D. J now returns and also enters the playhouse.
(138)	J–DR:	Batgirl's downstairs.	J points down at Debbie. D and R now begin jumping on the bed and do not respond to J.
(139)	J–DR:	Batgirl's down there.	J now moves to top of stairs and points down again.
(140)	D–R:	( ) way to go.	D and R continue jumping until R hits his head.
(141)	R:	OW!	R moves toward J, holding his head
(142)	R–J:	I bumped my head.	
(143)	J–R:	Batgirl's down there.	J again points down at Debbie.
(144)	R–J:	Where are the batgirls?	
(145)	J–R:	Down there.	J points again.
(146)	R–J:	I will catch them quickly with my bear.	R picks up a teddy bear and starts downstairs with J. D now stops jumping on the bed and follows J and R downstairs. The episode ends at this point.

In this sequence, the children's threats and references to "poo-poo," like most routines in peer culture, are *embedded in episodes of peer play*. As a result, the interpretation of this routine must be guided by its place and function in this particular episode. In this episode, Richard and Denny have created a game—taking turns tossing the slinky down the stairs—which they would like to protect from the intrusion of other children (see Chapter 4). Although successful in warding off the access attempts of several children, Richard and Denny are unable to overcome Joseph's persistance. Unable to dissuade Joseph with simple warnings (e.g., lines 100, 102, 109), the boys turn to physical threats.

These threats exhibit some of the same features isolated by Brennis and Lein (1977) in their sociolinguistic analysis of the arguments of first grade children. For example, the boys used *repetition,* in that some threats were countered by similar threats (e.g., lines 114–115, "I'll punch him in the eye," "I'll punch you right in the nose") and *escalation,* in that in some exchanges successive statements were stronger and often longer and more complex syntactically than preceding statements (e.g., lines 119–125).

Although the data in this episode are similar to the findings of Brennis and Lein (1977), there are some important differences. These differences are primarily the result of how the data were collected. In Brennis and Lein's (1977) study, the data were elicited by asking children to "role play" situations which would lead to arguments or disputes. For example, dyads were asked to have an argument about who was the smartest (Brennis and Lein, 1977:50). Although children may certainly argue about who is the smartest in real-life situations, such arguments are embedded in naturally occurring peer activities. Features of interactive events like the nature of the ongoing activity (e.g., "playing a game," "talking about friends," etc.), where the dispute occurred in unfolding activities, the number of people involved, etc., are important both for children's participation in disputes of this type and for researchers' analysis and interpretations of the behavior.

In Example 5.12, the more complex threats emerged as a result of Joseph's persistence in gaining access to the play shared by Richard and Denny. In fact, Richard and Denny had verbally remarked that they were "sharing" the slinky and would not allow others to play before any child attempted to gain entry. As a result, this episode contained a pattern typical of peer culture in the nursery school, "defenders versus intruders" (see Chapter 4).

Given Joseph's persistence, a triadic sequence developed involving Denny and Richard defending the play area against Joseph. This pattern of two defenders against one intruder led to the interesting sociolinguistic feature of several of the threats; that being the "indirect" nature of many of Richard and Denny's verbal threats. For example Richard and Denny threaten Joseph by *telling each other* what they plan to do to him (112, 114, 116, and 117). These indirect speech acts served two functions in this content. First, the boys were able *to threaten* Joseph and attempt to counter his access attempt. Second, the indirect threats were used to *build solidarity* in the defender dyad by *marking the team effort* of their attempt to dissuade Joseph.

A final interesting feature of the indirect threats is Richard's use of metaphor in (119). Richard notes that: "and he'll [Joseph] be bumpety, bumpety and punched out all the way down the stairs." Richard is implying that Joseph (after he is punched out) will go bumpety, bumpety all the way down the stairs like the slinky he and Denny had been playing with. Again it is important to note that this interpretation of the complexity of Richard's threat was based on having information on the whole episode in which the threatening exchanges were embedded.

We now come to the final part of the episode and the children's references to "poo-poo." Almost all disputes in the nursery school were settled without physical aggression. Disputes would often escalate to a given point and then be *relieved* by some action, such as one or the other party giving in or teacher intervention. A form of *relief* I often observed was the production of a cue or signal that the dispute was, after all, *part of play* and should not be taken too seriously. In Example 5.12, and in numerous other disputes involving verbal threats, the signal which brought about relief to an escalating series of threats was a reference to "poo-poo."

In Example 5.12, Joseph escalated the dispute (120) by threatening to poke out Richard's eyes with a gun. Denny repeated Joseph's reference to a gun, but hesitated in escalating the dispute. Richard then noted (122) that he had a gun too, but he did not directly threaten Joseph. Denny, often taking time to think about a response to Joseph, claimed he had a bigger gun (123) and that his gun would "poo-poo down." Although Denny's meaning is not clear, it seems he is saying that his gun will shoot poo-poo. Nevertheless, Denny's reference to "poo-poo" lead to laughter and relief from the escalating dispute. After the laughter, Richard again told Joseph to leave. Joseph, however, countered with a threat (125) that also contained a reference to "poo-poo." Joseph's threat can be seen as a positive response to Denny's earlier attempt to end the dispute. At (127), Richard again threatens Joseph, who responds in kind. But shortly thereafter, Joseph, Denny, and Richard play together in the upstairs playhouse, and the three boys eventually leave together to play in another area of the school.

Denny's reference to "poo-poo" in Example 5.12 is similar to the complex use of such references in children's humor observed by Wolfenstein (1978) and McGhee (1979). As I noted earlier, these theorists of child humor maintained the school-age children, unlike preschoolers, did not see the mere mention of "poo-poo" or "pee-pee" as funny. The older children did, however, incorporate these references into dirty jokes. Denny, like the school age children in Wolfenstein's and McGhee's research, extended the function of references to "poo-poo" beyond the simple attempt to be silly. He incorporated the reference into a dispute as a way of relieving the build up of threats and of avoiding possible aggression. In peer culture, "being funny" is valued, but so is one's ability to relieve and settle a dispute without *overtly* backing down or giving in. Denny's reference to "poo-poo" brought laughter to a threatening situation and eventually led to the settlement of the dispute.

Approach–Avoidance Routines

Much of the children's play in the outside yard of the nursery school involved running and chasing routines. These routines are similar to what Blurton-Jones (1976) has described as "rough-and-tumble" play. According to Blurton-Jones, rough-and-tumble play consists of seven movement patterns: "running, chasing and fleeing; wrestling; jumping up and down with both feet together ("jumps"); beating at each other with an open hand without actually hitting ("open beat"); beating at each other with an object but not hitting; laughing and falling on the ground, a soft object, or each other" (Blurton-Jones, 1976: 355). Although rough-and-tumble play may appear to be hostile, Blurton-Jones maintains that it seldom results in actual physical aggression and that it is quite different from disputes over possession of objects.

In early field notes, I, like Blurton-Jones, focused on the ethological features of the play routines. I recorded many of the same patterns (especially chasing, fleeing threatening gestures, and laughter), and, given the alternation of the pursuer–pursued roles and persistent laughter, I also was convinced that the behavior was not hostile in intent. I did, however, find that Blurton-Jones's description of rough-and-tumble play fit some types of activities much better than others. For example, when playing superheroes, the children (almost always boys) often chased each other around the yard and engaged in wrestling and "mock" fights. These activities were much in line with Blurton-Jones's findings. On the other hand, I also witnessed other running and chasing routines in which children pretended to be wild animals and monsters. These routines contained a feature which was not described by Blurton-Jones. This feature was the children's consistent display of "feigned fear" when they adopted the "pursued" or "threatened" role in the play.

Feigned fear was often displayed by way of fleeing behavior, screeches, screams, and attempts to hide. On several occasions, children in the "pursued" or "threatened" role hid behind me and asked me to protect them from their pursuers. The pursuers were labeled as monsters or wild animals, and they did seem to be somewhat frightening. Therefore, I responded much the same way teachers did in the situations: I simply asked the attackers to stop scaring their apparently frightened playmates. Moments later, however, I saw the same children (but now in reversed roles) repeating the same performance with one of the teaching assistants. Repeated experiences of this type led me to believe that apparent victims were really not afraid and attackers were really not frightening; *but it was important to the children that these routines be seen as involving real threats and real fears.*

To pursue this interpretation further, I collected several videotaped episodes involving this play routine. The transcription and micro-analysis of these data led to the discovery of a basic theme. In nearly all the videotaped episodes of this play routine (running, chasing, etc.), *there was a threatening enemy or foe (real or imagined) who was both approached and avoided.*

Approach–avoidance routines were either embedded in or totally comprised interactive episodes. In either case, the routines were composed of three distinct phases: identification, approach, and avoidance. The identification phase occurred only once in a given routine, while the approach and avoidance phases were generally repeated several times. The identification phase involved the children's discovery and their mutual signaling of a threat of danger. Identification always preceded the initial approach phase, but it was not always the first phase in an approach–avoidance routine. On some occasions, the identification phase followed avoidance. For example, one or more children might be threatened by other children and those under attack would flee to avoid their pursuers. After such avoidance behavior, however, the children might then identify the nature of the threat and then approach their attackers. Regardless of sequencing, the identification phase was important because it served as an interpretive frame for the activities which followed. That is, identification of a shared threat was a signal that the approach–avoidance routine was now under way and that emerging activities should be interpreted in line with the particular play theme.

As I noted previously, the initial approach phase followed the identification of a threat or danger. This phase quite simply entailed the careful approach of the source of the danger. There were a variety of approach strategies, but they all shared one common feature. It was essential to approach with *caution*. The children's behavior during the approach phase exuded caution. They would advance slowly, quietly, cautiously, but with determination to confront the danger. Other children pretending to be wild animals or monsters (i.e., the source of danger) would, at first, purposely fail to notice the approaching children. But then at some unexpected (but totally predictable) moment the dangerous animals, monsters, or villains would detect the approach of their counterparts; and with a shocking reaction (e.g., a growl, an evil laugh, or a diabolic threat) signal the beginning of the avoidance phase of the play routine.

Behaviors during the avoidance phase were the most similar to Blurton-Jones's description of rough-and-tumble play. Children in the attacker role would chase after their fleeing playmates while growling, yelling threats, and beating at (without actually hitting) their victims. As I noted earlier, the pursued children feigned fear by screeching, screaming, and attempting to hide. In some cases, the fleeing children would actually be captured by their pursuers, and brief shoving and wrestling matches would ensue. Such activity, however, was usually short-lived. Eventually, the attackers would move away and the danger would diminish. At this point, the play routine would end or the pursued children would initiate a new approach phase. In some cases, the approach and avoidance phases were repeated several times, with a large number of participants entering into and exiting from the play routine.

Approach–avoidance routines were embedded in several types of fantasy role play (e.g., monsters, wild animals, mad scientists, etc.) and, for the oldest children, the routines frequently emerged in cross-gender play. I will discuss each of these patterns in turn and then go on to consider the importance of approach–avoidance routines for peer culture in the nursery school.

Wild Animals. As we saw earlier in Chapter 3, the children, at times, pretended to be wild animals and in some cases even enacted animal family activities with specific roles (mother, baby, etc.) assigned and adopted. When engaged in this type of fantasy play, the children pretending to be wild animals often became involved in approach–avoidance routines with other children who were playing in the outside yard. The following example illustrates a typical approach–avoidance routine involving wild animals.

Example 5.13
Field Notes
Outside, near climbing bars
Participants: Mark, Peter, Graham, Denise, and Eva

Denise and Eva are in the climbing bars. Mark and Peter crawl up to the bars, growling loudly. The girls screech and climb higher in the bars. The two boys stop growling momentarily and announce: "We are lions!" The girls now climb higher in the bars and Denise yells: "No lions allowed!" Peter yells back: "I'm a mountain lion."

"Well, no lions of any kind allowed!" responds Denise. Peter now says: "My first name is cougar—no—ah, that's my last name. My first name is mountain lion."

"Get away, you're scaring us!" yells Eva.

The boys now crawl away from the bars. Denise says to Eva: "Those dumb lions were scaring us." "Yeah," responds Eva. "Let's go get them." "Ok," replies Denise.

The girls get down and carefully move toward Mark and Peter, who have joined Graham in the large sandpile in the center of the yard. The boys pretend to dig with their hands (front paws) in the sand as if trying to find something they buried earlier. The girls now circle the sandbox very slowly; they are glancing back at each other and giggling in hushed tones.

The boys do not seem to notice the advance of Denise and Eva, who have now moved into the sandpile. Denise very carefully sneaks up behind Mark. She then reaches down and cautiously grabs the tail (a short piece of fur) Mark has placed in the back of his pants. Feeling his tail being removed, Mark whirls around and sees Denise. Denise speaks first and says: "You're bad." Mark growls and Denise flees from the sandpile, screeching loudly.

The other two boys now see what is happening and begin to chase Eva around the yard. Eventually, the girls run back to the bars. The boys growl at them for awhile and then move away to another area, still pretending to be lions. "That was close," says Eva. "Yeah," says Denise. "Let's do it again." "Ok," replies Eva. And, once again, the girls begin their careful approach. A short time later, they are again chased back to the bars by the lions.

The routine was repeated one more time before a teaching assistant intervened and told the boys to stop scaring Eva and Denise. After this, the girls went inside the school and the boys continued to crawl around, pretending to be lions until "clean-up time."

An important point to note in this example is the *spontaneity* with which the approach–avoidance routine is developed. There is *no direct negotiation* about when to begin the routine, what each child is supposed to do, or when the routine is to end. The mere presence of a possible threatening agent—in this instance, the boys pretending to be lions—is transformed into an approach–avoidance routine by the girls. The transformation is the result of two steps: (a) the girls first identify the threat (i.e., "Those dumb lions were scaring us"); and then (b) decide to approach the threatening agents (i.e., "Let's go get them").

Once the girls' approach is noticed by the boys, they too become part of the routine. But note again that there is not explicit negotiation. The boys do not discuss among themselves or with the girls what they are to do. They simply enact their parts in the routine: they chase the girls who avoid them by running to the bars. Once the girls reach the bars, another implicit understanding is activated and employed without negotiation (i.e., the bars are defined as a safe area or "home base"). Given this understanding, the boys do not pursue the girls into the bars. The boys do, however, continue to threaten the girls from the ground, but they eventually move away and leave the girls with the option of recycling the routine.

We need to consider a final point about wild animal approach–avoidance play before moving on to the monsters and mad scientists. Although there was an obvious gender difference across the pursuer–pursued roles in Example 5.13, this difference was not fully representative of wild animal approach–avoidance routines recorded in field notes or on videotape. Groups of girls often enacted the pursuer or threatening roles in the routines. In fact, pretending to be wild animals was a favorite activity of several girls in the afternoon group. When girls pretended to be wild animals, they frequently entered into approach–avoidance routines with other girls or with groups including girls and boys. However, there were no instances in the data where a group of girls pursued or threatened a group of boys (i.e., a sex role alignment which is the exact opposite of Example 5.13). I will return to discuss the implications of this finding when I examine cross-gender approach–avoidance routines below. But now, on to the monsters.

Monsters and mad scientists. It was not surprising to find that the children in the nursery school—like most kids—liked and frequently talked about monsters. After all, monsters, goblins, and other evil villains frequently appear in fairy tales, movies, television programs, and other media events created by adults for young children. What I found most interesting is how the children incorporated monsters and other evil creatures and villains into peer culture; that is, how the children made monsters a part of their fantasy play. Earlier, we saw that monsters and other threatening agents or events were often a part of basic themes in spontaneous fantasy play. Monsters appeared even more frequently in approach–avoidance routines, and, more importantly, the monsters were often embodied in playmates.

Monster approach–avoidance routines often emerged unexpectedly in peer play, and in some instances children would find themselves literally *thrust* into the monster role. For example, in one videotaped episode, several boys from the morning group (Denny, Jack, Joseph, and Martin) were playing in the upstairs playhouse. At one point, a wrestling match ensued with all four boys pushing, wrestling, and giggling on the bed. As they become unentangled, Joseph pointed at Martin and yelled: "Watch out for the monster!" Denny and Jack responded: "Oh, yeah, watch out!" Then the three boys ran downstairs, pretending to flee the monster.

Martin was at first a bit bewildered by this turn of events. He moved to the stairway to see where the others had gone, and, then, not seeing them, returned near the bed and peered down into the school. Meanwhile, the other three boys huddled together in the downstairs playhouse out of Martin's view. They giggled and pretended to be afraid. Denny suggested: "Jack go see where the monster is." Jack cautiously moved out of the playhouse, looked up, saw Martin, and then ran back inside screeching loudly. Martin now began to move down the stairs, eventually turned the corner, and saw the other boys in the playhouse. The three boys then screamed and ran back upstairs. As they passed Martin, Joseph yelled: "You can't get us, monster."

At this point, Martin began walking mechanically (somewhat like a "mummy") and followed the other boys back upstairs. The approach–avoidance routine was then recycled several times, with Denny becoming the monster later in the episode.

In another approach–avoidance routine that emerged in the morning group, a girl (Rita) who was wearing a dress with an apple print walked by several children (Glen, Leah, Denny, and Martin) who were playing in the outside sandpile. Glen yelled: "Hey, there's the apple girl!" Denny then shouted: "Watch out! She'll get us!" Rita then moved into the sandpile and the other three children ran out and toward the climbing bars, shouting: "Watch out! It's the apple girl!" Rita continued after them toward the bars, and the approach-avoidance routine continued and was recycled several times.

Although monster approach–avoidance routines often emerge unexpectedly, they do not always involve the identification or labelling of the threatening agent by children who adopt the pursued role. In some cases, the role of threatening agent is self-defined and even embraced. Consider the following example.

Example 5.14 "The Mad Scientists"
Tape 21
Afternoon Episode 9
Participants: Peter, Graham, Lenny, Jonathan, Steven, Lisa, Antoinette, Dominic, Sue, Eva, and Denise, Researcher
Peter (P) and Graham (G) are painting with brushes and water on the blacktop near the climbing bars. They also have colored chalk and, since the chalk is wet, it is coloring their hands red and green. Noticing this the boys refer to the red as blood and to themselves as mad scientists. I (R) am standing nearby with a microphone.

Transcription		*Description*
(1) G–R:	We're mad scien-tists. Don't get near us or I'll—	
(2) R–G:	I'm standing way over here.	R is some distance away from G and P.

Transcription, cont'd		*Description, cont'd*
(3)	P–R: We'll get 'ya!	P and G hold out their hands, which are covered with red dye, in a threatening manner. Their speech is also threatening and low pitched and guttural, with an evil tone.
(4)	R–P: Don't—Don't do that!	R does not want P or G to get the dye on his clothes.
(5)	G–R: Don't get near us!	Approaches R and uses threatening tone
(6)	R–G: I won't. I'm just gonna stay right over here and watch. You guys go ahead—	R wants to stay in microphone range to record the activity.
(7)	G–R: Get over there!	G points to a place further away.
(8)	R–G: Well, I want to stay this close—	
(9)	G–R: Get right here.	G points to a place on the ground.
(10)	R–G: All right.	R moves back to where G has designated.
(11)	P–R: I wanna get 'ya with (this blood).	P holds out his hands in a threatening manner.
(12)	R–P: Yeah, that's Ok. I'll stay right here. You and Graham go ahead and play.	P now moves closer to R.
(13)	R–P: Go ahead. I'm watching. Put blood on the ground.	R is concerned about getting dye on his clothes. P returns back near buckets and G.
(14)	G–P: I'll make bl—ood!	G reaches into the bucket and gets his hand wet. Then G and P wet the red chalk and draw on the ground. P then moves away toward bars then comes back and says:
(15)	P–G: Let's go get that girl!	P is referring to Eva (E) and Denise (D), who are standing near the bars. P now moves toward the girls holding out his hands which are covered with red chalk

Transcription, cont'd	Description, cont'd
(16) E, D–P: Stop! Stop!	The two girls run off away from P. P runs after them a short distance, but then returns to the buckets, where G is still painting. P is laughing diabolically, as if a monster or mad scientist.

In the first phase of this monster approach–avoidance routine, we see that the boys have *identified* themselves as "mad scientists" and go on to threaten those around them. It is important to note that this identification and the later approach–avoidance sequence emerge spontaneously. There is no formal plan or proposal like, "let's play monster and scare the other kids." Rather, the boys move through three steps: (a) They notice how the dye from the red chalk is coloring their hands; (b) They decide that the red dye on their hands is blood and then link this designated image to the character "mad scientist" which they had probably seen on television or at the movies; and (C) They eventually begin to threaten others by holding out their bloody hands and making menacing sounds. However, the movement through these steps is not uniform, since at first only Peter threatens other children, while Graham is more concerned with keeping me at a distance. In this episode, it is again clear that, although I am accepted more than other adults, I am still not able to enter fully into all types of play. Graham wants to keep me at distance, and I was concerned about their threats not because of any fear of mad scientists, but because (like any adult) I did not want the dye to get on (and possibly ruin) my clothes. This practical, adult-like concern was not what motivated the girls to flee (16). For them, Peter was indeed a mad scientist and a threat to be avoided. Let's now pick up the interaction later in the episode.

Transcription	Description
	Lenny (L) now enters play area and sits with P near the bucket and brushes. L had been playing with P and G earlier.
(30) L: Can I try to help put that on there.	Referring to painting the ground with the brushes.

Transcription, cont'd

(31)	G–L:	Nǫo!

Description, cont'd

We now move to a later point in the episode—from utterance 31 to utterance 101—where the children are about to leave the area where they have been painting on the ground. First P, and then, later, G and L, leave the area where they were painting and moved to the climbing house area, where they threaten several children: Lisa (Li), Dominic (D), Antoinette (A), and Sue (S).

(101)	Li–P,G,L:	Don't you dare!

Another boy Steven (St) now approaches P.

(102)	St–P:	Are you guys monsters?
(103)	P–St:	Yeah!

Meanwhile Li, D, and S have moved to upstairs of the playhouse and begin to resist the threats of P, G, and L.

(104)	Li–D:	Dominic, you guard the slide. You guard the slide.

Li now looks down at P, G, and L.

(105)	Li–P,G,L:	You can never come in! Never come in!

Li is taunting the boys.

(106)	P:	Grr! Grr!
(107)	A–P,G,L:	Go away! And stop that this minute!
(108)	Li:	Nobody ever gets in here.

P now begins to climb up a rope to the upstairs of the house. Li and S shriek loudly at P's attempt to enter.

(109)	A–P:	Oh, no, you can't!
(110)	G–A:	Oh, yes, we can

Transcription, cont'd			Description, cont'd
(111)	G:	I'm gonna paint.	G brushes the house with the paint brush he is carrying.
(112)	A–GP:	Stay down!	P moves down the rope, but then immediately begins to climb a ladder into the house. D and A move to block his path while Li and S screech loudly, pretending to be afraid.
(113)	Li–D,A,S:	Don't let him in!	D kicks at P and he backs down the ladder.
(114)	A–P:	What are you doing here?	
(115)	P–A:	We're scientists.	
(116)	G–P:	No! We're mad scientists! Mad Scientists!	
(117)	P–D:	Quit it! Stop it!	D continues to kick at P. But P resists and moves into the top of the climbing house. Once in, P whispers in D's ear and explains that they are pretending to be mad scientists.
(118)	P–D:	Want to play?	
(119)	D–P:	Ok.	
(120)	Li–D:	Stop him, Dominic!	Screaming.
(121)	D–Li:	They're just scaring us.	
(122)	A:	They're scaring me.	A backs away from P and joins Li, S, and D near the firepole. P approaches them and the girls scream and Dominic goes down the pole.
(123)	P–Li,S,A:	I'm Spiderman now. I'm Spiderman. Don't be scared. I'm Spiderman.	P moves near girls and they back away and P goes down the pole. The girls continue to scream and look down the pole. Now Jonathan (J) enters the top of the playhouse and the girls again scream.

Transcription, cont'd

(124)	J:	We're scientists. We're scientists.
(125)	A–Li,J:	This way! This way!
(126)	A–J,G:	You can't get us!
(127)	G–St:	Are you a mad scientist?
(128)	A–Li:	What shall we do?
(129)	A–Li:	I know where it's safe.
(130)	G–A,Li:	I'm up! I'm up!
(131)	A–Li:	Lisa, go down here!

Description, cont'd

(124) Lenny now enters and goes down the pole. When L gets to the bottom, he runs up to P, who says "Spiderman." Then the two run off together. G now enters the climbing house and the girls scream. G goes down the pole just as Steven (St) moves into the house with Dominic.

(125) Great deal of screaming as the girls pretend to be afraid. A goes down the pole and Li goes down the slide. S follows and, on the ground, J, G, and St threaten the girls. The girls move away but A looks back and taunts the boys.

(126) J reaches for A, who screams and moves away, joining Li, who is climbing back up into the house. G and S follow while St, J, and D stay below.

(128) G is moving toward A and Li on the ladder. A pushes Li toward the slide.

(129) But they discover that St is climbing up the slide. The girls run toward the fire pole while St and G enter the house.

(130) G holds out colored hands in a threatening manner. St moves toward the girls. He places his finger in his mouth and stretches it, making a monster face. The girls scream and move away.

(131) A goes down the pole. Li moves toward the pole with St following. Meanwhile, G goes down the slide.

Transcription, cont'd	Description, cont'd
(132) S–Li: A monster!	Li screeches and goes down the pole. At bottom, she joins A and they run off into the school, and the episode ends.

We see in (30–31) that Lenny has now joined Peter and Graham and that he quickly adapts the "mad scientist" role. In fact, Lenny joins Peter in chasing several children around the yard, something Graham has yet to do. To this point, the three boys have identified themselves as "mad scientists" and several other children have fled and displayed feigned fear in response to the boy's threats. However, the threatened children have not as yet resisted the boys threats, nor have they returned to approach the threatening agents. Therefore, the approach–avoidance routine has still not fully developed.

It is not until near the end of the videotaped episode (101–131) that the approach–avoidance routine is fully enacted and then re-cycled. The interaction here is quite dense, with several children adapting and relinquishing the various roles (threatener and threatened) in the routine. At (101), we see the first resistance on the part of the threatened children with Lisa saying "Don't you dare!" in response to Peter's attempt to move into the climbing house. This resistance becomes more organized at (104–107), and both Lisa and Antoinette actually taunt Peter and Graham at (108 and 109).

At this point, the threatening agents have been identified and approached by way of resistance and taunts. However, when Peter actually moves into the climbing house, only the girls avoid him while Dominic continues to resist. As a result, the approach–avoidance routine is not completed. In fact, Peter abandons the mad scientist role, works out on agreement with Dominic, and the two of them leave the area together. At this point, Jonathan enters the scene, assumes the mad scientist role, and, along with Graham and Steven (another newcomer), begins to threaten the girls. The girls now begin to scream loudly and move away from the boys and eventually flee the area (125). Once the girls get away, however, they quickly decide to return to the climbing house. With Antoinette's taunting of the boys (126), the approach–avoidance routine is recycled, with Graham and Steven pretending to be mad scientists and Lisa, Antoinette, and Sue in the threatened role (126–132).

There are two things to note about Example 5.14. First, the play is loosely structured and may appear to be disorganized from an adult perspective. This unstructuredness is fairly typical of approach–avoidance play where there are often false starts, abortive enactments of the basic routine, and a great deal of coming and going among the children involved. Although the play appears somewhat chaotic, it does revolve around the children's creation of and reaction to threatening agents ("mad scientists"). Eventually, the children go beyond the identification of threatening agents to the performance of approach–avoidance routines.

A second and related aspect of Example 5.14 is that the threatening agents identify *themselves* as mad scientists. Since they are self-identified, the mad scientists are *dependent* on the appropriate reactions of those threatened for the full enactment of the routine. Early on in the episode, the threatened children displayed fear and moved away from (or avoided) the mad scientists, but they did not approach. In fact, it is not until near the end of the episode that the mad scientists are approached (i.e., actively resisted and taunted) and the routine is fully enacted. The pattern is quite different in play where the threatening agents are labelled as such by other children (see the earlier descriptions on pages 117–118 and Examples 5.15 and 5.16).

It is an interesting feature of approach–avoidance play that the children in the threatened role have more control over the performance of the routine than those children who adopt the role of threatening agent. Although it may appear that those threatened are equally dependent on the threatening agents for enactment of the routine, this is not the case. Those threatened can identify, approach and avoid, and pretend to fear almost any response displayed by those identified as threatening agents. In fact, as I noted earlier, threatening agents are often thrust into their role. To pursue this point and to develop further the importance of approach–avoidance routines for peer culture, it is useful to present and examine two additional examples of monster approach–avoidance play.

In the first example, two children, Vickie and Brian, are pretending to be rabbits. Brian has crawled into a cage which had previously housed a real rabbit in the school. Once Brian was in the cage, Vickie closed the door and said that Brian was in an oven. We pick up the episode at this point.

Example 5.15 "The Eating Princess"
Tape 17 Episode 1
Afternoon
Participants: Vickie (V), Brian (B), Researcher (R), Cameraperson (C)

Transcription		*Description*
(1)	V–B: You're hot enough.	
(2)	B–V: What?	
(3)	V–B: Hot. Get out!	V begins to open the cage door.
(4)	B–V: No. Turn it off.	
(5)	V–B: Ok.	V now closes door again and then pretends to turn off oven by pressing on top of my microphone, which is positioned with some other equipment on top of the cage.
(6)	B–V: I want to stay in.	
(7)	V–B: You're gonna get cooked.	
(8)	B–V: I'm a rabbit in a cage.	
(9)	V–B: You're a rabbit in the stove.	V now picks up microphone and pushes it, saying "boo, boo."
(10)	V–B: Now it's on. I'm gonna push this button.	V fiddles with equipment
(11)	B–V: Stop! No! I don't wanna be burned!	
(12)	V–B: You are!	
(13)	B–V: No! I'm hot enough. Turn it off.	
(14)	V–B: Ok.	V pretends to turn off the stove.
(15)	B–V: I just wanna be in here. Cooked.	
(16)	V–B: I'm gonna make you into a bird	V again fiddles with the equipment.
(17)	B–V: A-a-a-y. Turn me back into a rabbit.	B pretends to cry.
(18)	V–B: No!	
(19)	B–V: Ye—es.	
(20)	V–B: I'll turn you back into a alligator.	V again manipulates the equipment

Transcription, cont'd	*Description, cont'd*
(21) B–V: No. I want to be a rabbit	V now begins to dance around excitedly, and B pushes open the door of the cage/oven.
(22) V–B: Yikes! There's an eating princess. Let's bite her.	V points to a woman who is operating the camera.
(23) B–V: Yeah.	B now gets out of the cage.
(24) B–V: Yikes! Let's get her. Get the princess.	B pulls V's arm to come with him as he approaches the cameraperson.
(25) V–B: You have to help.	B approaches the cameraperson (C, eating prince/princess) and then quickly jumps back as if afraid.
(26) V–C: Hey! I'm gonna bite you!	V stops short of C and then pushes B toward her.
(27) V–B: Come on. Let's do it.	
(28) V–C: Bite!	V moves up near C and pretends to bite. C makes a face at V and B and they screech loudly and run off.
(29) V–B: Hey, come here. Come here.	B joins V and they slowly approach C again, but get scared before they reach her, and run off again laughing. They then turn and begin a third approach.
(30) B–C: Biting Princess.	
(31) V–C: I'm not going to race away.	V and B again move close to C. C looks at them and they race off again but stop and then quickly return for a fourth approach. But again, the princess (C) looks at them and they race off. On their fifth approach, B asks V:
(32) B–V: Are you a baby rabbit? Am I a baby rabbit?	V does not answer as they move close to C then yell "yikes" and race off again.
(33) B–V: Am I your baby rabbit?	

Transcription, cont'd	*Description, cont'd*
(34) V–B: Yes.	V and B now start their sixth approach.
(35) V–B: Let's go! Let's go!	C has now moved from behind the camera and is sitting on a sandbox. V and B approach her.
(36) B–V: Yeah. Cause we're three buck rabbits. We can go faster than the whole wide world, right?	
(37) V–B: Right!	V reaches out toward C, who looks over to V and B. V and B run off screeching. But V abruptly turns and starts back.
(38) V–C: Now you can't not get me.	V moves close to C
(39) V–C: Nohow! Nohow! Nohow! Nohow! Nohow!	C now leans closer to V.
(40) V–C: That doesn't scare me at all. Yikes!	V now runs off, with B following, and they stand some distance from C.
(41) B–V: Let's go back to her. Let's go back. Let's go back. Let's go back.	B pats V on the head to get her attention. B and V now approach C for the eighth time.
(42) V–C: I'm not scared of you.	Spoken in singing, taunting voice. C now growls at V and B and they run off giggling loudly.
(43) B–V: Let's go. You go with me.	
(44) B–V: I'll go with you. I'll protect you. I'll tell her not (to do it).	B and V move further away from C.
(45) V–B: That was too scary.	
(46) B–V: I'll protect—I'll go with you. I'll go with you.	V pushes B towards C.
(47) V–B: Oh, no. Ok. But one more time.	B starts toward C. Half way to C, B says:

Transcription, cont'd　　　　　　　*Description, cont'd*

(48) B–C: Now be nice to us, princess, Ok, princess?

(49) B–C: Ok, princess. Will you be nice to us?

(50) B–C: Yes?　　　　　　　　V backs away as B cautiously moves closer to C.

(51) B–C: And don't bite us. Cause we're just (rabbits) and this is our house.

(52) C–B: Are you going to be good children?

(53) B–C: Yes!　　　　　　　　V now quickly moves forward next to B.

(54) B–C: Well, anyway, call us rabbits cause we're really rabbits. And I'm a baby and she's my mother.

(55) C–B: Be good rabbits and, yes, I won't bite.

(56) B–C: Ok. Yea! Yea!　　　　B and V hop off as very happy rabbits.

(57) B–V: We're good rabbits, right?

(58) V–B: Right!

　　　As was the case in the earlier examples of approach–avoidance play, we see that the routine develops spontaneously in Example 5.15. There is no formal negotiation. Rather, the children extend their earlier fantasy play involving rabbits and magic (e.g., Vickie's changing Brian into different animals) by labelling the cameraperson as first an "eating prince" (22) and then an "eating princess" (24). Immediately after this identification phase is accomplished, the children quickly complete one cycle of the approach–avoidance routine (24–28) and then they recycle the routine nine times. After the third repetition, I suggested to the cameraperson that she play along but in a restrained way. The fact that the cameraperson was somewhat new to the setting (she had been working with me for only 2 months and was at the school only twice a week) may have influenced the children's identification of her as the threatening agent. The children were still somewhat curious about her and her presence in the school (see Chapter 1). By involving her in a routine which they controlled, the children were able to quell their curiosity in an indirect and symbolic way. In short, the children were able to deal with this new person in their environment by making her a part of peer culture. A final point: It is clear that the identification, approach, and avoidance of the threatening agent is *jointly accomplished*. The children are performing with and for each other. They are enjoying the performance while at the same time coping with the uncertainty of a new person in their setting. And they *are doing all these things together*.

This tendency on the part of the children to deal with uncertainties in their environment by jointly integrating them into peer culture is even more apparent in Example 5.16.

Example 5.16   "The Walking Bucket"
Tape 18 Episode 10
Afternoon, outside yard
Participants: Beth (Be), Brian (B), Mark (M), Steven (S), and Frank (F)
This episode involves three children (Be, B, and M) playing on a rocking boat. After about 10 minutes of rocking, Be notices Steven, who is walking around the school yard with a bucket (large trash can) over his head.

	Transcription		*Description*
(1)	Be:	Hey, a walking bucket! See the walking bucket.	Be has noticed S walking with the bucket on his head. B and M can not see S because they are facing in the opposite direction of Be.
(2)	M–Be:	What?	
(3)	Be–M:	A walking bucket. Look!	Be points at S walking with the bucket over his head, and both M and B turn, look, and see Steven.
(4)	B:	Yeah. Let's get off.	B, M, and Be stop the boat, get off, and slowly and carefully approach S. When they reach S, B and M push the bucket. S responds by flipping the bucket off his head. B, M, and Be quickly run back to the rocking boat with S pursuing them.

Transcription, cont'd		*Description, cont'd*
(5)	B:	Wh-a-a-oo!	
(6)	M:	Wee—Yikes!	S approaches the rocking boat, flailing his arms in a threatening manner. B, M, and Be pretend to be afraid, screech, and move to the far side of the boat. S stops at the empty side of the boat and rocks it by pushing down on the boat with his hands. S does not actually climb onto the boat, nor does he try directly to get at B, M and Be. S then returns to his dropped bucket and places it back over his head. B, M, and Be watch from the boat, giggling and laughing.
(7)	M–B,Be:	Let's kick him.	M says this as he and B move over toward S while Be remains on the boat. When they reach S, M kicks him in the shins. B also kicks at S but seems to miss. Then B and M run back to the boat, where they are joined by Frank. After being kicked, S flips off the bucket, but does not pursue B and M. Now B, M, Be, and F rock on the boat while S walks around the yard with the bucket over his head.
(8)	Be:	Whee! Faster! Faster!	The children now rock the boat faster.
(9)	Be:	Hey, He's coming!	Be is referring to S, who is still walking with the bucket over his head. S is now somewhat closer to the boat than he was earlier.
(10)	B–S:	Hey, you big poop butt!	M, Be, and F laugh loudly at B's name-calling.
(11)	Be–S:	Hey, you big fat poop butt!	S does not respond to these taunts, so Be jumps from boat and runs toward S. B follows close behind Be, but Be then runs off to the

Transcription, cont'd	*Description, cont'd*
	right as B continues toward S. When B reaches S, he pushes the bucket, knocking S to the ground. F and M have followed B and stand close behind. S now flips the bucket off, and B and M act afraid and flee back toward the boat. F and Be flee to another area of the school. S chases B and M back to the boat and then returns to pick up the bucket. B and M yell at S.
(12) B,M–S: Fat butt!	Once S places the bucket over his head, B and M again approach. But before they reach S, he flips the bucket off and takes a fighting stance. B begins to run back to the boat as M first chases, and then is chased and grabbed by, S. At this point, I signal for aid and a teacher intervenes. After the teacher separates them from S, M and B run inside the school.

In Example 5.16, we see that the routine again develops spontaneously and that the threatened children have the most control over its enactment. Brian, Mark, and Beth had been rocking on the boat when they noticed Steven walking with the bucket over his head. Steven had not threatened them at this point. In fact, Brian, Mark, and Beth initiated the routine by first identifying Steven as the threatening agent (1) and then approaching and taunting him (4–5). Steven reacts in accordance with the developing routine by flipping the bucket off his head and chasing the other children back to the boat. Once the two reach the safety of the boat, Steven threatens them briefly but does not climb up onto the boat. Steven them returns to the bucket and one cycle of the routine is completed. It is clear that the children share an understanding of the underlying rules of approach–avoidance play. The routine is readily enacted without any formal negotiation about who is the threatening agent, who is threatened, or the fact that the boat can serve as home base.

However, this example is not a typical monster approach–avoidance routine. The labelling of Steven as the monster or threatening agent has a special significance for both the development of the routine and the eventual physical conflict which ends the sequence. Steven was the oldest child in the afternoon group. He was also physically the biggest child. Steven primarily played alone, with Jonathan, or with two or three of the other older boys (Lanny, Larry, and Dominic). Even when playing with other children, Steven's participation was often limited. He would frequently play for awhile, often take a peripheral role, and then leave the play activity after a few minutes. Only when playing with Jonathan (see, for example, Chapter 4, Example 4.10 involving "police" role play) would Steven become highly involved and continue to participate over the entire course of an interactive episode. Steven felt, and often voiced his feelings to his mother and the teacher, that he was too old for nursery school. Early in the year, he often seemed bored and played alone. Near the end of the term, however, he became more involved in peer interaction, but still tended to remain on the periphery, except when playing with Jonathan.

Given Steven's age, physical size, and his rather aloof interactive style, it is not surprising that many of the younger children were *both apprehensive and curious* about him. They often watched Steven from a distance, and, when Steven would become involved in interactive episodes with them, they seemed to closely monitor his actions.

In Example 5.16, Steven at first readily embraces his role as the threatening agent and Brian and Mark seem to greatly appreciate his performance. In fact, with Steven as the threatening agent, the approach–avoidance routine takes on a new dimension. The play routine now becomes intertwined with reality in that the feigned fear of Brian, Mark, and Beth now has a tinge of real apprehension. It may be this apprehension which causes Brian and Mark to alter the routine. After the completion of one cycle (1–6), Brian and Mark escalate their taunts on the second approach by kicking Steven. This physical attack on the threatening agent did not occur in any other approach–avoidance routine. Although Steven seems a bit upset with the kicking, he adheres to the threatening agent role by chasing the children, but respects the underlying agreement of not pursuing them onto the boat (home base). Later, Brian, Mark, and Beth increase their taunting by calling Steven a "big poop butt" and a "big fat poop butt." The children seem to be testing their control over a bigger and older playmate, a peer of whom they are both curious and apprehensive. But once again Steven adheres to his role and does not react to the escalation of the taunts. Finally, however (12), Steven flips off the bucket from his head in the midst of Brian and Mark's approach, and then he grabs and twists Mark's arm. The end result is a mild scuffle which is eventually settled by the teacher.

Examples 5.15 and 5.16 both illustrate the children's tendencies to extend an enjoyable play routine in such a way as to deal with real fears and curiosities. In this sense, approach–avoidance play is similar to spontaneous fantasy where the children manipulate objects to bring to life basic themes (lost–found, danger–rescue, and death–rebirth) which reflect some of their basic concerns and anxieties. In both types of play, we again see that the children cope with the circumstances of their everyday life world by integrating them into the peer culture of the nursery school.

Cross-gender approach–avoidance. Over the course of the school year, I observed marked differences between the morning and afternoon groups regarding the gender composition of play groups. The younger children (morning group) primarily played in mixed-gender groups. In addition, there were only two clear activity preferences by gender in the morning group. The girls never participated in firefighter role play, while the boys often took part in family role play but refused to adopt female roles ("mommy," "wife," etc.). In contrast, I observed much more same-gender play and clear preferences of activity by gender in the afternoon group. The boys in the afternoon group seldom engaged in family role play and showed definite preferences for more physical types of play (superheroes, police, construction work, play with trucks and wagons, etc.) in the outside yard. The girls, on the other hand, frequently engaged in human and animal family role play, and also displayed a preference for arts and crafts activities inside the school. In short, the older children (afternoon group) were manifesting the beginnings of separate peer cultures for boys and girls (see Dweck, 1981).

Having begun to grow apart over the course of the school term, boys and girls in the afternoon group began to view each other in a new way. They were no longer just playmates, they were now *boy and girl playmates*. In short, gender now made a difference, and, near the end of the year, it began to affect how the children related to one another. The most striking incidence of this development was cross-gender approach–avoidance play. I will begin by presenting an example of this variant of approach–avoidance. I will then go on to provide an analysis and to discuss the importance of children's participation in the approach–avoidance routine for their development of social knowledge.

Example 5.17   Boy vs. Girl Approach–Avoidance

Tape 26 Episode 3 Afternoon

Participants: Peter (P), Larry (L), Antoinette (A), Lisa (Li), and the Researcher (R).

Peter (P) and Larry (L) have been playing in the climbing bars. They have ropes which are tucked into their pants. Antoinette (A) and Lisa (Li) are nearby and have been playing in an overturned pipe. L has moved down from the bars near where the girls are playing. I (R) am standing near the pipe.

Transcription			Description
(1)	P:	Dun . . . Du . . . Dunt . . . Dunt!	In the bars, swinging his rope.
(2)	A–L:	You can't get us!	L is near pipe while A and Li are in pipe.
(3)	L–A:	Oh, yes, I can!	
(4)	P–A:	I can whip you.	P is still in the bars, but now begins to move down.
(5)	A–P:	Oh, no, you can't!	
(6)	P–A:	Oh, yes, I can!	
(7)	A–P:	No, you can't!	
(8)	P–A:	Yes, I can!	L circles the pipe while P gets down from the bars and moves near the pipe swinging his rope.
(9)	P–A,li:	Dun . . . Dun . . . A . . . Dunt . . . Dunt!	P swings rope near the girls
(10)	A–L:	Come on. Let's get down!	A and Li jump down in pipe and out of view. L and P move over to pipe just as Li pops back up.
(11)	P–A,Li:	A rattlesnake.	P and L had been pretending to be snakes while in the bars.

Transcription, cont'd		*Description, cont'd*
(12) A–P:	Get out of here.	P hisses at A and Li as if he were a snake. A now climbs out of the pipe and moves toward P.
(13) P–L:	Whip your rope!	
(14) P:	Dun . . . Dunt . . . A . . . Dunt . . . Dun!	As he whips his rope.
(15) A–Li:	Let's go.	A runs off with L and P chasing after her. Li now moves out of the pipe.
(16) L–P:	I whipped her bottom.	Laughing, and referring to A, whom, he swung at with his rope but missed. A now circles the yard, with L and P pursuing her.
(17) Li–A:	Antoinette!	Li motions for A to return to the pipe, which she does.
(18) L–P:	She's charging for us.	Referring to A as she runs by him as she returns to the pipe. A now starts to get into the pipe, when P returns riding a broomstick horse, and chases her away. Li and A screech loudly, pretending to be afraid.
(19) Li–A:	Get in!	A now again circles the yard, with P in pursuit.
(20) A–L,P:	It's (only suppose to be)	
(21) L–P:	Now she's charging for us. She's charging for us.	L runs away from A as she runs near him, and the approach-avoidance pattern is momentarily reversed.
		A moves to climbing house and starts up the slide, while Li has left the pipe and climbs up the ladder near the slide. L and P, meanwhile, have left the area in front of the pipe and have gone over near the sandbox, where there is another group of children.

244 • *Friendship and Peer Culture in the Early Years*

Transcription, cont'd   *Description, cont'd*

(22) Li–A: We have to hide.   Li and A now return to the pipe.
             We have to hide.

(23) Li–A: Get down.   Whispering.

(24) A–Li: Where are they?   Sticking her head up to look for L
                                     and P.

(25) Li–A: Right there.   Points and still whispers.

(26) A–Li: How do you
             know?

(27) Li–A: (   ), they're   Li sees L looking at them from a
             coming!   distance. Li pulls A down into
                                     pipe and they both scream as if
                                     afraid.

(28) Li–A: Get down! Get   From inside the pipe.
             down!

(29) A–Li: Are they there?   A and Li pop back up.

(30) Li–A: No, they're not.

(31) A–R: Are they there?   R is standing behind the pipe,
                                     holding a microphone.

(32) Li–A: They're coming!   Li screeches, grabs A, and at-
                                     tempts to pull her down.

(33) A–Li: They're not com-   A resists Li's attempts to pull her
             ing.   down.

(34) A–L: Na . . . Na . . .   A sees L, who is some distance
             Nee . . . Na . . .   away, and she tries to get his at-
             Na!   tention.

(35) A–Li: He's not coming.

(36) Li–R: He's not coming.   Li asks R about his microphone.
             Hey, what you
             got?

(37) A–R: What you . . .   A turns to look at R, but is cutoff
                                     by Li.

(38) Li–A: That sure was   A and Li are now sitting on top of
             close. Boy, they   the pipe, facing each other.
             didn't get us.

(39) Li–R: Bill, you tell 'em
             we're not here, ok?

(40) R–Li: Ok.   R shakes head yes.

(41) A–R: And (surprise   ).

(42) Li–A: They're not sup-   Li seems to be referring to L and
             posed to run.   P.

Transcription, cont'd	*Description, cont'd*
(43) A–Li: Oh, they're com- ing! Get down!	A jumps down into the pipe.
(44) Li–A: No, they aren't.	Laughs and remains seated on the pipe. But then Li suddenly screeches and jumps into the pipe with A. A then sticks her head up and says to R:
(45) A–R: Bill, you—	R cuts A short and motions for her to get back into the pipe.
(46) R–A,Li: I'll tell them. Get down so they can't see you.	A and Li go back down into the pipe. Meanwhile, L has been slowly approaching and is now on the rocking boat near the sandpile, about 25 yards from the girls. P is still playing with some other children near the entrance to the inside of the school.
(47) Li–A: They're coming!	
(48) A–Li: He's coming!	Both A and Li peek out of the pipe and see L. A and Li now get back into the pipe as L moves closer.
(49) Li–A: He's coming!	In pipe.
(50) A–Li: He's coming!	A peeks out and sees L, who has now moved even closer. Li whispers to A and then they both peek out, see L, yelp, and drop back down into the pipe.
(51) L–P: Peter come here I see them. Peter come here.	L turns to talk to P, who is at sandbox near inside of the school. P does not respond.
	First Li and then A come out of pipe and look at L, who is now very near the pipe.
(52) R–L: They're not here Larry, they're gone.	Li gives R an exasperated look for saying such a dumb thing.
(53) L–R: Un-huh.	L now swings rope near girls, and Li screams.
(54) A–L: Uh-oh!	A holds up her hand to fend off the rope.

Transcription, cont'd		*Description, cont'd*
(55) Li–L:	Get out!	
(56) L–Li:	No, you get out!	L continues swinging rope and laughing while Li holds up her hand to fend off the rope. Li then grabs at the rope but cannot catch it.
(57) L:	Goo-od . . . she . . .	
(58) A–L:	Come on!	A starts to get out of pipe. A then gets out of pipe as L swings his rope against it.
(59) A–L:	You can't catch me . . . Ya knee . . . na . . . knee . . . na . . . a	A taunts L. L then chases after A, swinging his rope. Li is outside of pipe, but then gets back in as A returns to pipe with L chasing her.
(60) A–L:	Let's get out.	A says this as she climbs back up on pipe and joins Li, who is now sitting on top of the pipe. L comes up and Li swings her hand at him.
(61) Li–L:	I'm gonna kill you Larry.	
(62) L–Li:	Un-huh.	L shakes head "no."
(63) Li–L:	Un-huh.	Li shakes head "yes." L then swings rope but misses Li as she drops back down into the pipe.
(64) Li–L:	Miss me. Missed me. Now gotta kiss me.	L laughs and continues swinging a rope at Li but moves farther away from the pipe in response to Li's threat of affection.
(65) A–Li,L:	(I got out)	Li now sits on top of pipe, and A gets down, then begins to climb back up.
(66) L–Li:	You said you would kiss me, why don't you try.	L stands a short distance from the pipe and now seems to be inviting girls to try and get, and possibly kiss, him.
(67) A–Li:	Come on, let's get him.	A has now climbed down and is standing in front of the pipe. Li now begins to climb down.

Transcription, cont'd			Description, cont'd
(69)	Li–A:	No. Ouch! Don't step on my foot.	L now moves away toward sand-pile. Li meanwhile drops down into the pipe, and A is still climbing back in.
(70)	A–Li:	How do I get in?	
(71)	Li–A:	They're not coming.	
(72)	A–Li:	No, cause they're still scared.	
(73)	Li–R:	Bill, you tell them we're not here.	
(74)	R–Li:	Ok.	
(75)	Li–R:	And we'll get 'em.	A now climbs back on pipe, then drops in pipe and joins Li.

Prior to the sequence in Example 5.17, Larry and Peter had played with Graham in the climbing bars. While in the bars, the boys pretended to be wild animals (snakes and lions) and there was some discussion about which animal was the "toughest." The boys also looked over the fence into the adjoining school, and saw some children swimming in the outside sandpile, which ' ad been filled with water. The children in the adjoining school ιad removed their clothing before swimming. Since this type of swimming activity also occurred in their school, it was not unusual for the boys to see naked children. Nevertheless, the boys commented on the nakedness of the other children, and especially noted the naked girls. They pointed at the girls, giggled, and whispered things like: "There's a naked girl!" "Oh, there's her butt!" "I see her vagina."

Given this background information, it is clear that Larry and Peter were thinking about differences between boys and girls as well as male notions of toughness just prior to their contact with the girls. Unfortunately, I do not have similar data for Lisa and Antoinette, since I was monitoring the play of the boys. However, I did notice that the girls commented on the boys using their ropes as tails and whips. The girls also taunted the boys several times, and were ignored until the beginning of Example 5.17.

This background information is important because it aided in the interpretation of the approach–avoidance sequence as symbolic play which displays both the children's developing sense of what it means *to be boys and girls and how they should act toward one another*. I will pursue the symbolic aspects of the sequence in more detail shortly, but first let us review the development and enactment of the approach–avoidance routine.

The approach–avoidance sequence in Example 5.17 is initiated by Antoinette, who taunts Larry (2) and then receives an immediate response from both Larry and Peter (3–4). After several additional threats and denials (5–8), Peter approaches the pipe swinging his rope. The girls then display fear of the boys and attempt to avoid their advance by hiding inside the pipe. Peter and Larry continue to threaten the girls by swinging their ropes and pretending to be snakes. At one point, Antoinette leaves the pipe (12) and is pursued by Peter and Larry. Eventually, both Antoinette and Lisa flee to the climbing house, and the boys suspend their pursuit and move away from the pipe to the sandbox area at the opposite end of the outside yard.

Lisa and Antoinette then return to the pipe and begin to monitor the very slow advance of Larry. As they watch Larry, the girls display a great deal of symbolic behavior. They both feign fear of Larry's advance (27–28, 32) and taunt him in typical approach behavior (34).

At this point, the approach–avoidance routine moves to a more complex level, with the various roles in the routine becoming interlaced. Larry, who is unable to gain aid from Peter (51), now is both *threatening the girls and cautiously approaching them as if they were a threat to be avoided*. The girls also now take on dual roles *simultaneously taunting and approaching* the threatening agent, Larry, (34, 47–50, and 59), and also *threatening him as well* (51, 61, 64).

The complexity of this approach–avoidance routine is a reflection of the children's understanding about their developing knowledge of sex-typed behaviors. The children's behaviors display shared knowledge that girls are supposed to be fearful and timid. However, this knowledge and its concomitant expectations *must be articulated with* the demands of the interactive setting (Cicourel, 1974). As the children discover, the articulation process is often complex and there is seldom a direct link between developing concepts and the actual behavior of peers.

The complexity of this approach–avoidance routine first becomes apparent (18), where Larry displays some uncertainity regarding Antoinette's response to his and Peter's threats (i.e., "she's charging for us"). Although girls are supposed to be fearful and timid, Antoinette's behavior during the school year was anything but such. In fact, Antoinette was one of the "toughest" kids in the school, and she frequently participated in physical and aggressive activities with both boys and girls. Antoinette's behavior in the nursery school may very well be a carry-over from her experiences at home in her play activities with her three older brothers. In any case, it is apparent to Larry that, although Antoinette may be "playing along" in terms of the approach–avoidance routine, she can still be expected to deviate from the fearful or threatened role. In fact, Antoinette seems to do just this when she leaves the pipe and flees from Peter, and then runs up to Larry as if "charging him" and reversing the routine.

It is also interesting to note Lisa's behavior. She does not leave the pipe, seems upset when Antoinette does, and calls for her playmate to return (18). Later, she seems to serve as a model for Antoinette (32) by screeching and grabbing her playmate while attempting to pull her down into the pipe as Larry approaches. At one point, Lisa even tells Antoinette that "they're (presumably the boys) not suppose to run" (42).

However, even Lisa is uncertain on how exactly to respond to Larry's threats once he actually arrives at the pipe (53). Lisa first responds to Larry's threats in kind (55–56, 61), but then later counters with a threat of affection (i.e., "missed me. Now gotta kiss me," 64). This response momentarily throws Larry off balance. He first retreats a few steps (i.e., avoids Lisa's counterthreat), but then seems to decide that being kissed may not be so bad after all (65).

There is certainly a great deal going on in this sequence. The children are: (a) using developing knowledge of appropriate sex-typed behaviors; (b) discovering that this knowledge must be linked or articulated with local features of the interactive scene, including characteristics of participants and the social-ecological setting; and (c) refining and expanding their developing knowledge as a result of their interactive experience. In short, the children's developing social knowledge is both affecting and being affected by their participation in a behavioral routine that is an integral part of peer culture in this setting.

It is clear that approach–avoidance and the other behavioral routines are a reflection of the children's attempts to understand

and use information from the adult world within peer culture. In the next section, I present a discussion of another peer routine, Garbage Man, which seems to have emerged totally within the peer culture of the morning group at the nursery school.

Garbage Man

It was a beautiful November morning. In fact, it was much too nice a day to remain inside the school. So, like many of the children, I decided to spend some time in the outside yard. Once outside, I noticed Michelle, Jimmy, and Dwight moving toward the sandpile, and I decided to join them. While the bright sun warmed the back of my neck, I sat in the sand watching the children digging. I could not recall such a warm November morning in all my years growing up in the Midwest.

Suddenly, I heard a loud shout and turned to see Denny, Leah, and Martin in the climbing bars. Denny was shouting and pointing out over the fence toward Kelly Street. Something or other must be going on out there. At this point Leah shouted: "It's him! It's him!" My curiosity was now aroused, but not as much as Michelle's, Jimmy's, or Dwight's. The three children had abandoned their shovels and were running toward the bars. The digging episode over, I opted for joining them. Just as I reached the bars, several children began shouting: "Garbage man!" "Garbage man!"

I moved beyond the bars, peered out over the fence, and did indeed see a garbage man. In fact, there were two garbage men out there, along with a large garbage truck. One of the men sat behind the wheel of the truck which he had—I assumed—backed up in front of the dumpster near the apartment building across the street from the nursery school. The other man had moved to the rear of the truck and he seemed to be attaching the dumpster to a lift. He then yelled "Ready!" to his partner, and the dumpster began to rise from the ground accompanied by a loud "whirring" noise.

The children in the bars were now very excited and were imitating the noise of the truck lift: "Whirr!" "Whirr!" "Whirr!" I was surprised to see that there were now more children in the bars. Ten in all, with one more, Barbara, climbing up. I looked around the yard and noted that all but two of the children who had been playing outside were now in the bars. As the dumpster reached its apex and the trash tumbled into the truck, the children seemed to reach their own peak of excitement. They waved and "whirred" in near perfect unison. At exactly this point, the garbage man looked up and waved back to his admirers. The lift then lowered quickly and the dumpster hit the ground with a loud bang. The outside garbage man then unhooked the dumpster and quickly joined his partner in the truck. The children continued waving and shouting "Garbage Man!" as the driver pulled the truck away, gave a short beep of the horn, and steered the large truck down the street to the next stop, far beyond the sight of the children.

The truck out of sight, I noticed that most of the children had left the bars and returned to other play activities in the outside yard. Michelle, Jimmy, and Dwight were moving across the yard and went inside the school. I later saw them having juice in the meeting room. Meanwhile Denny, Leah, and Martin were still in the bars and were now playing police. Denny was the police chief and Leah and Martin were robbers. I decided not to join in this activity or others developing in the yard. Instead, I went into the school, stopped in the kitchen area, and wrote out some rather detailed notes about the event I had just witnessed. Having finished the description, I added the following personal note:

PN: I am surprised I had never noticed the garbage man routine before. I wonder how often it has occurred. Do the teachers know about it? Will it reoccur tomorrow?

The garbage man routine did indeed occur the next day, and 8 children participated. The following day, "Garbage Man" was again enacted with 5 children participating. In all, the routine was enacted every day for the 110 days I checked for its occurrence over the remainder of the school term (around 155 days). The number of children participating in the routine ranged from 2 to 13, and all but 2 girls participated in the routine at least once. Several of the children were regular participants, and were involved in about 30% of the garbage man routines I observed. Two of the teaching assistants and the head teacher were aware of the routine when I asked them about it. Only the teacher had paid much attention, and she remarked about how nice it was that the garbage man always waved to the children while making his pickup.

So we see that "Garbage Man" was a stable behavioral routine in peer culture. But what is its significance? Is it really any more than a few minutes of excitement for the children who happen to be in the area when the garbage men make their daily stop? It may not at first glance seem to be any more than this for an adult, but for the children involved it is an important aspect of peer culture.

The garbage man routine shares many characteristics with other elements of peer culture discussed previously. First, there is the sharing of *excitement and joy* that we saw in spontaneous fantasy, the childrens' chants about being bigger, group glee, and approach–avoidance routines. Second, the routine involves *group production* which builds and reaches a climax at an appropriate moment. This sequential pattern in group activity was also apparent in spontaneous fantasy play and in the children's mocking chants directed towards adults from the climbing house and bars. Finally, the routine is enacted in an area of the school (high in the climbing bars) that the children see as their own, and which is generally off-limits to adults. Further, the routine emerges in reaction to something that has a special appeal: the loud "whirring" and "clanging" of a big, and, to the children's eyes, beautiful machine (the garbage truck). In this sense, the garbage man routine, like other features of peer culture, is a *reflection of the children's values and concerns.*

At a more abstract level, "garbage man" is different than other elements of peer culture. For in this activity the children literally *reach out beyond* the physical boundaries of the nursery school to the adult world, and transform a mundane everyday event (the collection of garbage) into a routine of peer culture which they jointly produce and enjoy. And, at an even deeper level, the routine is significant because the children are *successful at procuring the participation of adults* (who wave and beep a horn) *in an event which the children create and control and of whose significance adults have only a surface recognition.*

But what are the children learning about the social world or each other through their participation in this routine? Does the routine contribute to the children's social development in specific ways? Such questions cannot be addressed without qualification. I cannot claim, for example, that specific types of learning actually occur just because the children do participate. However, the children's consistent involvement in the routine surely results in an awareness of specific types of societal and cultural knowledge which are important for social development.

First, the children are becoming aware of basic characteristics of occupations and work. They see first hand that work involves the cooperation of generally two or more individuals to accomplish a goal. They see also that work often involves the organization of a task into coordinated sequences or phases. The garbage collection task is relatively simple and repetitive. It consists of backing the truck up, attaching the lift, dumping the garbage into the truck, returning the dumpster, and driving away. But it is just this repetitiveness, although tedious and perhaps alienating to the workers, which is so attractive to the children. The activity occurs again and again, at the same time every day, in this sequence, with these noises. And, further, the routine is symbolically marked for the children by the workers themselves.

So the children may learn a bit about work, the accomplishment of goals in work, and the cooperation of workers. But, more importantly, the children are learning about routines, that things get done in a certain order in a certain way. In fact, by making the worker's routine a part of their own routine, the children have made it a part of their peer culture. However, it is not the particular content of the routine which is most important. The children may forget much about "garbage man" and how they enjoyed the routine soon after the school term ends. But the children will carry with them a notion of ritual and ritual events which is very important in understanding and participating in everyday life.

The wave of a hand, the "whirr" of the lift of the truck, the beep of the horn as the truck departs are minor, some might argue trivial, cues in a very ordinary event. They were, however, organized and interpreted in a symbolic way by the children, and in that sense were part of their peer culture and the culture of the adults who participated as well.

There is a final note on the garbage man routine. Although my research in the nursery school was limited to 1 year, since I took a job in another part of the country, I did return during the next year for some limited observations. The morning group from the year before now attended afternoon sessions, and there was now a new morning group at the school. Since the garbage was collected in the morning on Kelly Street, I was anxious to see if the children in the new group had noticed the garbage collectors and had developed a routine similar to that of their couterparts from the year before. On the first day back in the school, I anxiously waited near the back fence for the garbage truck to appear. I was a stranger to the three boys who were playing in the bars, and they paid me scant attention as I awaited the truck. Finally the truck arrived and backed up to the dumpster. Then I heard it. Shouts of "Garbage Man!" from the children in the bars. Two boys and two girls quickly joined their peers in the bars and the routine was enacted: the whirring, the shouts, the wave of the hand, and the beep of the horn. The routine was repeated each day for the week I visited. Although I cannot be sure, I suspect that "Garbage Man" will probably live on in the school for many years to come.

Children's Conception and Reaction to Adult Rules: The Underlife of the Nursery School

In a brilliant essay in his book *Asylums,* Erving Goffman argued that, without something to belong to, individuals have no stable self, but total commitment to any social unit implies a kind of selflessness. For Goffman, "our sense of being a person can come from being drawn into a wider social unit; our sense of selfhood can arise through the little ways in which we resist the pull" (1961a:320).

In pursuing this view of the individual in society, Goffman introduced the notion of "secondary adjustments." Secondary adjustments are "any habitual arrangement by which a member of an organization employs unauthorized means, or obtains unauthorized ends, or both, thus getting around the organization's assumptions as to what he should do and get and hence what he should be." According to Goffman, "secondary adjustments represent ways in which the individual stands apart from the role and self that were taken for granted for him by the institution" (1961a:189).

Secondary adjustments are seen by Goffman as forming the *underlife* of social establishments. Goffman identified a number of types of secondary adjustments in his documentation of the underlife of an asylum, a highly restrictive institution. Goffman argued, however, that his work in an asylum led to findings regarding the individual's relationship to organizations that apply in some ways to all institutions. Furthermore, Goffman believed that the individual's tendency simultaneously to embrace and to resist institutional rules and expectations is a central feature of personal identity or self.

But is Goffman's work useful for understanding peer culture? Surely the nursery school is not a total institution as is an asylum or a prison. Further, it is difficult to argue that preschool children have developed the cognitive skills necessary to define their emerging selves in regard to both their embracement of and resistance to the organizations to which they belong. On the other hand, the nursery school, like all other organizations, involves a set of goals, rules, procedures, and expectations for its members. In this sense, Goffman's work has implications for understanding how children conceptualize and adapt to the rules and procedures of this particular social institution. And, although preschool children do not have a stable sense of self or the cognitive skills necessary to infer the implications of both embracement and resistance of organizational rules for personal identity, *they do have a clear notion of the importance and restrictiveness of the adult world as compared to children's worlds.* At this age, children have made a distinction between adults (''grown-ups'') and children. In fact, they can, and often do, distinguish between the adult world and their own peer world.

Although membership and participation in the adult world is important to nursery school children, their developing sense of who they are is also strengthened through their active resistance of certain adult rules and expectations regarding their behavior. In this sense, the children's joint recognition of adult rules, and their mutual resistance of certain of these rules, can be seen as stable elements of peer culture.

Nursery School Rules and Children's Secondary Adjustments

The university school, like all nursery schools, had a set of rules which embodied expectations regarding the children's behavior. Given my interest in peer culture, my concern is less with the rules themselves than with the children's conceptions of the rules and their strategies for evading them (i.e., their secondary adjustments). Therefore, I will not attempt to cover all the school rules. Instead, I will concentrate on those rules which were most burdensome to the children and which motivated them to invest a great deal of energy in devising evasive strategies.

Rules regarding play areas and materials. Early in the school year, the children learned that certain behaviors could occur in some areas and not in others, and that some play materials were to be used only in the areas in which they were stored and available.

One rule regarding the use of play areas in the school centered around the teachers' distinction between inside and outside play. Running, chasing, and loud shouting were defined as inappropriate behaviors inside the school and were restricted to the outside yard. Problems in adherence to this rule were most apparent when children became overly excited while playing indoors, or when disputes turned more physical and resulted in running and chasing. Normally, the teachers and TAs reacted quickly to such violations, and the children seldom resisted correction except to deny that they were indeed involved in the behavior ("I wasn't running!") or to claim that another child was responsible ("Peter was chasing me.").

The rule restricting more physical play to the outside yard was most troublesome to boys, especially the older boys in the afternoon group. The boys enjoyed physical play and often attempted to include physical activities (running, etc.) in play which normally did not involve gross motor behavior without breaking the general theme or frame of the ongoing activity. Before describing some of these attempts, which can be seen as secondary adjustments, I should note that the boys in the afternoon group faced an additional rule. Since the boys seldom played indoors during the first month of the school term, the afternoon teacher designated the outside area as "closed" for the first 45 minutes of the afternoon session. The teacher hoped that the rule would encourage the boys to become more involved in play activities inside the school. The rule was successful in this regard, but it also led to the emergence of a number of secondary adjustments as the boys attempted to get around the rule which limited running, chasing, and similar physical activities to the outside yard.

One type of secondary adjustment I observed in the afternoon group involved attempts to extend family role play. Boys who felt confined in the inside of the school would sometimes join other children engaged in family role play in the playhouse area. After joining the other children, the boys would often suggest new directions for the role play. For example, the boys would propose that the house was being robbed and take the roles of robbers and police. The police would eventually chase the robbers from the house and throughout the inside of the school. When the teacher or TAs reminded the boys that there was no running inside, the boys would claim that they were not running and explain that the playhouse had been robbed. When faced with this sort of explanation, the TAs would often compromise and allow the children a bit more latitude, but ask that they confine the chase to an area near the playhouse. On another occasion, I saw the role play extended when some boys suggested that the playhouse was on fire, and, more imaginatively, in another case a family was threatened by a wild lion which escaped from the zoo. In this instance, one boy exuberantly adopted the lion role while another boy became a lion trainer, chased the lion from the playhouse, and eventually captured him.

On other occasions, boys who felt confined inside the school entered the playhouse and, finding it unoccupied, were at a loss what to do. In one instance, two boys (Graham and Peter) decided to play house and, after some negotiation, one boy became a father and the other an uncle. But, after adopting these roles, the boys seemed to have no idea what an uncle and father might do together. So they roamed around the playhouse and eventually overturned the kitchen table. To their surprise, they saw that the table was an overturned waste can with a round piece of plywood attached to the top. Now, upside down, the table became a race car as Peter climbed inside the waste can and Graham pushed him across the floor of the playhouse. Neither the teacher nor the TAs noticed this unusual bit of family interaction involving the uncle and father.

These types of secondary adjustments were not confined to the afternoon group. On one occasion, two boys (Denny and Martin) and one girl (Leah) from the morning group were in the upstairs playhouse but soon became bored with family role play. Denny found a piece of string and, lying flat on the floor of the house, dangled the string through the bars and announced that "he was fishing." Leah and Martin ran downstairs, got some string, and soon joined Denny at his fishing hole. Soon other children and several TAs noticed the trio. The TAs were so impressed with this ingenious use of the upstairs playhouse that they overlooked this mild violation of proper inside behavior. In fact, the TAs helped some of the children in the downstairs playhouse tie toy animals to the dangling fishing lines. Denny, Leah, and Martin ended up catching a lot of fish.

These secondary adjustments were quite complex in that they involve the active cooperation of several children, and they can be seen as extensions or elaborations "of existing sources of legitimate satisfactions" for private ends. They are what Goffman has referred to as examples of "working the system" (1961a:210).

There were other secondary adjustments regarding use of play materials which were less complex, but just as effective. For example, children often violated the rule about moving play objects (blocks, dishes, toy animals, etc.) from one area of the school to another simply by concealing them on their persons during transport. On one occasion in the afternoon group, Daniel took a suitcase from the playhouse, carried it to the block area, and filled it with blocks and toy animals. He then carried the suitcase outside, dumped the blocks and animals in the sandpile, and buried them. Shortly thereafter, a TA noticed the suitcase in the sandpile and told Daniel to return it to the playhouse. He did so, but then quickly returned to the sandpile to play with the blocks and animals. At clean-up time, Daniel abandoned the secretly transported objects and went inside. When a TA discovered the objects in the sand during clean up. she asked two children in the area how they got outside. They responded with a typical preschooler answer: "We don't know." Which in this case was true, but not believed by the TA.

The concealment strategy was also used consistently to evade the rule about not bringing toys and other personal objects from home to school. This rule was necessary because personal objects were attractive to other children just because they were different from the everyday play materials in the school. As a result, the teachers, were constantly settling disputes about sharing the personal objects. Therefore, the rule specified that objects should not be brought and, if they were, they must be stored in one's locker until after school. Early in the school term, the children began to evade this rule by bringing small personal objects which they could conceal in their pockets. Particular favorites were small toy animals, along with candies and chewing gum. While playing, a child would often show his or her "stashed loot" to a playmate, and they would carefully share the forbidden objects without catching the attention of the teacher or TA. Although such small deceptions may seem insignificant to an adult, as they were to the TAs who would often chuckle and ignore them, they were not trivial to the children and were important moments in the sharing of peer culture.

Rules against guns and shooting. There were no toy guns in the school, nor were the children allowed to bring guns and similar toys to the school. There was also a general rule against the use of pretend guns and shooting. However, many of the children, in almost all cases boys, would employ what Goffman has termed "make-dos" to get around the no-guns rule. That is, the children would use "available artifacts in a manner and for an end not officially intended" (Goffman, 1961a:207). For example, boys would often shoot at each other from a distance simply by pointing their finger and cocking their thumbs. The "hand gun" was just one of many weapons created by the children. They also often used shovels, blocks of wood, and broomstick horses as rifles. As we saw earlier in Example 3.7 involving the "hunters," the children would go to great lengths to avoid detection in evading the rules about guns and shooting. In the hunter example, the boys created rifles by flipping over their broomstick horses, used crackers for bullets, and shot at objects which could not shoot back (targets and children from the adjoining school). As a result, they almost avoided detection, and, when they were discovered by a TA, they received only a mild warning. A warning they promptly ignored and continued with their hunter play.

I should note here that I am in no way negatively evaluating the school rules regarding guns or shooting or the teachers ability to enforce the rule. My point is that the children's strategies to evade the rule, their secondary adjustments, *can become as important aspects of peer culture as the children's original interest in guns themselves.* In fact, the children's resistance of the rules is another symbolic marker distinguishing the adult world from peer culture.

Rules prohibiting bad language. Many of the rules the children encountered in the nursery school were the same as those they followed at home. At school as well as in the home, the children were expected to obey adults, share their toys with others, and were not to fight or swear. The children seldom used bad language in school. But there were occasions when a child would become upset and say "damn" or "shit" or some other swear word. There were also instances where verbal disputes would escalate into cursing and name calling. In every instance where swearing occurred, the children involved or nearby would look around and check to see if an adult were present. If a teacher or TA was in earshot of a child who said a bad word, the child would always be corrected and told not to repeat the word again. In short, the children knew that swearing was bad and, therefore, refrained from the behavior or were careful to confine their swearing to places in the school where adults would be unlikely to hear them.

However, just because swearing was bad or taboo, it had a certain appeal to the children. This attraction to bad or taboo words was shared by the children and was thus an element of peer culture. The appeal of swearing was best expressed through routines where children rattled off strings of bad words. The bad words were spoken, not because the children were upset or arguing, but just in a sense "to be bad." However, in these instances the children wanted more than to be bad, they wanted to *be bad and not be caught*—in short, to put something over on their adult caretakers, and, in Goffman's view, maintain a sense of self through secondary adjustments.

I observed several of these swearing routines in both groups over the course of the school year. In every case, there were two to four children involved, and the routines always occurred in peer-dominated areas of the school (e.g., in the climbing house, climbing bars, or upstairs playhouse). One instance was especially interesting and involved two girls in the morning group.

The two girls, whom I will just refer to as A and B, had been playing in the outside yard. We were videotaping their play, which involved climbing up on a large wooden spool and jumping to a mat on the ground below. I was sitting near the spool holding a microphone. After several jumps to the mat, A walked behind the spool and then called out: "B, hey, B! Look here!" B came around to look and I followed close behind with my microphone. When we found A, she was ducking into a small opening in the back of the spool. She then sat down inside the hollow center of the spool.

"Come on in," she said to B. B quickly joined her and, as I appeared in the opening, A said: "Not you! Go away and leave us alone." I said: "Ok, but can I leave my microphone?" B responded: "Ok, but you get out of here!" I set the microphone inside the spool and quickly left to join my assistant, who was operating the camera and monitoring the audio.

I was anxious to hear what the girls were talking about, so I motioned for my assistant to let me use one half of the headset and we listened together. The first thing I heard was a banging of the microphone as A picked it up and said: "I'll talk first." She then said "you !!XX, XX, XX!!, !!XX, !X!X, ———!" The string of curses was 14 words long and contained some words I had heard only a few times, and two or three I had never uttered in my life. I should add here that I am not a prude. I have been known to cuss every now and then. Many of these words were references to sexual activity and curses which had to do with the legitimacy of one's parentage. When A finished, B said: "Let me talk to the dummy!" B, who seemed to be referring to me, took the microphone and said: "You !X!X, XXX, ———!" Her string repeated several of the bad words A had produced, but she also added a few of her own. I must admit that I was a bit shocked that these two little girls could repeat such words, but I was sure that they had no idea what most of them meant. They simply knew that they were bad words.

The routine continued for three more rounds, with the girls producing many of the words over and over and giggling at their bit of naughtiness. They then emerged from the spool and I approached and asked them why they were calling me bad names. "You couldn't hear us," said A. I said that I had, and B said: "We weren't talking to you, anyway!" "Yeah," said A, "you didn't hear us anyway." They both turned and walked away, but B looked back and said: "Don't tell teacher!"

It is not clear whether the girls knew that I could hear them or not. They probably did not. It is clear that the main aim of this routine was to be naughty. The children found themselves a hideaway, a hideaway in which they were momentarily concealed from the adult world. In this situation, they decided to engage in forbidden behavior and commenced to enunciate every bad word they had probably ever heard. In doing so, they were not really being bad. They were producing a ritual that they would repeat many times in their youth, a ritual which symbolizes one of children's most cherished desires: *to defy and challenge adults, share the experience, and not be detected.*

Clean-up time. Of all the rules of the nursery school, the ones must actively resisted by the children pertained to proper behavior during clean-up time. Shortly before meeting time in both the morning and afternoon groups, the teacher and TAs would move throughout the school calling: "Clean-up time!" When the clean-up announcements were made, the children were expected to do three things: (a) stop their ongoing play activities, (b) help the TAs return the school to its proper order by replacing all the materials they were using in their proper places, and (c) move to the back room of the school for meeting time. Although the children enjoyed meeting time, they often did not want to stop playing and they frequently resisted cleaning up. During the first half of the school term, when clean-up time was announced in the morning group, the children would often ask if they could keep playing for a while longer. The following excerpt from field notes is a typical example of the children's attempts to prolong play activities.

Example 5.18
October 22
Morning Episode 1
Scene: Inside, Block Area
Participants: Cindy, Ellen, and Jack

FN: Cindy, Ellen, and Jack have been building in the block area for around 20 minutes when a TA, Catherine, comes over and announces clean-up time. "Oh, no, not yet!" Jack protests. "We're not finished," says Ellen. "Well, you still must clean up now," says Catherine, and then adds: "It's almost time for our meeting." "We don't want to go to meeting yet," says Cindy. "We have a special story today. You like stories, don't you, Cindy?" asks Catherine. "Yes, but we want to finish our building first!" Cindy responds. "No, you can build another one tomorrow, now let's start putting the blocks away," says Catherine as she picks up several blocks from the floor and places them on the shelf. Catherine then asks Jack: "Come on and help me. Hand me that block there by your foot. We have to hurry." Jack hands her the block, and all three children begin placing the blocks on the shelf. The children move slowly, but soon the area is in order and the three children run to the back room to hear the promised story.

PN: The children seem to want to continue playing and go to the meeting as well. They do not seem to understand why the meeting cannot be delayed. The adult notion of time and scheduling seems arbitrary to the children. It seems to me that Catherine was successful because she simply initiated clean up rather than continuing to discuss "why" the children should stop playing.

Example 5.18 illustrates both the children's apparent lack of understanding of the rationale for "why" they are asked to stop their play, and the common strategy of verbal resistance. The example also illustrates how the TAs successfully overcame such resistance. In the second half of the school term, children in the morning group seldom verbally resisted the implicit request in the clean-up time announcement to cease their play activities. Having learned the futility of asking to play longer, the children virtually abandoned verbal resistance, and, like their counterparts in the afternoon group, they immediately employed one of several strategies to evade clean-up time.

Before considering these secondary adjustments to the rules of clean-up time, it is useful to consider how the children conceptualized and felt about the rules. The children seldom discussed the rules of the school among themselves, but they did talk about cleanup much more than any other adult rule. From their discussions, it is clear that the children felt clean-up time was dumb and redundant. Consider the following example from field notes.

Example 5.19
November 9
Afternoon Episode 10
Scene: Outside, Sandpile
Participants: Peter and Graham

FN: Peter and Graham had been shoveling sand into their dumptrucks in the sandpile. They then hear a TA, Willy, announce clean-up time in another part of the yard. Anticipating Willy's arrival, Peter looks at Graham and frowns. Graham says, "Clean-up time! Ain't that dumb! Clean-up time!"
"Yeah," responds Peter, "we could just leave our dump trucks here and play with 'em tomorrow."
"Yeah," says Graham as he turns over his truck and shakes out the remaining sand, "clean-up time is dumb, dumb, dumb!"
Just then Willy arrives, makes the announcement to the boys. They seem to ignore him, but after a brief delay they put away their trucks and go inside.

PN: There is a certain logic to the boys' complaints. The rule does seem dumb on the surface, but there are very good reasons for clean up. The children are thinking about the reasons. But are they thinking about them in the right way?

After I recorded my notes on November 9, I was careful to listen for other comments about clean-up time and other adult rules. I heard similar comments to those in Example 5.19 espoused by children in both groups on several occasions. One boy from the morning group, Richard, extended Graham's point by arguing that putting the toys away meant that we would "just have to take 'em out all over again." From the children's point of view, clean up is just not work that they don't want to do. It was not that the children were lazy. To them, clean up was unnecessary. It was dumb work that interfered with fun play.

Given the children's conception of clean up, it is not surprising that they had some fairly elaborate strategies to evade it. In the first part of the school term, the children in both groups often relied on what I will call the "relocation strategy." When employing this tactic, children would move from one area of the school to another immediately after hearing the clean-up time announcement. When asked to clean up in the new area, the children would claim that they had not been playing there and that they had already cleaned up elsewhere. Since the children had indeed not been in the new area and may have worked elsewhere, the TAs would often soften their demands. They would not insist the children clean up, but they would suggest that the children help. The children would often agree, but do very little, and the TAs and children who did not relocate would do the bulk of the work. Although a successful tactic in the first part of the school year, the TAs soon figured out the ruse or were informed of it by the head teacher. From that point on, children who employed the relocation strategy were told that everyone had to clean up regardless of where or what they played during the day. If children insisted that they had cleaned up elsewhere, the TAs merely said "good for you, but you must work here too." Not surprisingly, the "relocation" strategy was employed much less frequently during the second part of the school term.

The children employed a second strategy to evade clean up which I will refer to as the "personal problem delay." When using this strategy, children claim they cannot help clean up for one of a number of personal reasons. The problems include such things as feigned illness or injury (e.g., "I got a stomach ache," "I hurt my foot," etc.), pressing business (e.g., helping another TA clean up in another part of the school, or role play demands). Although these strategies are seldom completely successful, they do delay the start of work. As a result the children involved often have less work to do once they do begin to clean up. Some of the most interesting personal problems I heard the children offer had to do with role play demands. A child in the mother role may claim she has to finish feeding her baby; a child pretending to be a lion may claim she cannot use her hands; a fireman may claim that he has to put out a fire in another part of the yard.

In one instance, when I was observing in the afternoon group, I witnessed the following sequence. Brian lay on the ground in the outside yard when clean-up time was announced. Shortly thereafter, a TA, Marie, told Brian to start cleaning up, but he did not respond and continued to lay motionless. Marie then said, "Brian, quit pretending to sleep and start helping us clean up." Brian still did not move, but Vickie, who was cleaning up, spoke for him. "He can't help. He's dead, killed by poison," Vickie told Marie.

Marie looked over to me and we both laughed. For some reason, I found the phrase "killed by poison" to be funny, and Marie seemed to as well. However, Marie was not about to let Brian escape from work. She knelt down next to him and pretended to pour something into his mouth.

"There," said Marie, "I gave Brian the antidote to the poison. He will now come back to life."

Brian, however, still remained motionless, and Vickie said, "The antidote didn't work."

"Yes it did," responded Marie who began to tickle Brian. Brian giggled and squirmed away from Marie.

"See, he's all alive now and is going to help us clean up," said Marie. Brian got to his feet and began to help, not killed by poison after all.

A final strategy the children consistently employed to evade clean up was deceptively simple, but highly effective. I will refer to this strategy as "pretending not to hear." When employing this strategy, the children, upon hearing the clean-up time signal, would merely continue to play as if the announcement had not been made at all. The TAs would then repeat the announcement in a louder tone of voice. The children still would not respond. Then the TAs would generally repeat the signal, still louder, for from one to seven more times and receive no response. Finally, the TAs would stop their own work and insist that the children begin to help. At this point, the children would say "ok," as if hearing the announcement for the first time, and begin to work. However, the strategy was often effective because there was normally little work remaining to be done after several repetitions of the announcement. In fact, the "pretending not to hear" is often more effective than the other two strategies, because the children's failure to respond is a less noticeable tactic than the active offering of a reason for not cleaning up.

All three types of secondary adjustments to the clean-up rule are excellent examples of what Goffman calls "working the system." The children have discovered that the TAs need to get the school in order so that meeting time can begin. In short, the TAs must meet organizational demands regarding the scheduling of activities. As a result, the TAs tend to do more than their share of the work when the children delay. In fact, the TAs were often so intent on finishing clean up that they were not aware of how much of the job they—as opposed to the children—were doing. The children were working the system in that they exploited a routine of official activity—cleaning up in a certain period of time—to meet their personal ends (i.e., keeping their own clean-up work to a minimum). These secondary adjustments are impressive because "to work a system effectively, one must have an intimate knowledge of it" (Goffman, 1961a:212).

But do the children actually share an awareness of these secondary adjustments to the clean-up time rules? In other words are the secondary adjustments really a shared element of peer culture? I believe they are, even though I have little direct data to substantiate my belief, since the children seldom discuss secondary adjustments. However, the following example from field notes does provide direct support for the claim that the children share an awareness of at least one of the secondary adjustments to the clean-up rules.

Example 5.20
December 4
Morning Episode 3
Scene: Outside, Swinging Tire
Participants: Barbara and Betty

FN: Barbara and Betty are playing in outside yard near climbing house.
   Barbara is swinging in a tire suspended from the roof of the enclosed
   area of the outside yard. Betty is standing in front of her, and I am

sitting nearby on the ground. As Barbara swings, Betty bends over and looks down at her and says:

"It's clean-up time!" Barbara smiles, ignores Betty, and keeps swinging. Betty repeats in a louder tone of voice, "It's clean-up time!" Barbara ignores Betty and keeps swinging. Betty then repeats "It's clean-up time!" seven times and keeps raising her voice. She is practically shouting right into Barbara's face during the last repetition. But Barbara continues to smile and to swing and to ignore Betty. Suddenly, Barbara stops swinging, jumps from the tire and says, "Now it's my turn." "Ok," says Betty and she quickly replaces Barbara in the swing. The girls then repeated the routine.

PN: Although I was not sure at first, it became clear with the role switch that the children were "playing teacher." In a sense, they were mildly mocking the TAs, who seem unaware of the delaying nature of the children's strategy of pretending not to hear the clean-up time signal.

Conclusion. It is clear that the children's secondary adjustments can be seen as makeshift means to obtain ends or needs which are restricted or denied by adult rules. But as Goffman maintained in his work with adults, I feel that such an explanation "fails to do justice to these undercover adaptations for the structure of self" (1961a:319). As I noted in the introduction to this section, Goffman sees secondary adjustments as essential elements for the maintenance of self and *individual identity*. It is my thesis that, for the nursery children, secondary adjustments are best seen as a way of developing and maintaining *group identity*. In collectively resisting adult rules, children develop a sense of community and "we-ness," which is extremely important in their acquisition of a sense of social structure (Cicourel, 1974). For, by sharing a communal spirit as a member of peer culture, children come to experience how being a member of a group affects both themselves as individuals and how they are to relate to others. Through secondary adjustments, children come to see themselves as part of a group (in the nursery school, a peer culture) which is in some instances aligned with, while in others opposed to, other groups (in the nursery school, adult rules and culture). In resisting adult rules through cooperative secondary adjustments, children not only develop a sense of group identity, they also acquire more detailed knowledge of adult norms and organizations. The acquisition of such knowledge is essential for children's movement through a succession of peer cultures, and their eventual entry into the adult world.

Conclusion

Throughout this book, I have argued that childhood socialization involves children's acquisition and use of social interactive and communicative skills and social knowledge in their everyday life worlds. In this chapter, I have identified and described stable elements of peer culture in the nursery school. I also discussed the significance of features of peer culture for understanding children's social development, and, more generally, the significance of the concept of peer culture for socialization theory.

Regarding children's social development, there is a need for the integration of information on children's life-worlds—discovered in micro-ethnographies of the type employed in this study—into interactionist or constructivist theories of human development. According to constructivist theories like those of Piaget, Mead, and Vygotsky, children acquire skills and knowledge through interaction with the environment. If children contsruct social knowledge and acquire interactive skills by acting on the environment, there is then a need to examine these actions within their social context (i.e., within the lifeworlds of children).

In this chapter, I have addressed how specific experiences resulting from participation in peer culture may affect the children's acquisition of interactive skills and social knowledge. The main features of the analysis are summarized in Table 5.1, where I have linked the various features of peer culture to specific types of learning.

Although actual developmental processes can not be fully substantiated without longitudinal data, the findings summarized in Table 5.1 identify potential sources of the development of a wide range of communicative skills and types of social knowledge. More importantly, these findings identify what is often missing in clinical interviewing studies of children's social development. In these studies (see, for example, Damon, 1978; Piaget, 1965; Selman, 1980; Turiel, 1978b; Youniss, 1980), researchers identify levels or stages of skills and knowledge—an important contribution to socialization theory—but they often gloss over *how* skills and knowledge are acquired with general references to disequilibrium

Table 5.1   Peer Culture and Children's Development of Social
Knowledge and Interactive Skills

Features of Peer Culture	Types of Social Knowledge	Interactive Skills
Values and Concerns		
Social participation and the protection of interactive space	Friendship; social norms and conventions	Access rituals; cooperative sharing
Concern for the physical welfare of playmates	Personal attributes and emotions	Empathy; social perspective taking
Concern with physical size	Status, power, and group identity	Independence; communal support
Themes in spontaneous fantasy	Story schema; morality; death or mortality; role expectations	Turn-taking; feedback cues; cooperative sharing; empathy
Behavioral Routines		
Children's humor	Joke and riddle structure and routines; humor	Humor as an interactive skill; performance skills
Insult routines	Insult structures; status and power	Competitive skills; tact
Approach-avoidance	Story schema; personal attributes; sex-role concepts; role expectations	Cooperative sharing; discourse skills; indirect action plans; sex-typed skills
Garbage man	Social time; ritual structure; occupational roles	Cooperative sharings; communal support
Secondary adjustments to adult rules	Social norms and conventions; status and power; role expectations; group identity	Independence; adaptive behavior; communal support

and the child's activity on the environment. The findings summarized in Table 5.1 can be seen as some of the sources of disequilibrium which are intricately interwoven in the peer culture of the nursery school.

The identification of features of peer culture is important for reasons beyond their implications for the children's social development. These findings help us to better understand children, how they construct and participate in their peer world, and how they view the adult world. Childhood socialization theory must go beyond an identification of the steps or stages children move through to become adults. Socialization theory should also involve an understanding of the life worlds of children.

Socialization is not merely a process by which children become adults. It is, rather, a process in which children participate in and successively move through a series of peer cultures. Full understanding of childhood socialization depends upon the documentation of elements of peer cultures and the continual points of contact between peer cultures and the adult world.

CHAPTER 6

Conclusions And
Implications For Early
Childhood Education

In early infancy, children, through participation in everyday interactive routines with their mothers, develop basic communicative skills and a sense of agency. Later in the infancy period, children initiate and take a more active role in interactive processes with adults. During this period, children begin to develop interpretive skills and acquire a central categorization of the childhood period; that is, children come to see themselves as "children" who are different from "adults." With this recognition, children begin to note differences between the adult and child world and also begin to establish relations with peers. Attendance in nursery school, participation in organized play groups, and informal activities with playmates and peers all lead to children's joint production of an initial peer culture, and launch them on a path involving participation in and the production of a series of peer cultures throughout childhood and adolescence.

In this book, I have focused on peer culture in the preschool period. I identified several stable features of peer culture and examined the relation between peer culture and the children's development of specific types of social knowledge (e.g., friendship, status, roles, and norms). Although I discussed a number of important findings, there were *two central themes* in the peer culture of the nursery school which capture the theoretical significance of this research for childhood socialization. Peer culture in the nursery school was characterized by the children's persistent attempts to gain *control* over their lives through the *communal production* and *sharing* of social activities with peers.

Control and Communal Sharing in Peer Culture

These themes of control and communal sharing were often interrelated and were apparent throughout the analyses of peer interaction presented in Chapters 3 through 5. In Chapter 3, we saw that the children's role play activities were not simply imitations of adult models, but rather involved the children's reproduction of their perceptions of the adult world within peer culture. These reproductions often centered around the display of power and control. Family role play, for example, often involved the enactment of a series of "discipline scripts" in which subordinates (babies, pets, etc.) purposely misbehaved to initiate discipline and control from superordinates.

Role play also involves communal sharing. During role play, children are dependent upon the reciprocal activities of peers for the ordered production of social events (i.e., mothers are dependent on babies to act like babies, etc.). Communal sharing is most apparent in cases where children expand or "stretch" routine role play activities (family activities, firemen, cowboys and Indians, etc.) to meet the needs of peer culture. The examples of wild animal family role play, and of the boys pretending to be hunters to evade adult rules regarding guns, presented in Chapter 3, demonstrated the importance of communal sharing in two ways. First, the sharing of peer values as background knowledge is essential for the joint production of play activities which are not based on specific adult models (e.g., wild animal families). Second, the production of role play episodes which involve the evasion of adult rules (as in the hunters example) is in and of itself a communal event. In such activities, the children share both something they like to do and the belief that they are "fooling" their adult caretakers.

In Chapter 4, we saw that the themes of control and communal sharing were apparent in the children's strategies for gaining access to play groups, their tendency to protect interactive space, and their developing conceptions of friendship. Establishing and maintaining peer interaction is not an easy task for young children, since they are in the process of developing the linguistic and cognitive skills necessary for communication and discourse. The nursery school is an ideal setting for facilitating children's development of social skills. It is a setting in which children not only learn to initiate and construct interactive events with peers, but also where they attempt to maintain these events admist a wide potential of possible disruptions.

This need on the part of the children to maintain peer activities despite frequent disruptions from numerous sources (other children, teachers and other adults, and other ongoing events in the school) is a reflection of the central themes of control and communal sharing. The initiation, construction, and maintenance of interactive events is a joint production which demands the active cooperation of participants. Although adults may often take such cooperation for granted in everyday events, the production of social order depends upon participants' use of a number of shared interpretive procedures (Cicourel, 1974; Garfinkel, 1967) and conversational or discourse maxims (Grice, 1975). For young children, the joint production of peer interaction is an immediate and highly conscious *shared* event. Given the development of *communal sharing* the children attempt to maintain *control* over what they have established (and share): (a) by the use of verbal claims of ownership of objects, areas of the school, and the unfolding events themselves (see Chapters 4 and 5); (b) by "saving" or "guarding" the place or position of playmates during their temporary leave-taking (see Chapter 5); and, most dramatically, (c) by their tendency to resist the access attempts of other children (see Chapter 4 and Corsaro, 1979c).

On the surface, these features of the children's protection of interactive space may seem selfish or uncooperative. In fact, as I noted in Chapter 5, the teachers often reacted negatively to such behavior and emphasized the importance of sharing play materials and areas of the school. But it is not that the children are resisting the idea of sharing. On the contrary, they wish to continue to share the interactive experience with each other. In short, the children want to maintain *control* over their *communally constructed and shared* play activities.

Recent work on children's friendships (Asher and Gottman, 1981; Damon, 1977; Selman, 1981; Youniss, 1975) has been primarily based on clinical interviewing and has shown that preschool children's conceptions of friendship are generally based on thinking which focuses on propinquity. For example, Selman found that, for young children, "a close friend is someone who lives close by and with whom self happens to be playing at the moment" (1981:250). The results of the present study are generally in line with these findings. As I noted in Chapter 4, an examination of children's spontaneous references to friendship demonstrated that the children often referred to friendship in the course of ongoing events (i.e., a friend is a person with whom you happen to be playing), and that the children's references seldom displayed a recognition of enduring personal characteristics of playmates. However, as I also emphasized in Chapter 4, the children's emerging conceptions of friendship were embedded in the social contextual demands of peer culture. For the children in this study, friendship often served integrative functions (such as gaining access to, building solidarity and mutual trust in, and protecting the interactive space of play groups) in the nursery school. It is this relation between social knowledge and concepts, and the everyday life worlds of young children, which cannot be captured by way of clinical interviewing.

These findings again demonstrate the importance of the two basic themes of control and communal sharing in peer culture for the social development of young children. Furthermore, this interpretation of children's developing conception of friendship, as well as the interpretation of the protection of interactive space as a reflection of the children's desire to control communally shared events, rests firmly on attaining an understanding of children's behavior and culture by becoming a part of children's worlds.

In Chapter 5, the themes of control and communal sharing were evident throughout the discussion of specific features of peer culture in the nursery school. Regarding the children's values and concerns, I have already discussed how the protection of interactive space illustrates both the children's desire to control their activities while at the same time sharing ongoing events with each other. The themes of control and sharing were also apparent in the children's concern for the physical welfare of their playmates, in their desire to be bigger, and in their enactment of underlying themes in spontaneous fantasy play.

We saw in Chapter 5 that the children closely monitored incidents where a playmate was or appeared to be injured, and that the children often talked to each other about the nature of the possible injury as they watched the teachers comfort the child in distress. In these conversations, the children not only revealed their concern for the physical welfare of their playmates, but also displayed empathy by recalling past injuries of their own which were seen as similar to that of their peer. These events involve an interactive alignment in which the children observe, talk about, and reflect upon the well-being of a fellow playmate, and, therefore, are in the process developing empathy skills. Most importantly, we see that the children's concern for the physical welfare of playmates and their development of empathy skills are communally shared elements of peer culture.

In Chapter 5, we also saw that the children valued "growing up" and "getting bigger." For young children, the primary distinguishing characteristic between themselves and adults is that adults are bigger. Young children also come to realize early on that adults are in control. It is adults who are the bosses and who have the power to tell children what they can and cannot do. This value of being bigger was best displayed by the children's attraction to, and patterns of play in, certain areas of the nursery school. The children preferred areas of play (the upstairs playhouse, the climbing house, and the climbing bars) where they were literally bigger and to a very real degree temporarily out of the control of adults. In these areas, the children were able to gain more control of their lives and their play. This sense of control was best illustrated in the nature of the children's play in these areas of the school. The play often involved group singing and chanting in which the children would challenge and taunt those below, including other children and adults (see Examples 5.4, 5.5, and 5.6). Here again we see the interrelation of the two central themes of control and communal sharing. The children gain control by climbing high into these areas and challenging others (especially adults), and then communally share this sense of control and the value of "being bigger" by way of group chants and taunts. The simple and oft-heard chant "We are bigger than anybody else" nicely captures the themes of control and communal sharing for this element of peer culture.

In spontaneous fantasy play, the children's concerns and values can be inferred from the underlying themes or schemata which the children share and employ to frame ongoing fantasy play. The three basic themes (lost–found, danger–rescue, and death–rebirth) which appeared in children's spontaneous fantasy play all share a basic structure which involves the generation and resolution of tension. These tensions, in turn, reflect very real fears in the lives of young children—the fear of being lost, of encountering unforeseen dangers (e.g., storms, fires, wild animals, monsters, etc.), and the uncertainty of death. In spontaneous fantasy play, the children cooperatively construct fantasy events in which they communally share the tensions associated with such fears as being lost, encountering danger, and thinking about death and dying. In these same play events, the children also share the relief of these tensions in the enactment and resolution of the fantasy episodes. In this way, the children gain control of their fears and uncertainties, and at the same time communally share this sense of control and the resolution of the tension generated in the spontaneous fantasy play. Again we see the interrelations of the themes of control and communal sharing as the children attempt to deal with fears, ambiguities, and uncertainties they first encounter in the adult world, but which they come to control and share within peer culture.

The central themes of control and communal sharing were also apparent in the children's behavioral routines. As I noted in Chapter 5, these routines can be seen as elements of peer culture because they involve activities that the children consistently produce together. In short, the routines are peer activities which are recurrent and predictable. The routines discussed in Chapter 5 include: children's humor and ritual threats and insults, approach-avoidance routines, and a routine that occurred consistently among the children in the morning session at the school which I termed "Garbage Man."

It was clear from the examples and discussion in Chapter 5 that the children were developing rudimentary conceptions of humor. However, the main feature of the children's humor was not the nature or structure of a joke or riddle, but rather the infectious and repetitious group laughter or glee (see Sherman, 1975) which resulted from a performance. What seemed most important to the children was the *sharing* of humor or laughter. The joke or riddle was something that was produced (sometimes correctly and sometimes incorrectly) to trigger the shared laughter. In short, for these children humor was a communally shared event. However, the children were beginning to develop a recognition that this shared event could be controlled (or set in motion) by an individual performance (i.e., the telling of a joke or riddle).

The recognition of the ability to control the reactions of others is best seen in the children's tendencies to, at times, use humor to reduce the build up of tension in a series of insults or threats. We saw in Example 5.11 that insult/threat routines can often emerge during attempts to protect interactive space. During the process of the routine, threats are exchanged as a way of controlling access to shared events. In addition, the actual threats themselves often build solidarity within groups while at the same time generating tension between groups. As we saw in Example 5.11, humor can be incorporated into a dispute as a way of relieving the build up of threats and of avoiding possible aggression. In sum, the introduction of *shared* humor and laughter is a device that can be used to relieve the tension or conflict which may result from attempts to *control* the behavior of others.

Approach–avoidance routines can best be described as a type of pretend play in which a threatening enemy or foe is identified, approached, and avoided. Several types of approach–avoidance routines were identified in Chapter 5: wild animal, monster, and cross-gender (see Examples 5.12–5.16). Approach–avoidance play is similar to spontaneous fantasy in that the children attempt *jointly* to gain *control* over real fears, concerns, and anxieties. In both types of play, the children cope with circumstances of their everyday life worlds by integrating them into a shared peer culture.

Approach–avoidance play differs from spontaneous fantasy in that the children physically act out the dangerous and threatening events rather than manipulating toy animals or dolls. In approach–avoidance play, the threatening agents are more actively personified, and, as we saw in Examples 5.14, 5.15, and 5.16, the threatening agents may be personified by individuals whom the children are actually afraid of or at least curious about. However, even though threatening agents and danger may seem more real in approach–avoidance play, it is also true that the children in the threatened role have more control over the performance of the routine than those children who adopt or who are assigned the role of threatening agent. In spontaneous fantasy, on the other hand, the danger is often unexpected and never directly approached or aroused. In spontaneous fantasy, danger (or being lost or dying) is always something that happens to the objects the children animate, and this danger is to be avoided or evaded. In approach–avoidance, the children, who are threatened, approach and initiate the routine. These children discuss and arrive at a mutual plan of action for approaching the danger, and this anxiety-filled and cautious approach *is shared as it is performed.*

In sum, both spontaneous fantasy and approach–avoidance involve: (a) attempts by the children to control the fears, concerns, and curiosities of their everyday lives; and (b) the communal sharing of the building anxiety and tension of the threat and the relief and joy of the avoidance or escape. However, in approach–avoidance routines the children seem to be moving toward a clearer recognition of their developing abilities to gain control over the uncertainties of their lives.

Although the behavioral routine, "Garbage Man," appeared only among the children in the morning group and cannot be readily generalized to other peer settings, it does share with the other elements of peer culture a reflection of the basic themes of control and communal sharing. First, there is *sharing* of excitement and joy as the group production of the routine builds and eventually reaches a climax at the appropriate moment. This group production and sharing of the build up and relief of tension was also apparent in spontaneous fantasy, the children's group chants from the bars and climbing house, and in approach–avoidance play. Second, the routine is enacted in an area of the school (the climbing bars) which the children see as their own and which is generally inaccessible to adults, an area of the school where the children feel in *control*. In fact, during the enactment of this routine, the children literally reach out beyond the physical boundaries of the school to the adult world and transform an everyday event (the collection of garbage) into a routine of peer culture. The enactment of the routine gives the children a strong sense of control, in that they are successful at procuring the participation of adults in an event which the children create and control and of whose significance adults have only a surface recognition.

The final element of peer culture discussed in Chapter 5 was the children's secondary adjustments to adult rules. Goffman's notion of secondary adjustments centers around the individual's attempts to gain a sense of self by resisting the control of social institutions. Secondary adjustments are, according to Goffman (1961a), ways in which the individual stands apart from the role and self assigned for him or her by the institution. As I noted in Chapter 5, the children in the nursery school did not display a stable sense of self or the cognitive skills necessary to infer the implications of the embracement or the resistance of organizational rules for personal identity. The children did, however, display a clear understanding of the importance and restrictiveness of the adult world as compared to children's worlds. In the nursery school, the children develop a group identity in which they often attempt to overcome the power of adults and what they often see as the arbitrary nature of adult rules.

In the process of resisting adult rules through a number of ingenious secondary adjustments (see Chapter 5, especially Examples 5.17–5.19), the children come to develop a sense of community and a group identity. In addition, the children's resistance of adult rules through cooperative secondary adjustments enables them to gain a certain amount of control over their daily lives. As I noted in Chapter 5, the children's secondary adjustments symbolize one of their most cherished desires: to challenge and defy adults, to share the experience, and to get away with it (i.e., avoid detection by adults).

As we can see, the themes of control and communal sharing underlie (to some degree) all the elements of peer culture. It is clear that control and sharing are central features in the lives of preschool children. If we are to understand the socialization process, that is, how children acquire adult knowledge and skills and eventually reproduce the adult world, we must study this process as it occurs in children's worlds. For preschool children, the acquisition of knowledge and skills is embedded in their attempts to gain control over their lives and to share this sense of control with their peers.

Theoretical Implications

In Chapter 2, I argued that the theoretical basis of this study, what I have termed an interpretive approach to childhood socialization, is in line with but also extends the constructivist views of Piaget, Mead, and Vygotsky. The interpretive approach extends the constructivist view in maintaining that children not only act on their environment, but also participate in a social world. The main findings of this study support the interpretive approach, in that we saw that the children help to shape (and *share* in) their own developmental experiences through their interactions with peers, and that the children attempt to gain *control* over their social worlds through the use of language and discourse.

The findings of this study are in line with the views of Piaget in that the features of peer culture are, to an important degree, a reflection of the children's level of cognitive development. For example, the children's consistent display of communal sharing and their reliance on a collective identity generally corresponds with Piaget's position regarding the limited perspective-taking abilities of preschool children. The ability to distinguish between general categories (i.e., child versus adult) and to share a collective identity with peers is cognitively less demanding than the ability to differentiate the individual self from others in regard to a wide range of social and personal characteristics or traits. Also in line with Piaget, we saw that much of the children's behavior was spatially and temporally bound. For the nursery school children, the features of peer culture were shared primarily *at the time of production; that is, during the actual unfolding of peer interaction.* It was clear that the children did not share this knowledge at a more abstract level. The children could not readily reflect upon behavioral patterns in their everyday lives and conceptualize and summarize these patterns in ways necessary to be able to talk about them (i.e., abstracted away from the actual events) with each other or adults. It is for this reason that clinical interviews can only capture surface features of the life-worlds of preschool children. Finally, my interpretation of the developmental implications of the study are generally in line with Piaget's concept of equilibrium or equilibration. Like Piaget's, the interpretive perspective offered here holds that learning should be viewed as a process of compensation resulting from children's continual attempts to deal with problems, confusions, and ambiguities in their life worlds. However, the interpretive perspective, in line with Vygotsky (see below), argues that these processes of compensation are often themselves practical activities which are embedded in children's life-worlds.

The interpretive perspective extends the views of Piaget in two ways. First, the interpretive approach focuses on the sources of disequilibrium in children's worlds, and attempts to document the processes through which children create and share social order in their life worlds. From this perspective, development is an interactive process which is situated in a social world. Children not only develop social skills and knowledge as the result of interactive experiences, *they actually use their developing skills and knowledge to create and maintain social order in their life worlds.*

Secondly, the interpretive approach attempts not to specify stages in children's acquisition of adult skills and knowledge, but rather to reach an understanding of children's life worlds on their own terms. Rather than viewing children's abilities and knowledge as egocentric or incomplete, the interpretive theorist attempts to discover children's use of their skills and knowledge to create and share a peer culture. From the interpretive perspective, socialization is not merely the children's attainment of adult skills and knowledge, but is viewed rather as children's eventual reproduction of the adult world as a result of their active production and movement through a series of peer cultures.

The findings in this study are also in line with G. H. Mead's views regarding the development of self-consciousness. It is clear that most, if not all, of the nursery school children were in Mead's play stage. The children consistently participated in activities in which they adopted roles that were embedded in an organized social structure. In so doing, the children not only took the role of another but also responded to the reactions of others to their behavior. However, the children seldom participated in organized, competitive games with explicit rules, and had yet to develop a firm grasp of society or what Mead termed "the generalized other."

Although Mead outlined a series of developmental stages of self, he did not overlook the important positive functions of certain activities within each stage. It was clear from the findings in the present study that the children's participation in role play and other routines provided important positive functions for self-development. We saw that, in peer play, the children jointly produced socially ordered events which involved people, objects, and ideas of which the children lacked a firm cognitive grasp. As Mead suggested, during the course of play children gain a sense of understanding and control over the vague forces and personalities which influence their lives.

The present study can be seen as an extension of Mead's views, in that there is an attempt to probe for a deeper understanding of the positive functions and general characteristics of children's peer culture during the play stage. For example, I argued that Mead's comparison of children's role play and the myths and rituals of primitive people was important, because it draws attention to the ritual and communal nature of children's activities in the play stage. During the course of peer play, children, like primitive peoples during the production of ritual events, experience a sense of communal sharing and group identity. For primitive peoples participation in rituals or myths was a way of collectively dealing with the forces of nature, while for young children participation in peer play is often an attempt to deal with the adult world. But in both cases the activities are communally produced and lead to the development of a collective identity.

This position implies that children, through participation in peer culture in the preschool years, come to see themselves as different from adults and as sharing with each other a range of characteristics and values. Later, through participation in organized, competitive games in peer culture during the preadolescent years, children begin to perceive differences among themselves. However, they also recognize that they can cooperate despite these differences to reach a common end or goal, and in the process they develop a generalized other (i.e., a sense of their place as individuals in society). The children's previous acquisition of a collective identity can be seen as an important step in the transition to the preadolescent years where group and individual comparisons and competition become a central part of their everyday lives.

As I noted in Chapter 2, the interpretive approach offered in this study has been influenced by the recent theoretical work of Aaron Cicourel. In fact, the findings from this study help to develop or "flesh out" theoretical notions first presented by Cicourel. As Cicourel has suggested, the child's activities are always embedded in social context, and their production depends on the child's acquisition and use of language and interpretive abilities. However, to date we know little about the role of peer interaction and culture for children's development of interpretive skills. The sociolinguistic analyses of peer play presented in Chapters 3 through 5 demonstrate how the children's participation in peer culture depends upon and facilitates the further development of the children's language and interpretive abilities. It was clear in these analyses that the children continually relied on their interpretive abilities to link specific contextual cues (voice intonation, facial expression, physical movements) to shared knowledge of both peer culture and the adult world, to participate competently in everyday peer events.

Consider, for example, the complex cross-gender approach–avoidance sequence in Chapter 5 (Example 5.16). The microanalysis of this sequence revealed that gender was becoming an important membership category in peer culture and that the children were beginning to recognize the relationship between gender and norms and behavioral expectations in the adult world. The children's behavior in this example indicated that they shared knowledge of sex-typed behavioral expectations (i.e., girls are supposed to be fearful and timid, while boys are supposed to be strong and aggressive). However, as Cicourel has suggested, such knowledge must be articulated with the demands of unfolding interactive scenes. In example 5.16, the children discovered that the articulation process is complex and that there is seldom a direct link between emerging concepts about the adult world and the actual behavior of peers. It is through repeated experiences of this type that children generate childhood conceptions of social structure and develop and sharpen their communicative skills and interpretive abilities. Over time, children create and move through a series of peer cultures and eventually acquire the knowledge and abilities necessary to gain a sense of, and reproduce, social structure in the adult world.

As I noted in Chapter 2, the present study has benefited from the revival of interest in Vygotsky's theoretical approach to human development. In the last few years, this renewed interest has led to the translation and interpretation of much of Vygotsky's theoretical work (see Hood, Fiess, and Aron, 1982; Lee and Noam, 1982; Vygotsky, 1978; Wertsch, 1979, 1981). Three important and interrelated concepts in Vygotsky's work are stressed throughout these recent translations and interpretations. First, in line with general Marxist's views, Vygotsky stresses the importance of practical activity for psychological change and development. This emphasis on practical activity in social contexts is crucial for understanding how Vygotsky's approach to psychological development differs from that of Piaget. Although both theorists view development as resulting from the child's activities on the environment, for Piaget development is primarily individualistic (i.e., the result of child-environment equilibration), while for Vygotsky development is always social or collective (i.e., the child's practical activities within social contexts).

The findings from the present study are in line with, and in some respects extend, Vygotsky's views regarding the importance of practical action for human development. In Chapters 3 through 5, I recorded and analyzed the children's key practical activities in their interactions with peers and adults in the nursery school. Many of these activities involved the children's attempts to initiate and maintain social events in line with the demands of peer culture, while others involved the children's strategies for coping with problems, fears, curiosities, and restrictions from the adult world. For example, in Chapter 4 we discussed the relation between the children's practical attempts to generate, organize, and protect peer events and their development of interpersonal skills and conceptions of friendship. In Chapters 3 and 5, we saw that the children's everyday play routines (role play, spontaneous fantasy, approach–avoidance, etc.) had important implications for the children's development of communicative skills and social knowledge. Finally, in Chapter 5, we saw that the children's practical attempts to evade what they viewed as arbitrary restrictions (i.e., their secondary adjustments to adult rules) resulted in the children's firmer grasp of both the nature and necessity of rules, while at the same time contributing to their development of a sense of collective values and identity. These findings are in line with and extend Vygotsky's views in that they result from the *direct observation* of children's practical activities as they are produced in the children's everyday life-worlds.

A second important concept in Vygotsky's work is his notion of *internalization,* which he defines as the external reconstruction of an external operation. Vygotsky's conception of internalization fits nicely with his emphasis on practical activities, in that he argues that every psychological function "in the child's development appears twice, first on the social level, and later on the individual level; first *between* people (interpsychological) and then *inside* the child (intrapsychological)" (1978: 57, emphases as in original).

The findings from the micro-analyses in Chapters 3 through 5 demonstrate the importance of peer interaction and culture for Vygotsky's conception of internalization. While Vygotsky impressively traced the process of internalization in his work on the development of inner speech, he did not adequately specify *the types of interactive events in children's worlds* in which psychological functions first develop (on the interpsychological level), nor their gradual internalization by the child (the intrapsychological level). The findings from the present study suggest that there are two important types of social relations in the internalization process. Children are first exposed to the social world in their interactions with adults. Through repeated everyday activities with adults, children come to develop a sense of social structure as well as a sense of their place in the social world as active members of society (see Corsaro, 1977, 1979b; Wertsch, 1979). However, the process of internalization is gradual and continuous throughout childhood. In their interactions within peer culture, children practice, work out, and eventually acquire a firm grasp of the knowledge and skills which first emerged in interactive events with adults. In this sense, the children's practical activities within peer culture can be seen as a mediational phase in the internalization process. The information and psychological functions first produced in adult–child activities are now reproduced within peer culture before eventually becoming part of the psychological makeup of the child.

A third important concept in Vygotsky's approach is his emphasis on the child's socio-historical appropriation of culture. As Lee and Heckman note, Vygotsky saw language "as both a social institution and a communicative system," and, therefore, believed that "its development socializes thought at two levels—the child joins a socio-historical system and a world of others to whom he speaks" (1982: 374). For Vygotsky, the child, in acquiring language, becomes a member of his or her culture or socio-historical system.

Vygotsky's concept of appropriation of culture is a major contribution to theories of human development. However, his conceptualizations of historical and cultural aspects of the socialization process are not fully developed. Vygotsky attempted to capture the importance of history and culture in his theoretical work and research on the relationship between language and thought. Although this work is impressive, Vygotsky did not specify how socio-historical change nor shared culture directly affects human development. If the child is born into a socio-historical world, we must investigate how specific features of given historical periods (e.g., attitudes toward children and child rearing, educational policy, technological innovation) affect the socialization process (see Aries, 1965). In addition, if the study of language and thought is abstracted away from everyday cultural contexts, a full understanding of the effects of language on the developmental process is not possible. Recently, some psychologists have displayed an appreciation of the importance of culture for child development, and have demonstrated the need for cross-cultural research (see Cole, Gay, Glick, and Sharp, 1971; Cole and Scribner, 1974; Super and Harkness, 1980). To date, however, the importance of peer cultures for child development has been all but ignored. In the present study, I have argued that children become members of their society through their construction of, and participation in, a series of peer cultures. To reach a valid understanding of the socialization process, it is essential that we identify stable features of peer cultures. If, as Vygotsky argued, the developmental process is deeply rooted in the links between the individual and social history, then changes in children's life-worlds influence or bring about cognitive change and development. Child development, then, cannot be fully documented unless it is studied as it occurs in the life-worlds of children.

Implications for Early Childhood Education

I began my research at the child study center with only limited knowledge of early childhood educational philosophy or programs. Although I knew that many early childhood education programs were grounded in the perspectives of theorists of human development such as Piaget, my main interests were not specifically in education. I wished to reach a better understanding of childhood socialization by entering children's worlds and observing peer interaction in a natural setting. During the course of field entry and data collection, I not only gradually became aware of what it was like to be a child in this setting, I also began to understand better the life of the nursery school teacher. Throughout the year, I had numerous conversations with the teachers and teaching assistants, and I regularly sat in on the teacher-staff conferences each day. We frequently discussed problems I encountered in data collection and, near the end of the school term, I reviewed initial findings with the teachers and teaching assistants and I often asked them to view and comment on videotaped episodes of peer play.

It was during the viewings, discussions, and interpretations of videotaped data that I first became aware of some of the specific implications of my work for early childhool education. During these sessions (which I referred to as examples of indefinite triangulation in Chapter 1), I came to realize that not only my specific research interests were being pursued. The teachers and teaching assistants often actively took control of the discussion, focused in on the educational significance of the data, and asked for my reactions and suggestions. On these occasions, I in no way felt my control of the situation had been usurped. To the contrary, I found myself carefully thinking about and reacting to the questions of the teachers. I also did not hesitate to offer suggestions. These suggestions were sometimes accepted and actually employed by the teachers in programs and projects to improve the educational experiences of the children. On the other hand, I should note that many of my suggestions and ideas were of little merit, and these were immediately dismissed by the teachers or kindly noted only to be forgotten shortly thereafter.

In this last chapter, I present the key features of those discussions and interpretations which emerged in the indefinite triangulation sessions that have a direct bearing on early childhood education. I should warn the reader at the outset that the ideas and suggestions I offer are not recipes or scientific formulas for meeting educational goals in preschool settings. Nor are the suggestions in any way comparable to the carefully developed strategies and projects offered in early childhood education manuals such as the one by Almy and Genishi (1979). What I have offered throughout this book is an attempt to understand the children's worlds—their values and concerns and their point of view. In this last section, I offer some general guidelines for how this information may be used by the preschool teacher. It is my hope, of course, that teachers will go beyond these suggestions to develop their own ideas and strategies to best meet the demands of their particular classrooms and students.

The Importance of Peer Culture

In my numerous discussions with nursery school teachers, I have been struck by their strong belief that important learning experiences occur during children's spontaneous peer play and their frustration over being unable to specify these learning experiences to the satisfaction of many psychologists. Prior to this study, I shared both this belief and frustration. I was convinced that young children acquired communicative skills and social knowledge in interaction with peers, but I was often frustrated with the difficult task of identifying the connection between a specific experience and the manifestation of subsequent learning. During the course of this study, I discovered that the source of the problem was my attempt to impose a linear view of learning onto the insight of the importance of children's practical activities for their social development. Like nursery school teachers, I had grown accustomed to assessing development almost totally in terms of individual progress in attaining specific skills and knowledge. This tendency is in line with what I earlier termed "the linear view of development" (see Chapter 2). The linear view emphasizes children's passing through stages or specific experiences in preparation for adulthood. On the other hand, the reproductive view of development presented in Chapter 2 maintains that children enter into a social nexus and through interaction with others build up social understandings. From this interpretive perspective, development is viewed as a productive–reproductive complex in which an increasing density and reorganization of knowledge marks progress. To understand childhood socialization, then, it is necessary to observe children's everyday activities as they are embedded in their life-worlds. For nursery school children, as I have demonstrated in this study, such an understanding depends upon observing children as they create and maintain a peer culture.

In Chapters 3 through 5, I attempted to capture an interpretive understanding of peer culture and its importance for social development. First, I noted that the children displayed a wide range of social skills and concepts during spontaneous peer play (see Chapters 3 through 5, especially Table 5.1, for a summary of these skills and concepts). Second, and most important, I argued that these social skills and concepts are developed, refined, and used by the children to produce and maintain a peer culture. Although social skills and knowledge develop within peer culture, peer culture is a production that exists over and above the skills and knowledge of its members. The nursery school children's peer culture is a reflection of their understanding, production, and reorganization of social structure. In short, peer culture is a manifestation of the children's sense of social structure at this point in their development.

But what is the value of this information about peer culture in a particular nursery school for early childhood educators in general? First, I hope that this information about peer culture can help teachers to develop a better understanding and appreciation of children's point of view. Such an understanding is essential for the design, application, and evaluation of preschool programs. Second, the research identifies a wide range of peer activities that have important learning potential that are often overlooked. Third, I hope the information is useful for teachers who wish to encourage the development of peer culture in their preschool programs.

Structuring the Development of Peer Culture

Although young children are able to create and participate in peer culture to some degree in any setting, the preschool can be structured to encourage the development of those features of peer culture which have the best potential for learning. Given my emphasis on the importance of spontaneous play for social learning, one might suspect that I would argue for highly unstructured programs. After all, is it not in spontaneous play where most of the features of peer culture emerge and are shared by the children? The answer to this question is, yes and no. Peer culture does most often emerge in spontaneous play, but its emergence is often a reaction to the adult world. Adult ideas, materials, rules, and restrictions can be seen as frames or boundaries within which features of peer culture emerge and are played out. Some of these frames or boundaries are carried to school in the children's perceptions and understandings of the adult world. Others are more tangible and are built up and maintained by teachers. In fact, the emergence of peer culture in the nursery school depends on and reaches its fullest potential in response to teachers' boundary maintenance.

Consider an example from the data on children's protection of interactive space (see Example 4.3). Two girls reject the access attempt of a playmate. The rejected child goes to a teacher for aid. The teacher asks the girls to allow their peer to play. The girls refuse, arguing that the other girl is not their friend. The teacher responds to this resistance by suggesting that the children must share and that they all three can be friends. The end result is that the two original playmates become frustrated with the teacher's intervention, reject this more general conception of sharing, and opt to leave the play area.

In Chapter 4, I argued that the children were frustrated because they felt they were already sharing. They were sharing the activity with each other and wished to protect this shared event. Such a conclusion does not, however, mean that I feel teachers should refrain from intervention in such cases. There may have been better or worse strategies of intervention in this case, but intervention was necessary. Intervention can be seen as a boundary that children react to and often resist. But this resistance, this attempt to preserve peer culture in response to the adult world, is an important source of learning. The children are induced to think about how their views differ from those of adults. Over time, repeated experiences of this type can lead to a recognition of both differences between peer culture and the adult world, and *the reasons* for these differences. In short, boundary contacts are crucial for development. But teachers should not expect immediate results. Children continually bump up against the adult world for long periods of time before they acquire a full sense of, and reproduce, adult culture.

To return to the question of types of preschool programs that facilitate learning within peer culture, the issue is not one of structure versus nonstructure, but rather one of boundary maintenance. Good programs are ones which provide: (a) structured (adult-directed) activities, (b) opportunities for spontaneous play, and (c) numerous instances of boundary contact between peer and adult culture in all situations.

In the nursery school where the present research was conducted, both the ecological structure of the school and the nature of the curriculum program provided for teacher directed activities and opportunities for spontaneous play. The inside and outdoors areas of the school were divided into smaller subareas, which were set up to promote either teacher-directed activities or spontaneous peer play (see Chapter 1, and also Cook-Gumperz and Corsaro, 1977). The sub-areas contained materials and props which encouraged a range of activities for groups of varying size. Also the school day was divided up into periods where free play, teacher-directed activities, and group meetings occurred on a specific schedule. Throughout the school year, the teachers attempted to make special note of what I have termed "boundary contacts," and devised and tested out strategies to improve the learning potential of both teacher-directed and peer activities. Some of these strategies resulted from the teachers' use of a systematic observation procedure which they employed at my suggestion (see below).

Systematic observation is essential for the assessment of any early childhood education program. Information obtained from the systematic observation of children allows the teacher to estimate the frequency and effectiveness of boundary contacts. In this way, such information can be the basis of curriculum development, evaluation, and refinement.

Systematic Observation in the Nursery School

Teachers as Observers

Recently, there has been a growing interest in ethnographic research in educational settings (see Green and Wallat, 1981). Some ethnographic studies have focused directly on applied implications and have involved the participation of teachers as coresearchers (Mehan, 1979; Wallat et al., 1981). Others have called for naturalistic observation as a key method for the evaluation and improvement of early childhood programs (see Almy and Genishi, 1979; Day, Perkins, and Weinthaler, 1979). Undoubtedly, the direct observation of children in the nursery school environment is important for developing teaching strategies and for setting and meeting educational goals.

But what is the best way to utilize naturalistic observation and ethnography to improve educational programs? First, direct observation should not in itself be confused with ethnography. Observation is but one of the data collection techniques employed by ethnographers. It should be remembered that ethnographers with to enter into and achieve an interpretive understanding of the worlds of the people they study. Nursery school teachers have different goals. They are concerned with effective teaching, that is, with providing children with important learning experiences. In attaining these goals, it certainly helps for teachers to understand children's worlds. It is for this reason that I feel most of the findings in this monograph are of direct value to teachers. But I would not expect, nor would I suggest, that teachers should become ethnographers in their own classrooms. Such an expectation is unrealistic, given the multiple demands teachers face in their classrooms. Teachers can, however, work with ethnographers or more practically borrow a basic tool of the ethnographic method. Teachers can become systematic observers.

But what is meant by systematic observation? Systematic observation involves the careful watching and recording of naturally occurring events. Systematic observation involves more than simply monitoring children's activities. First, teachers must be concerned with the naturalness of their observations. Here, the notion of the "interactive episode" as a basic unit of collection (see Chapter 1) is important. Teachers, like researchers, must be concerned with the validity of their observations, and should attempt to observe behavior within its social context. Although all teachers may not find my definition of the interactive episode applicable in their settings, they should attempt to make observations in line with theoretically relevant units of interaction.

Secondly, teachers must preserve their observations through the use of some sort of recording device or devices. Given the limitations of human memory, it is necessary to record observations if they are to be of use beyond the immediate situation.

Although some teachers may have access to audiovisual equipment and will be able to record events on videotape or film, most teachers will have to rely on some sort of field notes. Here my discussion of field notes presented in Chapter 1 is most relevant. Given the multiple demands teachers face in their classrooms, it is unrealistic to expect that teachers can routinely record in-depth field notes. However, the sheer detail of field notes is less important than their organization and validity. Teachers may find that less detailed field notes, coupled with carefully documented personal, methodological, and theoretical notes are more than adequate to meet their needs. The crucial factor is to link personal and methodological (or applied) interpretations as closely to actual events (as summarized in field notes) as possible. Such a procedure can help teachers avoid the common tendency to expand or "fill the gaps" in what must be incomplete field notes, to make interpretations and evaluations fit together after the fact.

A Proposed Observational Routine

In this section, I offer an observational routine which is a modification of one the teachers used in the child study center where the present research was conducted. What I offer is a general model for systematic observation which can be altered, within limits, to meet the specific demands of particular preschool programs. In the procedure, a teacher, teaching assistant, or adult aide (parent, student, etc.) assumes the observer role. The observer, on one or a number of consecutive days, removes his or herself from normal instructional duties. The observer's primary responsibility is to watch episodes of interaction, and then to record observations into field notes.

Prior to the initiation of the routine, the observer must decide on a specific definition of his or her collection unit. This definition should reflect both theoretical approaches to human interaction and specific social-ecological features of the preschool setting (see my discussion of the interactive episode in Chapter 1). Also, the observer should decide on a representative range of events (i.e., type of peer play, teacher-directed activity, meeting time, etc.) he or she wishes to observe before beginning the routine.

Once in the setting, the observer should watch events from a distance which is close enough to see and hear all the activity, but which is far enough away so as not to disrupt ongoing events.

It is important to note how the proposed positioning of the observer differs from my strategies for field entry and data collection in the present study. Instead of watching from a distance, I physically entered into play areas and often was drawn into the events as a participant observer. But it should be remembered that this participant observation was based upon my ability to enter the children's worlds and to be defined as an atypical adult (i.e., an oversized playmate who was not a teacher, parent, or experimenter). Such a procedure is not possible for teachers who have been defined by the children to meet certain expectations (i.e., to fit the teacher role). Therefore, the teacher's presence in the peer activities would alter the normal course of the events. In a sense, the observer would be best off employing a strategy the children often employ to gain access to ongoing play—that is, to watch from a distance, occasionally changing position to remain unnoticed by the participants of the event under observation (see Chapter 4 and Corsaro, 1979c, for a discussion of these access strategies, which are termed "nonverbal entry" and "encirclement").

Once positioned, the observer must then decide what to observe and later to record. As a particular event unfolds, the observer should attempt to process what is happening in a literal, noninterpretive fashion. For example, if Jonathan pushes Graham in a resistance to Graham's attempt to gain access, the observer should attempt to mentally make note of the events that occur, and their order of occurrence, and refrain from thinking about why certain things occur (e.g., "why" Jonathan pushed Graham) or their potential consequences. This mental recording of events serves as a basis for the explicit composition of field notes at the end of an episode. While attending to an interactive episode, the observer should remain uninvolved and detached. The only exception to this general rule would be in cases where it is necessary to offer needed information to other teachers. Such instances normally occur when a teacher must enter into a peer activity to settle a dispute. In these cases, it is best for the observer to offer the information quickly and, if possible, out of the immediate presence of the children involved.

Once an episode ends, the observer should move to a part of the school were initial notes can be recorded without distraction. Most schools have a kitchen, work shop, or office areas which are generally "off limits" to the children, and are, thus, ideal for recording notes. The observer should begin by recording field notes. As I noted in Chapter 1, field notes are literal descriptions of events (who did and said what with whom, etc.). While recording field notes, the observer will experience personal feelings as well as ideas and evaluations regarding the significance of the field notes for the preschool program. The observer should refrain from inserting these feelings and ideas into the field notes or from stopping to record them separately. Once field notes are composed, the observer should review them, this time stopping when necessary to jot down feelings and ideas under the headings: PN (Personal Notes); MN (Methodological Notes), and TN (Theoretical Notes). Once this process is complete, the observer has the option of returning to the field or moving on to the next step in the recording and organization of notes. I would recommend returning to the field and moving through steps 3 through 5 at the end of the day, either alone or with other teachers in a staff meeting. Regardless of when they occur, steps 3 through 5 involve writing out and expanding ideas previously jotted down under personal notes (step 3), methodological notes (step 4), and theoretical notes (step 5). Table 6.1 provides a general description of the four types of notes, along with a summary of the recording procedure.

As we see in Table 6.1, the last step in the process involves the development of the educational implications of field and personal notes by expanding methodological and theoretical notes. This step best occurs in staff meetings where the observer can present field and personal notes to other teachers and ask for their reactions and suggestions. In a sense, the last step in the procedure involves the generation of ideas for the application of information from systematic observation, to meet the instructional needs or goals of particular preschool programs.

Some Potential Applications of Observational Information

Individual student assessment.. Since teachers are primarily concerned with learning and development, one of the most common uses of observational data is to evaluate the progress of individual students. The value of the observational method outlined here is that the teachers acquire information on the children's behaviors as they are embedded within their natural contexts. This method has definite advantages over observing individual children employing some sort of time-sampling procedure. Instead of hav-

Table 6.1 Categories for Observational Notes and
Note-Recording Procedures*

Field Notes (FN)	Field Notes describe events which were experienced directly by watching and listening. They contain as little interpretation as possible, and are best recorded during or shortly after the observational period.
Personal Notes (PN)	Personal Notes attempt to capture the observers feelings and personal reactions to specific features of the events observed. These personal reactions may involve responses to the feelings or behaviors of specific participants in the observed events.
Methodological Notes (MN)	Methodological Notes generally involve evaluations of, and instructions for improving, methods of observational data collection. Methodological notes can be expanded to include specific evaluations of, and advice or strategies to improve, teaching effectiveness.
Theoretical Notes (TN)	Theoretical Notes represent attempts to develop the general theoretical significance of one or a set of field notes. In the case of educational programs, these notes represent attempts to estimate the effectiveness of instructional methods and evaluate general program goals.

Steps in Note Recording Procedure

1. Write out field notes, refraining from including personal feelings or interpretations.
2. Review field notes, recording personal feelings, ideas, and interpretations in short phrases under one of three headings (PN, MN or TN).
3. Inspect all entries under PN heading, then expand and fully write out personal notes.
4. Move on to entries under MN heading and repeat process as in Step 3.
5. Move on to entries under TN heading and repeat process as in Step 4.
6. Alone or in staff meeting, review all field and personal notes for several days' observations, and expand methodological and theoretical notes.

*The categorical definitions for field, methodological and theoretical notes are a revised version of definitions presented in Schatzman and Strauss (1973).

ing a record of a large number of discrete behaviors pulled from their natural contexts, the method offered here provides information on the children's actions as they unfold in everyday events. Field notes of episodes involving the participation of a specific child can be reviewed so that teachers can evaluate the child's behavior over time in groups of differing size and across a range of interactive episodes.

If specific problems or needs are identified, teachers may wish to collect additional information by observing episodes in which the target child is a participant. Once such information is collected, the teacher can pose specific questions and look to the overall set of observational data for possible answers. Some possible questions which could be addressed include the following.

- Does the child regularly participate in a wide or narrow range of both peer and teacher-directed activities?
- Does the child have difficulty in entering and being accepted into peer activities?
- Does the child regularly participate in both large and small groups?
- Does the child regularly play with a number of different peers or rely on primarily one or two peers as interactive partners?
- Are the child's peer activities restricted primarily to same-gender groups?
- Is the child actively involved in peer culture?
- Does the child display a sense of group identity? Does the child display concern for the physical welfare of playmates? Does the child engage in recurrent peer routines?
- Is the child frequently involved in disputes and disagreements with other children?
- Does the child show boredom or disinterest in teacher-directed activities?
- Does the child resist attempts by teachers to encourage him or her to participate in teacher-directed activities?
- Does the child actively participate in organized group or meeting times?

Once questions such as these are addressed through analysis of observational materials, teachers can develop strategies to improve the learning experiences of children who demonstrate persistent problems. Later, these strategies can be evaluated by the collection and analysis of additional observational data. Take, for example, a child who confines nearly all of his or her free-play time to teacher-directed activities. He or she may be learning a great deal from these experiences, but not developing the skills and confidence necessary to interact successfully with peers. Furthermore, minimal involvement in peer culture can have negative effects on acquisition of social knowledge. The view of the world may seem complex and adult-like, but this knowledge may be fragile and not firmly grasped, since it relies primarily on imitation of or identification with adults rather than resulting from more active contacts between the adult and child world.

Strategies for dealing with individual problems of this sort depend on patterns isolated in the observational notes. Does the child have difficulty entering into play groups? Is he or she often rejected? Is he or she persistent when he or she encounters initial rejection? Does he or she play regularly with several playmates or confine his or her peer activities to one or two other children? If, for example, the child has difficulty entering groups, or gives up easily when he or she encounters initial resistance, then he or she may need direct aid from the teacher. The teacher can help by watching ongoing peer activities with the child from a distance and then discussing possible access strategies (e.g., "producing a variant of the ongoing play" see Corsaro, 1979c and Chapter 4). Or a teacher, upon seeing the child rejected, can encourage him or her to make a second attempt, or suggest he or she try to gain access to another group. Such strategies, if successful, can bolster a child's confidence. Also, the strategies themselves can be observed by another teacher who, because of his or her detachment, will have a more objective view of their success or failure than the teacher employing the strategy.

I could go on to pursue many additional possibilities here, but my purpose is to demonstrate the general potential of the observational procedure and the information it generates. Teachers should have no problem identifying the multiple uses of the observational method for individual assessment of students in their preschool programs.

Program assessment and evaluation.. In addition to evaluating the progress of individual students, nursery school educators are also interested in the overall effectiveness of their instructional programs. Here, teachers wish to estimate how well specific projects, strategies, and methods are accomplishing more general educational goals. To evaluate program effectiveness, teachers can look for general patterns in observational data with a number of questions in mind. Some possible questions which could be addressed include the following.

- What is the range of group size in peer and teacher-directed activities?
- What is the range of group composition (by gender and age) in peer and teacher-directed activities?
- How are specific areas of the school, materials, and props utilized by the children in peer play?
- Are certain areas of the school and peer activities more prone to disputes and conflicts than others?
- What is the range regarding the level of participation across individual children within teacher-directed activities and in group meeting times?
- Is there evidence of a sustained peer culture in the nursery school?
    Do the children display a sense of group identity?
    Do the children display a concern for the physical welfare of playmates?
    Do the children engage in recurrent peer routines?

Once teachers discover answers to these and similar questions in observational materials, they can develop strategies to address specific problems to improve the overall effectiveness of their educational programs. As was the case for individual assessment, these strategies can be employed and then later evaluated through the collection and analysis of additional observations.

Let us consider a common problem for nursery school teachers which has to do with playgroup size and composition (in terms of gender and age). Suppose, for example, that our systematic observations reveal that a large number of boys confine almost all their free-play time to one or two activities (e.g., superhero role play and construction play with large dump trucks), and play in relatively large, same-gender, and similar age groups. Suppose we also find that several girls confine their free-play time to teacher-directed activities and peer play in small, same-gender groups. Given this information, we wish to develop strategies which encourage the children to expand the range and nature of their free-play activities. If successful, these strategies will not only enrich the learning experience of the children involved, but also improve the overall effectiveness of the educational program.

In the present study, the teacher in the afternoon group faced a problem similar to the hypothetical one just described. She was somewhat concerned that several boys spent a good part of each session playing with large dump trucks and wagons in same-gender groups. Since these activities occurred exclusively in the outside yard, the teacher developed a strategy which involved a minor alteration of the daily schedule. When the children arrived for the afternoon session, they were informed that the first part of the free play period would be confined to the inside area of the school. As a result, the boys who favored the trucks and same-gender playmates were forced to consider other activities for the first part of free play.

The results of this strategy were mixed. The boys did indeed engage in more teacher-directed activities and in more mixed-gender peer play. The boys even engaged in some family role play, an activity they shunned in the past. After the first few days, however, the children seemed to sense and anticipate what was called "outside time." Several of the boys would often gather by the locked doors and ask the teacher, "Is it outside time yet?" Once the doors were opened at the appropriate time, the boys in particular would immediately terminate their ongoing activities and race to the outside yard. Once outside, they would inevitably head for the dump trucks and confine the remainder of the free play period to this activity. The strategy, then, was moderately successful in that it increased the boys involvement in teacher-directed activities and cross-gender peer play inside the school, but decreased the range of peer activities they engaged in while playing in the outside yard.

The main limitation of this strategy was that many of the children saw the new schedule regarding inside and outside time as just another arbitrary, adult rule. They, therefore, developed a secondary adjustment to the rule which involved biding their time and waiting near the doors for "outside time" to commence. My purpose in presenting this example is not to criticize the teacher; she was quite perceptive in recognizing the problem, and her strategy to deal with it was moderately successful. My aim, instead, is to expand the discussion of the value of systematic observation. It should be remembered that systematic observation provides information that can be used both to identify problems *and* to generate strategies to address them. One of the best ways to generate such strategies is to build upon information or knowledge about peer culture obtained through systematic observation.

I will now present a teaching strategy to deal with problems related to group size and composition. This strategy builds upon knowledge of peer culture of the children in the nursery school I studied. Although the strategy could be employed relatively intact in another setting, my purpose is to offer it as a general procedure for how information from systematic observation can be used to develop strategies to deal with specific problems. It is hoped that teachers can use the procedure to develop similar strategies to meet the demands of their specific programs.

I found in the present study that the children had a keen interest in wild animals and wild animal families (see Example 5.12 and Example 3.6). This interest can be used as a basis for a strategy to encourage children to engage in a wide range of activities in different-sized, mixed-gender groups. The strategy begins with a group meeting in which there is an attempt to build on and expand the children's interest in animal families. In the meeting, teachers introduce children to the notion of families of animals by displaying and talking about a phylogenic chart of various families or groups (i.e., mammals, birds, reptiles, fish, etc.). During the meeting, an observer should note the children's understanding of the family notion and the children's favorite animals.

After the meeting and after the children have gone home for the day, the teachers divide the children's names into groups which represent ideal distributions in terms of size, gender, age and other specific characteristics (e.g., an even distribution of shy and out-going children). Each of the three or four groups are given an animal family designate or mascot. The teachers then make different color cut-outs of animals from the different animal families. For example, lions, tigers, whales, etc. could all be red and represent mammals; sharks, octopi, etc. could all be blue and represent fish, and so on for reptiles and birds, depending on the number of subgroups desired. The animal cutouts are then placed in envelopes and put in children's lockers in line with the group division decided upon previously.

When the children arrive at school the next day, the teacher asks them to get the envelopes from their lockers and to bring them to the meeting room. In the meeting room, the teacher tells the children to open their envelopes and discover their animals, if they have not done so already. The teacher then asks all the red, blue, etc. colored animals to get together in separate groups. Once assembled, a teacher or teaching assistant will ask the children in their respective groups to identify their animals. The teachers will then briefly describe to the children what the animals of specific groups share in common. This discussion can build on information presented during meeting time on the previous day. After this discussion, the teacher for each group will tell the children that they are going to spend the day playing with members of their animal family. The teacher will also note that each family will play in different areas of the school at different times of the day (e.g., first outside and then inside). At the end of the day, the children can talk about what they did in their animal families during meeting time.

The entire procedure is most effective if repeated for several days with different group assignments. At first, the animal theme will undoubtedly affect the nature of peer play and perhaps even adult-directed activities (i.e., children drawing animals). This effect should, however, wear off over time, and the children will benefit from the smaller group size and, it is hoped, engage in a wide range of cross-gender activities. The animal family procedure can, of course, be observed and evaluated, and staff discussion of the observational notes could lead to refinements or expansions of the general strategy.

In closing this section, I should note that this procedure is just one of many that could be developed to deal with a common problem in nursery school programs. The nursery school teacher does, of course, encounter many additional problems in program development and evaluation. The proposed procedure does, however, demonstrate how teaching strategies can be based on information about peer culture. Furthermore, the procedure illustrates how knowledge of the children's peer culture can be linked to formal instructional procedures in group meetings.

Settling peer disputes and conflict.. One of the major reasons for nursery school teachers' intervention into peer play is to resolve disputes and conflicts. Since conflicts are often disruptive to the educational value of peer play, teachers wish to settle disputes as quickly and as fairly as possible. Teachers' interventions are also, however, important in and of themselves, because they represent what I earlier referred to as "contacts" between peer culture and the adult world. Successful interventions are ones that resolve conflict, take individual circumstances into account, and expose children to social norms and moral values. To meet all these objectives in one intervention is a tall order. Although I will offer some general strategies for intervention, it would be unrealistic to believe that every intervention can be totally successful.

Before turning to a consideration of intervention strategies, it is first useful to consider some common sources of disputes and conflicts in peer play. One source of conflict in nursery schools centers around children's attempts to gain access to playgroups. As I discussed in Chapter 4, the children's desire for social participation and their tendency to protect interactive space led to recurrent conflicts. Although the conflict resulting from access attempts may vary, given the number of children in a program and the physical size and ecology of the school, teachers are frequently called upon to help rejected children gain access to playgroups.

A second common source of conflicts has to do with the sharing of play materials. Unlike problems with access, which center around the protection of ongoing play, conflicts over play materials often emerge among participants during the course of play episodes. These conflicts normally occur when two or more children desire an object which cannot be shared at the same time. For example, if a group of children are making pretend pies and cakes around a sandbox, they will have no trouble sharing a community stove or oven. Disputes do, however, often emerge over rolling pins and muffin pans—which must be shared in a serial fashion through turn-taking. As I discuss below, this type of conflict provides excellent opportunities to introduce children to the notion of temporal sharing and turn-taking.

A third source of conflict is overly aggressive play. Here things begin innocently enough, but often get out of hand. A typical case is where several children (frequently boys) are involved in physical play like one of the varieties of approach–avoidance or superhero role play. In the process of running, jumping, and threatening each other, these children's activities often spill over into the play of others. These contacts or intrusions often result in confrontations and complaints to teachers. Another frequent occurrence is for conflict to develop within the physical play itself. Here, threats and playful pushes and shoves turn into real fighting (see Example 5.15 for such an occurrence in monster approach–avoidance play).

The general goal of any teacher intervention into children's disputes is not only to resolve the conflict but also to encourage the children to reflect upon the normative and moral significance of their actions. In such interventions, teachers are, in line with

Cicourel (1974), encouraging children to link specific features of unfolding action scenes with general norms and values. As I have argued previously, such contacts between adult and child culture are basic to the process of socialization. Teachers must remember, however, that, given their power and authority over children and the multiple demands of their everyday lives in the classroom, there is always a tendency to resolve disputes by simply imposing abstract rules upon the specific situation. Although the children may be frustrated in such cases and see the adult rules as arbitrary, the conflicts are resolved nonetheless.

To avoid this tendency, teachers need to have as much background information as possible about the events in which conflicts are embedded. Such information is often difficult to obtain from children. The information children contribute in this regard is often unreliable, due to underdeveloped cognitive abilities and the biased nature of their reports (e.g., "I had that and Peter hit me for nothing" or "She just fell, I didn't push her"). In such instances, general knowledge of peer culture and specific information acquired from systematic observation is highly useful.

Take, for example, disputes involving access to playgroups. In such cases, an understanding of the children's need to protect interactive space can be valuable in settling disputes and making children aware of the need for sharing play areas with others. Successful strategies in dealing with disputes over access often involve taking children's reasons for resistance seriously and suggesting ways in which the children attempting to gain access can easily join in the ongoing event. For example, in a dispute over access to the climbing bars (see Example 5.10) a teaching assistant (TA) intervened and first informed the defenders of the area (Jonathan and Steven) that they had to share the bars with Graham and Antoinette. The boys resisted, claiming that they were in the bars first and, further, that the bars served as their police station and were only for police. The TA countered by arguing that the bars were a public place which must be shared. The boys continued to resist, so the TA expanded her strategy somewhat by noting that all the police she knew were nice and would welcome visitors to their police station. Meanwhile, Graham and Antoinette slipped into the bars and Antoinette announced, "We're already in!" At this point, the TA decided to withdraw from the area. Jonathan and Steven continued to resist for a short time, but Jonathan then decided to give in and allow Graham and Antoinette to play. He then went on to convince Steven to let the other children play and to be a nice policeman. Later, Antoinette and Graham became robbers and the police role play continued for some time.

There are a number of interesting points in this example. First, notice that the TA first alluded to a general policy about sharing, but then later attempted to tie the idea of sharing to more specific features of the role play event (i.e., suggesting the boys be nice policemen and allow visitors into their police station). Although her suggestion was resisted at first, the boys eventually "talked it over" and agreed to be nice policemen. The TA was definitely on the right track in this example. Although she may have suggested a more active role for Antoinette and Graham (e.g., robbers rather than visitors), she did encourage the boys to link specific features of the play to a general rule, and her decision to withdraw when she did was a wise one. Her withdrawal gave the children a chance to work out the problem on their own. The result demonstrates how a teacher's suggestions may be resisted at first, but then are eventually accepted and employed by children later on.

In children's disputes over play materials, a frequently heard claim is "I had that first!" This claim exemplifies the strong temporal theme of disputes of this type. Since many young children have not often had to share their toys in the home, it is difficult for them to control their impulses regarding ownership of play materials in the school. The problem is really not one of sharing as such, but rather one of waiting while another child plays with a toy first. Children are not against sharing in these instances. They just do not want to be the first to share. A major problem for teachers in these instances is that it is often difficult to know who indeed had first possession of a desired object. One way many teachers handle this problem is to insist that it makes no difference who had first possession. In this strategy, teachers arbitrarily designate one child to play first. Teachers often make these decisions more palatable by occupying the waiting time of the first sharer. Teachers, together with the first sharer, make up waiting lists of children's names and, after certain periods of time, the desired objects are transferred and the lists are updated by crossing off some names and adding others.

Here I would suggest, from the children's point of view, that who had the object first does indeed matter. Children become very frustrated if they have to wait when they firmly believe that they have the right to go first. In instances of this type, teachers should try hard to gain the needed information. If an adult observer was present, the problem is easily resolved. If not, the teachers should tell the children that, since it is not known who had first possession, they will play a game to see who goes first. Perhaps the object could be hidden and the first child to find it gets to play first. This strategy may work well, because it nicely overlaps with the children's interest in lost–found themes discussed in Chapter 5. In any case, it is important that the decision of "who goes first" is not perceived as arbitrary by the children. In emphasizing the importance of "who goes first," I am not suggesting that formal turn-taking procedures through the use of waiting lists or other devices are unimportant. Children learn a great deal about formal rules as a result of such experiences. My emphasis is again on the need to articulate the feelings and concerns of peer culture with the norms and values of the adult world.

Before intervening in what appear to be disputes involving over-aggressiveness on the part of one or more children, teachers should first determine if the aggression was real or part of fantasy play. As we saw in Chapter 5, running, chasing, and threatening behavior are features of approach–avoidance routines. It is necessary in these routines that some children produce "feigned fear" while others take the role of aggressors. Upon first witnessing these events—or even after being asked for aid by a threatened child—teachers should closely watch the activity to determine if the threats or aggression are real before attempting to intervene.

On rare occasions, one of the many varieties of approach–avoidance play may erupt into real conflict. In these cases, intervention should be immediate and firm. The children involved are best taken aside for a discussion which emphasizes both "what was wrong" with their behavior and how the behavior developed. Regarding the latter, it is useful to attempt to reconstruct with the children the movement from play to aggression or conflict. It is especially important to identify specific acts or verbalization which are not normally part of play routines. In this way, children are encouraged to link mentally violations of moral rules (i.e., physically harming another) to specific actions in play which generated the undesirable behavior. Such discussions are also useful to teachers for responding to the often heard "I didn't mean to."

Teachers can temporally accept such accounts while encouraging children to identify and to accept responsibility for specific actions which led to the actual aggression.

The most common problem with physical play like approach–avoidance routines is that the participants sometimes intrude into and disrupt the activities of other children. In some cases, the problem is minor because the children have no real intent to disrupt. They have become overly exuberant in their play and are not aware of the disruptive effects of their running and chasing on other activities. The best solution in these cases is to remind the children of the rights of their peers regarding the use of interactive space, and to restrict the more physical play to certain areas of the school.

In other instances, the disruptive behavior is intentional and is an attempt on the part of the children involved in approach–avoidance play to recruit others to participate in the routine. Some children do not, however, appreciate these recruitment tactics. They may not want to join the routine and may actually be frightened of children who have assumed the role of threatening agents.

In these cases, teachers should attempt to make the children aware of ways in which play can accommodate the needs and desires of members of both groups. For example, in the present study I was once observing three girls engaged in family role play in the outside yard. During the course of their play, two boys ran into the area, knocked over some dishes, and yelled: "We are mean dragons!" The girls moved away from the boys and one shouted, "We don't want you, go away!" The boys left, but soon returned, chased after the girls again, and pretended to be "breathing fire." One of the girls yelled, "Stop, you will burn down our house!"

At this point, I suggested that the dragons should stop chasing the girls and help them. "How can dragons help a scared girl?" one boy asked. I was ready for this question and said, "Well it's cold in their house, so start a fire in the fireplace." "Hey, good idea!" he replied. He then pretended to breathe fire on a small, wooden box. The other dragon and the girls watched. When finished, the dragon said, "There, now you got a fire." The girls then pretended to warm themselves by the fire and one suggested that the dragons breathe fire on their plates to cook their food. One of the boys immediately did so and the girls shouted, "Good, now we can all eat!" The girls and the dragons sat down to eat.

Later, the dragons dried clothes and dishes, being especially careful (at the girls' insistence) not to burn them. After several minutes, the dragons ran off and were successful in initiating an approach–avoidance routine with three other children. The dragons did, however, stop back at the girls' house several times to restart the fire, eat some more food, and dry the dishes.

This example demonstrates how knowledge of peer culture is useful for rechannelling potentially disruptive behavior into enjoyable and inventive peer play. I do not claim that things will always work out this well, but the example does illustrate the importance of making children aware of the wide range of possibilities for engaging in cooperative peer play.

Early Childhood Education as a Reproductive Partnership

In Chapter 2, I argued that childhood socialization can be viewed as children's participation in, and production of, a series of peer cultures in which childhood knowledge and skills are gradually transformed into the knowledge and abilities necessary for participation in the adult world. The emphasis on peer culture does not deny the importance of adults in the socialization process. In fact, peer culture can be seen as primarily involving children's attempts to use, practice, and eventually more firmly grasp information first presented to them by adults. In terms of early childhood education, I stressed the importance of formal instruction and teachers' intervention into peer activities as important points of culture contact. It is during such contacts that children are encouraged to reflect upon the general social significance of their everyday activities. In this sense, nursery school teachers can be viewed as partners in children's movement toward their eventual reproduction of the social order.

In closing, I must note that culture contacts between teachers (and all adults) and children can be a two-way process. Adults can learn much from children. We can learn about the creative nature of spontaneity, the exuberance and awe of confronting a complex and mysterious world, and the sheer joy of sharing our lives with others. To understand childhood socialization, adults must see, hear, and appreciate the everyday life-worlds of children.

APPENDIX

Indefinite Triangulation Sessions With Graham And Jonathan

Graham, Indefinite Triangulation Session
Describing Tape 12 3/3/75 on 5/23/75
B = Researcher, Bill
G = Graham

(1) B: Now I want you to watch this and see if you remember. See, what happens is that I was watching this and I couldn't figure out what was happening. And I want you to watch and see if you can remember what was happening and tell me what was wrong, Ok?

(2) G: Ok.

(3) B: Ok. Here we go. Now watch.
(Plays tape)

(4) B: See yourself?

(5) G: Nope.

(6) B: Who's that right there?

(7) B: Who are those people?

(8) B: Who's this guy? (G smiles upon recognizing himself)

(9) G: (You know what) happening?

(10) B: Do you remember this?

(11) G: There's Bill. There's you.

(12) B: Um-Hum. (There I am).

(13) G: I'm tired.

(14) B: Let's watch it for a little bit. Ok? Cause I don—I want you to tell me something.

(15) G: Is Peter in this?

(16) B: I don't think so.

(17) G: (   ).
(18) G: This is a long, long time ago.
(19) B: Yeah. What's going on? Why did they—why did they knock you down? What's happening? Huh?
(20) G: I don't know.
(21) B: You don't know what's happening?
(22) G: Nope. (Tape plays)
(23) B: Why—why are you telling Tommy to do that?
(24) B: What's wrong? Why are those guys fighting you? Why—what are you trying to do?
(25) G: I don't know.
(26) B: (Laughs) You don't know? You can't tell me what you're doing? Why don't they want you to come in?
(27) G: (I don't—)
(28) B: Did you want to go in the bars?
(29) G: (Yeah).
(30) B: And what did you want to do in the bars?
(31) G: Climb.
(32) B: Climb? And how come—and they wouldn't let you in?
(33) B: Is that what was happening? (Pause)
(34) B: Is that why they were pushing you? (Pause)
(35) B: Why didn't you just go away then? (Pause)
(36) B: When they pushed you, why didn't you go away?
(37) G: I don't know?
(38) G: I wanna go.
(39) B: Well, just watch a little more, Ok? (Plays tape)
(40) G: Does that—keep on going like that forever? (Meaning tape)
(41) B: Well, till you're done playing.
(42) B: There you are. What are you doing to Jonathan? (Pause)
(43) B: You remember what happens next?
(44) G: No. (Plays tape)
(45) B: Does this happen a lot of times when you want to go in something and somebody says you can't come in there? Do they do that a lot?
(46) G: (Un-Uh). (Meaning no)
(47) B: Do you ever do that to anybody. Tell them they can't come in when you're playing?
(48) G: No.
(49) B: You always say: "Come on right in and play." Or do you say "No, we're playing here first."?
(50) G: No.
(51) B: What do you do?

(52) G: Peter says it. Sometimes (when)—I do at school.

(53) B: Um-Hum.

(54) B: If you and Peter are playing and somebody else comes over, do you sometimes rather they wouldn't play with you so you could play with Peter by yourself?

(55) G: If Peter—if they wanna—if—if Peter wants to play with them and play with them. And Peter—don't want 'em to.

(56) B: If Peter don't want 'em to then you tell 'em not to come and play?

(57) G: Yeah.

(58) B: Wonder if you want 'em to and Peter doesn't? What do you do then?

(59) G: I don't want 'em to and Peter (   )?

(60) B: Yeah, if you don't want 'em to but Peter does, what do you do then?

(61) G: I let 'em play. (Let 'em) play. But if he changes his mind and he don't want 'em to play—I don't want 'em to play (Instead)— —(of   ) play they have a fight.

(62) B: They have a fight? Who does?

(63) G: The people who wanted to play.

(64) B: And Peter doesn't want 'em to, so they have a fight?

(65) G: Yeah.

(66) B: Would you like to see one when you and Peter were playing or do you wanna go back?

(67) G: See one when Peter and me are playing.

(68) B: You wanna see another one of these when you and Peter are playing?

(69) G: Just one.

(70) B: Just one? Ok.

(71) G: A little bit.

(72) B: Ok. Well, it will take just a second for me to—for me to rewind this, Ok?

(73) G: I—I don't want to.

(74) B: Don't want to? Ok.

(75) B: Wanna go back?

(76) G: Um-Hum.

(77) B: So what—tell me though what was happening there. You and Jonathan, and—and Steven were having a fight. Because of what? Because they didn't want you to play with them? Do you think sometimes Jonathan and ah—Steven are like you and Peter? Since they don't want anybody to play with them?

(78) G: I (want to leave). Is this your house?

(79) B: This is where I work, yeah. Do you like it?

(80) B: Did you see my pictures?

(81) G: Who made those for you?

(82) B: Oh, lots of people. Vickie made that one. And Anita made that one. And you could make me one sometime and I'll put it up, Ok? Would you like to do that? Hum, Graham (Laughs) Would you like to do that?

(83) B: How do you like this one?

(84) G: Who made that one?

(85) B: A little girl that I know.

(86) G: Who is it?

(87) B: Her name's Iris.

(88) B: And this one is a little boy that I know.

(89) G: Who?

(90) B: His name's Buddy. He lives in North Carolina where I was before I came here.

(91) G: Who made that other one?

(92) B: This one?

(93) G: Yeah.

(94) B: I think Laura made that one.

(95) G: Who made that one?

(96) B: A little girl named Betty who goes to school in the morning, and she made this one too. And Vickie made this one, and Anita made that one. You'll have to make me one, Graham, and I'll put it right here, Ok? Maybe tomorrow? Will you do that? Huh?

(97) G: If I want to.

(98) B: If you want to? Ok.

(99) B: Want to take a short cut? (They leave room and taping stops)

Jonathan, Indefinite Triangulation Session Describing Tape 12

3/3/75 on 5/23/75

J = Jonathan

B = Researcher, Bill

(1) B: I want you to tell me what's going on. All right?

(2) J: Ok.

(3) B: Here we go. See if you remember when this was happening. (Tape plays)

(4) J: That's me and Steven.

(5) B: Un-Huh.

  (6) J: And that's you. You funny guy.

  (7) B: Yeah, that's me.

  (8) J: You silly koo-koo nut (   ).

  (9) J: That was a long, long time ago.

(10) B: Yeah.

(11) J: And that was you. You silly koo-koo nut.

(12) B: Who's this?

(13) J: I don't know—Graham.

(14) B: Um-Hum.

(15) J: And that's me.

(16) B: Yeah.

(17) J: Only I had a green shirt on then. Those are my police (clothes).

(18) B: Now what's happening there? Why—why ya doing that?

(19) J: Cause—we want to play police with nobody else in that except for when we put the people in jail.

(20) B: And wh—what was Graham doing that made ya mad?

(21) J: I didn't—Graham—Grah—

(22) B: Graham (Last name) (There is some confusion here, because Steven and Graham have the same first name in real life while I am using cover names in this report. So every time I asked about Graham or Steven, I had to use the same name, which caused problems. Therefore, I often used last names to clear up any misunderstanding)

(23) J: Well, cause—he—we wouldn't let him in the house.

(24) B: Un-Huh.

(25) J: That's what made him (   ). What are those little lines?

(26) B: Those are just lines that go through the picture.

(27) B: So you were already in the house. And they tried to come in? Was that it? And you were already playing police?

(28) J: Yeah. We—we meant it that time.

(29) B: You meant it? What do you mean, you meant it that time?

(30) J: Cause when they—when—

(31) B: Sometimes when people come in you really don't mean it when you say, you can't come in?

(32) J: (Un-Huh). I mean I *really* do mean it.

(33) B: You really do mean what?

(34) J: What I was saying.

(35) B: That you can't come in?

(36) J: (Yeah).

(37) B: Sometimes when you say that, it's Ok if they come in?

(38) J: Yes.

(39) B: Sometimes it's all right if they come in, and sometimes it's not. Is that right?

(40) J: (Shakes head yes)

(41) B: What times is it all right?

(42) J: When I say it.

(43) B: When you say, you can come in? (J Shakes head yes)

(44) B: Ok, Let's watch some more and you can tell me—see cause Graham. Let's watch some more and see what else is (in it).

(45) J: I wasn't mad at (first name)

(46) B: I mean (First name   last name) (We again have same problem with same first names in real life for Graham and Steven) (B and J watch tape; Graham is asking Tommy for help on tape)

(47) J: I got away in a quick escape, didn't I?

(48) B: Yeah. You were trying to get away without them grabbing ya?

(49) J: Yeah. I know just what to do when they tried to get me. I went— I went the quick escape way.

(50) B: I see.

(51) J: They couldn't get me. *Now* I'm trying to get them out of there.

(52) B: You don't want them in the box either, huh?

(53) J: No. Hey, there's you with your dummy microscope.

(54) B: Microphone?

(55) J: Yeah. And it's a dummy.

(56) B: A dummy microphone?

(57) J: Yeah.

(58) B: Now what are you telling Tommy?

(59) J: I told him (the jungle Jim is taken right now) (   ).

(60) B: Were you really gonna hit him?

(61) J: Yes (I was).

(62) B: Or were you just trying to scare 'em?

(63) J: I was trying to scare 'em.

(64) J: I don't want them to get in.

(65) B: Ok, Now we'll make it (the tape) go fast. (Moves tape up) and we'll look at something that happened later on.

(66) J: Ok. I want to see the rest of it right now.

(67) B: Ok, I'm gonna just move it up a little faster. Skip some of it, Ok. Here we go. (moves tape)

(68) J: Was that me going real fast?

(69) B: Um-Hum. And I think Antoinette's up there.

(70) J: That's (Name of Teaching Assistant). (Name of Teaching Assistant) is the friendliest (   ) in the yard. And you're still a dummy.

(71) B: Um-Hum.

(72) J: I (   ). Now you keep your mouth on your—

(73) B: What are telling Steven? You're whispering.

(74) J: I'm trying—I have a plan to get them. I don't know what the plan is. I (forgot).

(75) B: You have a plan to get them what? To get—

(76) J: To get them good and permanently.

(77) B: I see.

(78) J: I (had) to get them good and permanently.

(79) J: Watch me.

(80) B: Now watch. Antoinette is telling you something. Now here you're gonna tell Steven to have his lunch or something. Tell me what's going on.

(81) B: See, watch this part, Steven—a-ah—Jonathan.

(82) J: What?

(83) B: Watch this part.

(84) J: What did I do?

(85) B: Watch what you tell Steven.

(86) J: Steven who?

(87) B: Steven (Last Name) (We again have the same problem of same first names that I discussed above) (Tape runs through the part when Jonathan tells Steven to go have his lunch)

(88) J: That's not me, That's Steven (Last Name).

(89) B: Yeah, this is you. You said—you said: "You go on and have your lunch and I'll talk to Antoinette." Remember when you said that? What did you tell Antoinette when you talked to her? I think you were gonna—

(90) J: I—I forgot. That was a long, long, long, long time ago.

(91) B: (Laughs) Well, watch and see what you tell her.

(92) J: Can I have this red ball? (J picks up a ball from desk).

(93) B: Sure.

(94) J: I told Steven you eat everything (for your lunch). Can I keep this little thing too?

(95) B: Sure.

(96) J: Is this—is this suppose to be a (   )?

(97) B: Yeah, I guess it could be that.

(98) B: Now what—see here. Jonathan, look. Now, Jonathan—now, Steven said they couldn't come in. Were you changing your mind?

(99) J: Yes.

(100) B: You were saying they could come in? How come you changed your mind?

(101) J: Cause they wanted to come in.

(102) B: Un-Huh. But they wanted to come in at first too. When Graham did, and you didn't change your mind then.

(103) J: Because I thought they wanted and needed to come in, so I let them.

(104) B: So now after they tried to come in for a long time you thought they need—

(105) J: Now, I'm gonna have my *real* lunch. (Picks up candy bar from table)

(106) B: (Laughs) But you know why I have that? Because today is my birthday. And that is my birthday present. Did you know that?

(107) J: Know what?

(108) B: Today really is my birthday. Ok, Let's watch a little more and see. (Starts tape)

(109) J: Are there any things on these things (Desk) that I can have?

(110) B: On this table? You can have the candy bar.

(111) J: To keep?

(112) B: Yeah, sure.

(113) J: Ok.

(114) B: That's if you watch now. You're not watching.

(115) J: Next time on your birthday, I'll give you three—*six* presents and eight candy bars.

(116) B: Ok.

(117) J: For—for you someday if you're hungry and you don't have any lunch. (Both watch tape)

(118) B: See now, he (Steven) doesn't want her (Antoinette) to come in.

(119) B: See now, you changed your mind, and you said she could come in. How could you convince Steven that it's Ok?

(120) J: Well, I'd say:—Well I had a plan. I'd say: "Steven, well they *can't* come in." And then I'd whisper in their ears: (very softly) "But you could come in." I was tricking Steven.

(121) B: Um-Hum—what would you—then you thought once they got in there Steven might change his mind?

(122) J: Yeah.

(123) B: Ok. Let's—let's move it up a little bit. (Moves up tape) That candy melting?

(124) J: No, hasn't melted yet. Is there any garbage can around here?

(125) B: Yeah, right over there.

(126) J: You want me to bring it over here? (Moves can) My dad has a Sony television.

(127) B: Yeah.

(128) J: It's littler than that. It—it doesn't have very much (color) like that does.

(129) B: Ok, we'll just look at one more part and then go back. (Starts tape) I want to show you this part where you were trying to get Steven to let 'em come in. (Tape plays)

(130) B: It's a little farther. (Moves tape up)

(131) J: That's my (voice): We'll check every kid in the school. (Tape plays)

(132) B: Yeah, now—now see. Here you come.

(133) B: You said: "We need to talk about it."

(134) J: I said that they should talk about it.

(135) B: See now, watch.

(136) J: Hey, I see something. What is this?

(137) B: Aaah-(Nugget). I think that's what they call it. Why did you shake hands with—with, ah, Steven—with Steven (Last name) and not Graham (Last name) and Antoinette?

(138) J: What did I do when I shake their hands?

(139) B: See, you said—asked Steven to be a nice policeman and let them come in. And then he said Ok and then you said: "Let's shake on it." Why didn't you shake hands with Graham (Last name) and Antoinette and say: "You can come in now"?

(140) J: Cause I gave my agreement with him. (Meaning Steven)

(141) B: And they already were agreeing with you, so you didn't have to shake their hands?

(142) J: Yeah.

(143) B: How did they know it was all right for them to come in?

(144) J: Cause I (shaked) hands with Steven.

(145) B: I see. (Tape plays)

(146) B: Now that they're in there, wh-what—wa—ah—are they gonna be able to play with you guys? And what do they have to do?

(147) J: Be policeman if they lived here. Or—

(148) B: What else could they be?

(149) J: Or they could be the guards.

(150) B: The guards?

(151) B: How 'bout robbers?

(152) J: No. They don't like to be the robbers.

(153) B: Why not?

(154) J: Cause they just don't.

(155) B: Um-Hum.

(156) J: If you—if you put some paper in here, I'd spell something for you.

(157) B: Well, I—really can't do that right now. I will in a minute, Ok? Well, I guess that's all I have to ask you. Let me see if there's anything else. If you don't want somebody to come in, what do you say?

(158) J: I say: "Goodbye, please don't come in here."

(159) B: And wonder if you don't—wonder if you're playing in the bars and you really don't care if anybody comes in or not and you see somebody walking up?

(160) J: I'd say: Ok, you can come in. It's all right with me.

(161) B: Un-Huh.

(162) B: What if—if you say you can't come in and they keep trying to come in. When do you decide it's Ok and when do you just keep trying to get 'em out?

(163) J: Well, when I try to get them out I try to fight them out.

(164) B: Um-Hum.

(165) J: And when I decide to get 'em in, I try to tell Steven about.

(166) B: Um-Hum. We—what makes you decide it's Ok for them to come in when first you thought they shouldn't? What convinced you?

(167) J: I don't know.

(168) B: You don't know? Cause—cause you changed your mind but Steven didn't? So you asked him to, you don't know what changed your mind?

(169) J: No.
　　　　(End of Tape)

References

Almy, M. and C. Genishi (1979). Ways of Studying Children. New York: Teachers College Press.

Aries, P. (1965). Centuries of Childhood: A Social History of Family Life. New York: Vintage.

Asher, S. and J. Gottman (eds.) (1981). The Development of Children's Friendships. New York: Cambridge University Press.

Bandura, A. (1969). "Social learning theory of identificatory processes." In D. Goslin (ed.), Handbook of Socialization Theory and Research. Chicago: Rand McNally.

Barker, R. and H. Wright (1966). One Boy's Day. Hamden, CT: Archon.

Barnes, K. (1967). "Some ethical problems in modern fieldwork." British Journal of Sociology 14: 118–134.

Bateson, G. (1956). "The message 'This is play'." In Group Processes: Transactions of the Second Conference. New York: Josiah Macy, Jr. Foundation.

Becker, H. S. (1958). "Problems of inference and proof in participant observation research." American Sociological Review 23: 652–660.

Becker, H. S. (1964). "Problems in the publication of field studies." In A. Vidich, J. Bensman and M. Stein (eds.), Reflections on Community Studies. New York: Wiley.

Becker, H. S. (1970). Sociological Work. Chicago: Aldine.

Blurton-Jones, N. (ed.) (1972). Ethological Studies of Child Behavior. New York: Cambridge University Press.

Blurton-Jones, N. (1976). "Routh-and-tumble play among nursery school children." In J. Bruner, A. Jolly and K. Sylva (eds.), Play: Its Role in Development and Evolution. New York: Basic Books.

Brennis, D. and L. Lein (1977). " 'You fruithead': A sociolinguistic approach to children's dispute settlement." In S. Ervin-Tripp and C. Mitchell-Kernan (eds.), Child Discourse. New York: Academic Press.

Broen, P. (1972). The Verbal Environment of the Language Learning Child. Monograph No. 17, Washington, DC: American Speech and Hearing Association.

Bronson, W. (1975). "Developments in behavior with age-mates during the second year of life." In M. Lewis and L. Rosenblum (eds.), Friendship and Peer Relations. New York: Wiley.

Brown, R. (1965). Social Psychology. New York: Free Press.

Bruner, J. (1974). "The organization of early skilled action." In M. Richards (ed.), The Integration of a Child into a Social World. New York: Cambridge University Press.

Bruner, J. (1975). "The ontogenesis of speech acts." Journal of Child Language 2: 1–19.

Bruner, J. (1977). "Early social interaction and language acquisition." In H. Schaffer (ed.), Studies in Mother-Infant Interaction. London: Academic Press.

Bruner, J., A. Jolly, and K. Sylva (eds.) (1976). Play: Its Role in Development and Evolution. New York: Basic Books.

Bruner, J. and V. Sherwood (1976). "Early word structure: The case of peekaboo." In J. Bruner, A. Jolly and K. Sylva (eds.), Play: Its Role in Development and Evolution. New York: Basic Books.

Challman, R. (1932). "Factors influencing friendships among preschool children." Child Development 3: 146–158.

Cicourel, A. (1964). Method and Measurement in Sociology. New York: Free Press.

Cicourel, A. (1972). "Interpretive procedures and normative rules in the negotiation of status and role." In D. Sudnow (ed.), Studies in Social Interaction. New York: Free Press.

Cicourel, A. (1974). Cognitive Sociology. New York: Free Press.

Cicourel, A. (1975). Theory and Method in a Study of Argentine Fertility. New York: Wiley.

Cicourel, A. (1976). "Discourse and text: Cognitive and linguistic processes in studies of social structure." Versus: Quaderni di Studi Semiotici 133–184.

Cicourel, A. (1978a). "Language and society: Cognitive, cultural and linguistic aspects of language use." Sozialwiss. Annual 2: B25—58.

Cicourel, A. (1978b). "Interpretation and summarization: Issues in the child's acquisition of social structure." In J. Glick and A. Clarke-Stewart (eds.), The Development of Social Understanding. New York: Gardner.

Cicourel, A. (1979). "Field research: The need for stronger theory and more control over the data base." In W. Smizerk, M. Miller and E. Fuhrman (eds.), Contemporary Issues in Theory: A Meta-Sociological Perspective. West Port, CT: Greenwood.

Cicourel, A. (1980). "Three models of discourse analysis: The role of social structure." Discourse Processes 3: 101–132.

Cicourel, A. (1981). "The role of cognitive-linguistic concepts in understanding everyday social interactions." In R. Turner (ed.), Annual Review of Sociology (Vol. 7). Palo Alto, CA: Annual Reviews Inc.

Clausen, J. (ed.) (1968). Socialization and Society. Boston: Little, Brown.

Cole, M., J. Gay, J. Glick, and D. Sharp (1971). The Cultural Context of Learning and Thinking. New York: Basic Books.

Cole, M. and S. Scribner (1974). Culture and Society. New York: Wiley.

Cole, M. and S. Scribner (1978). Introduction. In L. Vygotsky, Mind in Society. New York: Cambridge University Press.

Connolly, K. and P. Smith (1978). "Experimental studies of the preschool environment." International Journal of Early Childhood 10: 86–95.

Cook-Gumperz, J. and W. Corsaro (1977). "Social-ecological constraints on children's communicative strategies." Sociology 11: 411–434.

Cook-Gumperz, J., W. Corsaro, and J. Streeck (eds.) (In press). Children's Language and Children's Worlds. New York: Cambridge University Press.

Cook-Gumperz, J. and J. Gumperz (1976). Context in Children's Speech. Working Paper No. 46, Language Behavior Research Laboratory, University of California, Berkeley.

Cooley, G. (1922). Human Nature and the Social Order. New York: Scribner's.

Corsaro, W. (1977). "The clarification request as a feature of adult interactive styles with young children." Language in Society 6: 183–207.

Corsaro, W. (1979a). "Young children's conception of status and role." Sociology of Education 52: 46–59.

Corsaro, W. (1979b). "Sociolinguistic patterns in adult-child interaction." In E. Ochs and B. Schieffelin (eds.), Developmental Pragmatics. New York: Academic Press.

Corsaro, W. (1979c). " 'We're friends, right?': Children's use of access rituals in a nursery school." Language in Society 8: 315–336.

Corsaro, W. (1981a). "Communicative processes in studies of social organization: Sociological approaches to discourse analysis." Text 1: 5–63.

Corsaro, W. (1981b). "Friendship in the nursery school: Social organization in a peer environment." In S. Asher and J. Gottman (eds.), The Development of Children's Friendships. New York: Cambridge University Press.

Corsaro, W. (1981c). "Entering the child's world: Research strategies for field entry and data collection in a preschool setting." In J. Green and C. Wallat (eds.), Ethnography and Language in Educational Settings. Norwood, NJ: Ablex.

Corsaro, W. (1983). "Script recognition, articulation and expansion in children's role play." Discourse Processes 6: 1–11.

Corsaro, W. and G. Tomlinson (1980). "Spontaneous play and social learning in the nursery school." In H. Schwartzman (ed.), Play and Culture. West Point, NY: Leisure Press.

Cottrell, L. (1969). "Interpersonal interaction and the development of self." In D. Goslin (ed.), Handbook of Socialization Theory and Research. Chicago: Rand-McNally.

Cross, T. (1977). "Mothers' speech adjustments: The contribution of selected child listener variables." In C. Snow and C. Ferguson (eds.), Talking to Children: Language Input and Acquisition. New York: Cambridge University Press.

Damon, W. (1977). The Social World of the Child. San Francisco: Jossey-Bass.

Damon, W. (ed.) (1978). Social Cognition. San Francisco: Jossey-Bass.

Davis, F. (1961). "Comment on 'Initial interaction of newcomers in alcoholics anonymous'." Social Problems 4: 364–365.

Day, D., E. Perkins and J. Weinthaler (1979). "Naturalistic evaluation for program improvement." Young Children 34: 12–24.

Denzin, N. (1977a). Childhood Socialization. San Francisco: Jossey-Bass.

Denzin, N. (1977b). The Research Act. Chicago: Aldine.

Dewey, J. (1938). Experience and Education. New York: Kappa Delta Pi.

Dweck, C. (1981). "Social-cognitive processes in children's friendships." In S. Asher and J. Gottman (eds.), The Development of Children's Friendships. New York: Cambridge University Press.

Eder, D. (1979). Stratification within the Classroom: The Formation and Maintenance of Ability Groups. Unpublished doctoral dissertation, University of Wisconsin, Madison.

Erickson, F. (1978). "Talking down: Some cultural sources of miscommunication in inter-racial interviews." In A. Wolfgang (ed.), Research in Non-Verbal Communication. New York: Academic Press.

Erickson, F. and G. Schultz (1982). Talking to the Man: Social and Cultural Organization of Communication in Counseling Interviews. New York: Academic Press.

Ervin-Tripp, S. (1976). "Is Sybil there? The structure of some American English directives." Language in Society 5: 25–66.

Ervin-Tripp, S. (1977). "Wait for me roller skate!" In S. Ervin-Tripp and C. Mitchell-Kernan (eds.), Child Discourse. New York: Academic Press.

Ervin-Tripp, S. and W. Miller (1977). "Early discourse: Some questions about questions." In M. Lewis and L. Rosenblum (eds.), Interaction, Conversation and the Development of Language. New York: Wiley.

Ferguson, C. (1964). "Baby talk in six languages." American Anthropologist 66: 103–114.

Fine, G. (1979). "Small groups and culture creation: The idioculture of little league baseball teams." American Sociological Review 44:733–745.

Fine, G. and B. Glassner (1979). "The promise and problems of participant observation with children." Urban Life 8: 153–174.

Fine, G. and S. Kleinman (1979). "Rethinking subculture: An interactionist analysis." American Journal of Sociology 85: 1–20.

Fitchner, J. and W. Kolb (1963). "Ethical limitations on sociological reporting." American Sociological Review 18: 544–550.

Flavell, J. (1963). The Developmental Psychology of Jean Piaget. Princeton, NJ: D. Van Nostrand Company.

Fortes, M. (1938). "Social and psychology aspects of education in Taleland." Africa 11.

Freund, J. (1952). Modern Elementary Statistics. Englewood Cliffs, NJ: Prentice-Hall.

Furth, H. (1969). Piaget and Knowledge: Theoretical Foundations. Englewood Cliffs, NJ: Prentice-Hall.

Gardner, J. (1981). The Quest for Mind. Chicago: University of Chicago Press.

Garfinkel, H. (1967). Studies in Ethnomethodology. Englewood Cliffs, NJ: Prentice-Hall.

Garnica, O. (1977). "Some prosodic and paralinguistic aspects of language acquisition." In C. Snow and C. Ferguson (eds.), Talking to Children. New York: Cambridge University Press.

Garvey, C. (1974). "Some properties of social play." Merrill-Palmer Quarterly 20: 163–180.

Garvey, C. (1975). "Requests and responses in children's speech." Journal of Child Language 2: 41–63.

Garvey, C. (1977a). "The contingent query: A dependent act in conversation." In M. Lewis and L. Rosenblum (eds.), Interaction, Conversation and the Development of Language. New York: Wiley.

Garvey, C. (1977b). Play. Cambridge, MA: Harvard University Press.

Garvey, C. (1979). "An approach to the study of children's role play." Quarterly Newsletter of the Laboratory of Comparative Human Development 1: 69–73.

Garvey, C. and D. Brendt (1975). The Organization of Pretend Play. The Annual Meeting of the American Psychological Association, Chicago, Ill.

Garvey, C. and R. Hogan (1973). "Social speech and social interaction: Egocentrism revisited." Child Development 44: 562–568.

Gelman, R. and M. Shatz (1977). "Appropriate speech adjustments: The operation of conversational constraints on talk to two-year-olds." In M. Lewis and L. Rosenblum (eds.), Interaction, Conversation and the Development of Language. New York: Wiley.

Ginsburg, R. and S. Opper (1979). Piaget's Theory of Intellectual Development. Englewood Cliffs, NJ: Prentice-Hall.

Glaser, B. and A. Strauss (1967). The Discovery of Grounded Theory. Chicago: Aldine.

Gleason, J. (1973). "Code switching in children's language." In T. Moore (ed.), Cognitive Development and the Acquisition of Language. New York: Academic Press.

Goffman, E. (1961a). Asylums. Garden City, NY: Anchor.

Goffman, E. (1961b). Encounters. Indianapolis, IN: Bobbs-Merrill.

Goffman, E. (1963). Behavior in Public Places. New York: Free Press.

Goffman, E. (1974). Frame Analysis. New York: Harper & Row.

Goody, E. (1978). "Towards a theory of questions." In E. Goody (ed.), Questions and Politeness: Strategies in Social Interaction. New York: Cambridge University Press.

Gottman, J. and J. Parkhurst (1980). "A developmental theory of friendship and acquaintanceship processes." In W. Collins (ed.), Minnesota Symposia on Child Psychology (Vol. 13). Hillsdale, NJ: Erlbaum.

Green, E. (1933). "Friendships and quarrels among preschool children." Child Development 4: 237–252.

Green, G. (1975). "How to get people to do things with words: The whimperative question." In P. Cole and J. Morgan (eds.), Syntax and Semantics. New York: Academic Press.

Green, J. and C. Wallat (eds.) (1981). Ethnography and Language in Educational Settings. Norwood, NJ: Ablex.

Greer, B. (1967). "First days in the field." In P. Hammond (ed.), Sociologists at Work. New York: Doubleday.

Grice, H. (1975). "Logic and conversation." In P. Cole and J. Morgan (eds.), Syntax and Semantics. New York: Academic Press.

Gumperz, J. (1976). "Language communication and public negotiation." In P. Sanday (ed.), Anthropology and the Public Interest: Fieldwork and Theory. New York: Academic Press.

Gumperz, J. (1977). "Sociocultural knowledge in conversational inference." In M. Saville-Troike (ed.), 28th Annual Roundtable Monograph Series on Language and Linguistics. Washington, DC: Georgetown University Press.

Gumperz, J. (1978). "Dialect and conversational inference in urban communication." Language in Society 7: 393–409.

Gumperz, J. (1982). Discourse Strategies. New York: Cambridge University Press.

Habermas, J. (1979). Communication and the Evolution of Society. Boston: Beacon Press.

Halliday, M. (1974). Learning How to Mean: Explorations in the Development of Language. London: E. Arnold.

Hartup, W. (1970). "Peer interaction and social organization." In P. Mussen (ed.), Carmichael's Manual of Child Psychology (Vol. 2). New York: Wiley.

Hartup, W. (1975). "The origins of friendship." In M. Lewis and L. Rosenblum (eds.), Friendship and Peer Relations. New York: Wiley.

Hays, W. and R. Winkler (1971). Statistics: Probability, Interface and Decision. New York: Holt, Rinehart and Winston.

Herron, R. and B. Sutton-Smith (eds.) (1971). Child's Play. New York: Wiley.

Holzman, M. (1972). "The use of the interrogative of three mothers and their children." Journal of Psycholinguistic Research 4: 311–336.

Hood, L., K. Fiess, and J. Aron (1982). "Growing up explained: Vygotskians look at the language of causality." In C. Brainerd and M. Pressley (eds.), Verbal Processing in Children. New York: Springer-Verlag.

Hood, L., R. McDermott, and M. Cole (1980). " 'Let's try to make it a good day': Some not so simple ways." Discourse Processes 3: 155–168.

Hudson, J. (1975). "The meaning of questions." Language 51: 1–131.

Hutt, C. (1971). "Exploration and play in children." In R. Herron and B. Sutton-Smith (eds.), Child's Play. New York: Wiley.

Hymes, D. (1978). What is Ethnography? Sociolinguistic Working Paper No. 45, Southwest Educational Development Laboratory, Austin, Texas.

Keenan, E. (1974). "Conversational competence in children." Journal of Child Language 1: 163–183.

Keenan, E. (1977). "Making it last: Repetition in children's discourse." In S. Ervin-Tripp and C. Mitchell-Kernan (eds.), Child Discourse. New York: Academic Press.

Keenan, E. and E. Klein (1975). "Coherency in children's discourse." Journal of Psycholinguistic Research 4: 365–380.

Kendon, A. (1977). Studies in the Behavior of Social Interaction. Lisse: DeRidder.

Kendon, A., R. Harris, and M. Key (eds.) (1975). The Organization of Behavior in Face-to-Face Interaction. The Hague: Mouton.

Kholberg, L. (1969). "Stage and sequence: The cognitive-developmental approach to socialization." In D. Goslin (ed.), Handbook of Socialization Theory and Research. Chicago: Rand McNally.

Kholberg, L., S. Yeager and E. Hjertholm (1968). "Private speech: Four studies and a review of theories." Child Development 39: 691–736.

Koch, H. (1933). "Popularity in preschool children: Some related factors and a technique for its measurement." Child Development 4: 64–75.

Labov, W. and D. Fanshel (1977). Therapeutic Discourse: Psycho-Therapy as Conversation. New York: Academic Press.

Lee, B. and G. Noam (eds.) (1982). Developmental Approaches to the Self. New York: Plenum.

Lewis, M. and L. Rosenblum (eds.) (1975). Friendship and Peer Relations. New York: Wiley.

Lofland, J. (1961). "Reply to Davis." Social Problems 8: 365–367.

Lofland, J. and R. LeJeune (1960). "Initial interaction of newcomers in alcoholics anonymous." Social Problems 8: 102–111.

Marshall, H. and B. McCandless (1957). "A study in prediction of social behavior of preschool children." Child Development 28: 149–159.

Martlew, M., K. Connolly and C. McCleod (1978). "Language use, role and context in a five-year-old." Journal of Child Language 5: 81–99.

McDermott, R., K. Gospodinoff and J. Aron (1978). "Criteria for an ethnographically adequate description of concerted activities and their contexts." Semiotica 24: 245–275.

McDermott, R. and D. Roth (1978). "The social organization of behavior: Interactional approaches." Annual Review of Anthropology 7: 321–345.

McDowell, J. (1979). Children's Riddling. Bloomington, IN: Indiana University Press.

McGhee, P. (1979). Humor: Its Origin and Development. San Francisco: Freeman.

Mehan, H. (1978). "Structuring school structure." Harvard Educational Review 48: 32–64.

Mehan, H. (1979). Learning Lessons. Cambridge, MA: Harvard University Press.

Mead, G. H. (1934). Mind, Self and Society. Chicago: University of Chicago Press.

Meullar, E. (1972). "The maintenance of verbal exchanges between young children." Child Development 43: 930–938.

Mitchell-Kernan, C. and K. Kernan (1977). "Pragmatics of directive choice among children." In S. Ervin-Tripp and C. Mitchell-Kernan (eds.), Child Discourse. New York: Academic Press.

Mueller, J., K. Schussler, and H. Costner (1977). Statistical Reasoning in Sociology. Boston: Houghton-Mifflin.

Newport, M. (1976). "Motherese: The speech of mothers to young children." In N. Castellan, D. Pisoni and G. Potts (eds.), Cognitive Theory, Vol. II. Hillsdale, NJ: Erlbaum.

Newport, M., H. Gleitman, and L. Gleitman (1977). "Mother I'd rather do it myself: Some effects and non-effects of maternal speech style." In C. Snow and C. Ferguson (eds.), Talking to Children. New York: Cambridge University Press.

Nucci, L. and E. Turiel (1978). "Social interactions and the development of social concepts in preschool children." Child Development 49: 400–408.

Ochs, E. (1979). "Transcription as theory." In E. Ochs and B. Schieffelin (eds.), Developmental Pragmatics. New York: Academic Press.

Omark, D., M. Omark and M. Edelman (1975). "Formation of dominance hierarchies in young children: Action and perception." In T. Williams (ed.), Psychological Anthropology. The Hague: Mouton.

Opie, I. and P. Opie (1959). The Lore and Language of School Children. New York: Oxford University Press.

Opie, I. and P. Opie (1969). Children's Games in Street and Playground. Oxford: Clarendon.

Parten, M. (1932). "Social participation among preschool children." Journal of Abnormal and Social Psychology 27: 243–269.

Peirce, C. (1957). Essays in the Philosophy of Science. New York: The Liberal Arts Press.

Piaget, J. (1950). The Psychology of Intelligence. London: Routledge and Kegan Paul.

Piaget, J. (1952). The Language and Thought of the Child. London: Routledge and Kegan Paul.

Piaget, J. (1965). The Moral Judgment of the Child. New York: Free Press.

Piaget, J. (1968). Six Psychological Studies. New York: Vintage.

Ratner, N. and J. Bruner (1978). "Games, social exchanges and the acquisition of language." Journal of Child Language 5: 391–401.

Raum, O. (1940). Chaga Childhood. London: Oxford University Press.

Reiss, A. (1971). "Systematic observation of natural social phenomena." In H. Costner (ed.), Sociological Methodology. San Francisco: Jossey-Bass.

Ritchie, O. and M. Koller (1964). Sociology of Childhood. New York: Appleton-Century-Croft.

Roth, J. (1962). "Comments on 'secret observations'." Social Problems 9: 283–284.

Rubin, Z. (1980). Children's Friendships. Cambridge, MA: Harvard University Press.

Rubin, K., T. Maioni and M. Hornung (1976). "Free play behaviors in middle- and lower-class preschoolers: Parten and Piaget revisited." Child Development 47: 414–419.

Rumelhart, D. (1975). "Notes on a schema for stories." In D. Bobrow and A. Collins (eds.), Representation and Understanding: Studies in Cognitive Science. New York: Academic Press.

Rumelhart, D. (1977a). "Understanding and summarizing brief stories." In D. LaBerge and S. Samuels (eds.), Basic Processes in Reading: Perception and Comprehension. Hillsdale, NJ: Erlbaum.

Rumelhart, D. (1977b). "Toward an interactive model of reading." International Symposium on Attention and Performance. Stockholm, Sweden.

Ryan, J. (1974). "Early language development: Towards a communicational analysis." In M. Richards (ed.), The Integration of a Child into a Social World. New York: Cambridge University Press.

Sachs, J. and J. Devin (1976). "Young children's use of age appropriate speech styles." Journal of Child Language 3: 81–89.

Sacks, H. (1972). "On the analysability of stories by children." In J. Gumperz and D. Hymes (eds.), Directions in Sociolinguistics. New York: Holt, Rinehart and Winston.

Sacks, H., I. Schegloff, and G. Jefferson (1974). "A simplest systematics for the organization of turn-taking in conversation." Language 50: 696–735.

Schank, R. and R. Abelson (1977). Scripts, Plans, Goals and Understanding. Hillsdale, NJ: Erlbaum.

Schatzman, L. and A. Strauss (1973). Field Research: Strategies for a Natural Sociology. Englewood Cliffs, NJ: Prentice-Hall.

Scheflen, A. (1973). Communication Structure. Bloomington, IN: Indiana University Press.

Scheflen, A. (1974). How Behavior Means. New York: Anchor Press.

Schutz, A. (1953). "Common sense and scientific interpretation of human action." Philosophy and Phenomenological Research 14: 1–37.

Schutz, A. (1955). "Symbol, reality and society." In L. Bryson (ed.), Symbols and Society. New York: Harper & Row.

Schwartz, U. (1983). Communication Analysis of Plot Structure and Plot Structure Generative Techniques in Young Children's Dyadic Pretend Play. Unpublished doctoral dissertation, School of Education, Indiana University.

Schwartzman, H. (1976). "The anthropological study of child's play." Annual Review of Anthropology 5: 289–328.

Schwartzman, H. (1978). Transformations: The Anthropology of Children's Play. New York: Plenum.

Selman, R. (1976). "The development of interpersonal reasoning." In A. Pick (ed.), Minnesota Symposia on Child Development (Vol. 10). Minneapolis, MN: University of Minnesota Press.

Selman, R. (1980). The Growth of Interpersonal Understanding. New York: Academic Press.

Selman, R. (1981). "The child as friendship philosopher." In S. Asher and J. Gottman (eds.), The Development of Children's Friendships. New York: Cambridge University Press.

Shantz, C. (1975). "The development of social cognition." In E. Hetherington (ed.), Review of Child Development Research (Vol. 5). Chicago: University of Chicago Press.

Shatz, M. (1981). "On mechanisms of language acquisition: Can features of the communicative environment account for development?" In L. Gleitman and E. Wanner (eds.), Language Acquisition: The State of the Art. New York: Cambridge University Press.

Shatz, M. and R. Gelman (1973). The Development of Communication Skills: Modifications in the Speech of Young Children as a Function of Listener. Monographs of the Society for Research in Child Development, 38, No. 152.

Sherman, L. (1975). "An ecological study of glee in small groups of preschool children." Child Development 46: 53–61.

Shotter, J. (1974). "The development of personal powers." In M. Richards (ed.), The Integration of a Child into a Social World. New York: Cambridge University Press.

Sluckin, A. and P. Smith (1977). "Two approaches to the concept of dominance in preschool children." Child Development 48: 917–923.

Snow, C. (1972). "Mother's speech to children learning language." Child Development 43: 549–565.

328 • *Friendship and Peer Culture in the Early Years*

Snow, C. (1977). "The development of conversation between mothers and babies." Journal of Child Language 4: 1–22.

Speier, M. (1973). How to Observe Face-to-Face Communication: A Sociological Introduction. Pacific Palisades, CA: Goodyear.

Stone, G. (1956). "The play of little children." Quest 4: 23–31.

Strauss, A. (1964). Psychiatric Ideologies and Institutions. New York: Free Press.

Strayer, F. and S. Strayer (1976). "An ethological analysis of social agonism and dominance relations among preschool children." Child Development 47: 980–989.

Super, C. and S. Harkness (eds.) (1980). Anthropological Perspectives on Child Development. San Francisco: Jossey-Bass.

Tomlinson, G. (1981). The Comedic Performance: An Interactive Analysis. Unpublished doctoral dissertation, Indiana University.

Turiel, E. (1978a). "The development of concepts of social structure: Social conventions." In J. Glick and A. Clarke-Stewart (eds.), Studies in Social and Cognitive Development. New York: Gardner Press.

Turiel, E. (1978b). "Social regulations and domains of social concepts." In W. Damon (ed.), Social Cognition. San Francisco: Jossey-Bass.

Vygotsky, L. (1962). Thought and Language. Cambridge, MA: M.I.T. Press.

Vygotsky, L. (1978). Mind in Society. Cambridge, MA: Harvard University Press.

Wallat, C., J. Green, S. Conlin and M. Haramis (1981). "Issues related to action research in the classroom: The teacher and researcher as a team." In J. Green and C. Wallat (eds.), Ethnography and Language in Educational Settings. Norwood, NJ: Ablex.

Wertsch, J. (1979). "From social interaction to higher psychological process: A clarification and application of Vygotsky's theory." Human Development 22: 1–22.

Wertsch, J. (ed.) (1981). The Concept of Activity in Soviet Psychology. New York: Sharpe.

Wolfenstein, M. (1978). Children's Humor: A Psychological Analysis. Bloomington, IN: Indiana University Press.

Youniss, J. (1975). "Another perspective on social cognition." In A. Pick (ed.), Minnesota Symposia on Child Psychology (Vol. 9). Minneapolis, MN: University of Minnesota Press.

Youniss, J. (1978). "Dialectical theory and Piaget on social knowledge." Human Development 21: 234–237.

Youniss, J. (1980). Parents and Peers in Social Development: A Sullivan-Piaget Perspective. Chicago: University of Chicago Press.

Author Index

Italics indicate bibliographic citations.

Subject Index

A

Abductive reasoning, 68–69
Access strategies, 122–150, 272–274, 289–290, 297, 303–304
Adult–child interaction, 56–57, 69–70
Adult rules, 278–279
  children's conception of, 254–268
Age groups
  in nursery school, 7–9
Applications of observational data
  by teachers, 294–307
Appropriation of culture, 58–59, 283–286
Approach–avoidance routines, 70–72, 219–250
  boys vs. girls, 241–250
  compared to spontaneous fantasy, 278–279
  monster, 224–241
  as a reflection of the themes of control and communal sharing, 277–278
  wild animal, 222–224
Audiovisual data
  cataloging of, 41–42
  micro-sociolinguistic analysis of, 47–48, 78
  organization of, 40–41
  transcription of, 42–47
Audiovisual recording, 34–38
  estimating obtrusiveness of, 36–38
  introducing videotape equipment, 34–36
  procedures, 34–36

B

Authority
  and status, 77–100
  of adults, 254–268

Behavioristic theories, 52
Boundary contacts
  between adult and peer culture, 289–290, 307
Boundary maintenance
  by teachers, 289–290

C

Childhood socialization, 51–75
Children's categorization of the social world, 1–2, 70–71, 271, 282–283
Children's play
  paradoxes of, 60–61
  as a reproduction of the adult world, 61
  as a shared feature of peer culture, 61
  as a stage of development, 63–66
  Vygotsky's views of, 59–61
Cicourel, A., 62, 66–72, 282–283
Clinical interviewing, 55–56, 273–274
Cognitive developmental theory, 53, 280
Communal sharing, 75, 176–177, 184–191, 208–209, 251–254, 271–279
Communicative functions, 78–85
Concern with physical size, 179–192, 275

333